TAKING
THE
ADVENTURE

TAKING
THE
ADVENTURE

A. B. MARSHALL

MICHAEL RUSSELL

First published in Great Britain 1999
by Michael Russell (Publishing) Ltd
Wilby Hall, Wilby, Norwich NR16 2JP

Typeset in Sabon by The Typesetting Bureau
Allen House, East Borough, Wimborne, Dorset
Printed and bound in Great Britain
by Biddles Ltd, Guildford and King's Lynn

Contents

Acknowledgements

Without my wife Mona there wouldn't have been much of a book at all. She will know that, in trying to produce some reasonable balance between business and family, there is, inevitably, a lot which has to give. I trust, however, that she and our children, who may, in their early years, have had something of a part-time father, will appreciate that I have tried to convey, albeit inadequately, my debt to them all. Thanks to Mona, Alastair, Gillian and James did not seem to suffer unduly and we are intensely proud of them – all happily married and, so far, two with growing families. Mona has supported me for forty years, understanding my failings and stiffening my resolve – I owe everything to her.

Betty Fairclough, who was my secretary over some seventeen years in all, has contributed enormously – typing, correcting, editing and, in addition, remembering, researching and criticising. She put my files in order and has maintained immaculate records, which have ensured that, twenty-five years after the events described, I could tell my part of the P&O story, confident of the accuracy of my data. She has given me unsparingly of her time and energy and such merits as this book may have will, to a high degree, reflect her input. I am immensely grateful. Opinions and comments, needless to say, remain my responsibility.

Andrew Best and his wife, Jackie, have been tireless in guiding a tyro through the complexities of first-time publication. I have learned a lot and wish that I had met them both a long time ago.

I thank Helmut Sohmen of World-Wide Shipping for allowing me to quote from his speech given at Lancaster University on 7 September 1980 (page 139) and also those who have helped with a number of the illustrations.

Many others have influenced me and befriended me over the years – I fear too many to be mentioned individually. I hope that the fact that I have had to forgo reference to them will be forgiven and that they will know they are not forgotten.

PART ONE
Early Years 1924–1971

I

Scotland

'Hello, sir!' Captain Mike Bradford greeted me warmly at the naming ceremony of P&O's new *Oriana* in 1995. 'Remember the old *Oriana* in '72?' I did indeed remember her, and the turbulent events of that year and the years that followed.

I had already, somewhat sporadically, been preparing this book. Now I was given a fresh impulse, for my wife, Mona, had just spotted a passage in the brief history of P&O which formed part of the commemorative book produced to mark the *Oriana* occasion:

> The difficulties of running a shipping company towards the end of the 20th century are formidable. They are made worse when the board of that company disagrees about what should be done. In 1972 events were set in motion that led to the resignation of the chairman, Ford Geddes, amid the boos and hisses of shareholders at an EGM.
>
> The events of 1972 were of passionate interest to the City and P&O shareholders. They are virtually incomprehensible to anyone else, but they had two important outcomes. The question of whether the shipping company should diversify – specifically by buying the construction and house-building group, Bovis, came to the fore and the 3rd Earl of Inchcape (grandson of the formidable James Mackay) became chairman of the P&O board.

This repeated the assertion first made in David and Stephen Howarth's book *The Story of P&O*, published in 1987, that the 1960s were 'the revolutionary years in shipping and difficult ones for P&O', yet glossed over the dramatic world events of the 1970s, events beyond the control of companies, even of nations, which threatened the survival of P&O and many similar enterprises. As chief executive of P&O, with Inchcape as my non-executive chairman for most of that period, I submit that the truly revolutionary and difficult years were the 1970s.

I have therefore felt justified, when writing about P&O from the inside, in seeking to make the events of 1972 comprehensible, and in so doing I necessarily go into more detail than a racy narrative would permit. In exploring this detail, I hope I may have done some service not only to those who took part in the hectic times of twenty-five years ago, but to any who may in future take an interest in what was a tumultuous decade for P&O, for British shipping and for the social fabric of Britain; a period during which the basis for much of P&O's future development was established and in which I had a guiding hand.

I want to say immediately that while a good deal of my story takes place in a business world where shipping predominates, this book is not a business history. It is about people – myself and others; how we challenge one another, how we respond, how we judge and how we deal. Yet given that business is about people, my story may be found to have relevance to the business world of today – to those who are active in it and to those who aspire to it.

George Mallory, lost on Everest in 1924, the year of my birth, said: 'The greatest danger in life is not taking the adventure.' It is because I had the confidence, based on stability and love throughout my life, that I had the courage, when challenges came, to take the adventure.

My father, David, was born in 1884, son of an Edinburgh lawyer who died young, leaving a widow and five children of whom my father, at fourteen, was the eldest. With his loss it was a struggle for my grandmother to make ends meet. The first priority was Father's education and the family stayed in Edinburgh until he completed his schooling at George Watsons, moving out to Dollar when he went up to Edinburgh University. At the turn of the century, his life was that of the typical Scottish student – walking miles on a Sunday night to catch the Edinburgh train, 'a bag of meal and an attic room' for the week and then home to help keep the family together.

Once qualified, he became a solicitor and notary public in Dunfermline. Having proved his worth he was soon associated with his uncle, Thomas Shaw, who was to become Lord Advocate and later, as 1st Baron Craigmyle, a Lord of Appeal at Westminster. During the First World War, Father served with the Fife and Forfar Yeomanry. They skirmished with the 'fuzzy-wuzzies' in the Sudan and then, dismounted, formed the Machine Gun Corps at Gallipoli, where he won the Military Cross and had his hearing severely damaged by gun blast. They remounted for Allenby's rapid advance through Palestine to Syria, where my father's war ended.

Ten years younger than Father, my mother, Madge Badenoch, was a daughter of the manse. Her war work was in a munitions factory. She always had a strong arm – a legacy of the heavy machinery the girls handled, and she never forgot her head being pinned against a wall by the foreman while he hoicked a metal splinter from her eye with his penknife.

My parents married in 1921, and had three children: James, eighteen months older than me, myself, born 31 December 1924, and Edith, three years younger. Our home, No. 9 Transy Place, Dunfermline, was newly built of stone and seemed designed for cold. So piercing were my memories of the cold that, years later, on my return from India, I gave my parents a large carpet threaded with electric wiring – a hazard by today's standards, but it served them well.

Transy Place provided great scope for the many children who lived there, near the country and close to the sea. David Goodall – my inseparable friend and classmate – and I walked across the park to Canmore primary school, where Miss Veitch from Stornoway taught us Gaelic songs and, if necessary, administered the ultimate punishment – the tawse: no great issue, simply a contribution to good discipline. As we boys grew up we learned to deliver the coup de grâce to a rabbit and gut and hang them in couples. We could spot a running pheasant or a clapped partridge, carry a hare (ungutted) and when father had a bit of rough shooting we were diligent beaters. In summer we learned how to guddle trout and to judge when the spate was good enough for a worm.

Church and Sunday school occupied Sunday mornings. We normally attended the Abbey – Father's affiliation – where he had secured the back pew fitted with a new-fangled hearing aid which he would snap *off* with a barely suppressed 'Nonsense' when the sermon didn't agree with his own straightforward views. Sometimes we were taken to St Columba's, my grandfather's charge, and it was there I met God. The congregation waited, with varying degrees of expectation, as the organ voluntary rolled out and lo, at 11 o'clock, a blue baize door high behind the pulpit opened and a bearded figure clothed in black with crimson facings descended, bible in hand, to greet his flock.

From Father I learned to appreciate the land and to love the freedom of the hills. Later, however short my wartime leave, Father always suggested 'a run up to the hills' to the Ochils above Kinross or up the Dunning Glen. We'd talk a little about the war and about mother keeping us all in contact. A long look out over the hills and father would say, with a gulp and a little abruptly: 'Drink it all in laddie, and hang on to it. It'll help to keep things in perspective.'

Alexander Shaw, Uncle Tom's eldest son, had married Margaret Mackay, daughter of the 1st Earl of Inchcape, and was now chairman of Peninsular and Oriental Steam Navigation Company (P&O). Father was his estate factor as well as his legal adviser. We boys were often taken to their splendid Borders house, Fairnilee, with its extensive gardens, an enormous staff and farms both home and tenanted. They were a kindly if somewhat Olympian family. As the factor's sons we tended to see as much of the head gardener, head gamekeeper, head groom, head chauffeur and the farmers as we did of the owners.

'Uncle' Alexander asked what was being done about our education. Father replied that while Edith would go to St Bride's, Helensburgh, his income simply would not run to anything comparable for us boys, who would attend Dunfermline High School. Soon afterwards he received a cheque for £1,000 (equivalent to about £30,000 today): 'David, this is to help with the boys' education.' And so we went to Glenalmond, one of Scotland's leading public schools. Shaw's act of generosity was very much in the Scottish ethos: education was valued most highly of the disciplines and such provision for a relative less fortunately placed was a fine tradition. It was not patronising; it was patronage. Above all, it afforded opportunity. What the recipient made of it was up to him.

During August 1939, the wireless played a significant part in our lives, and the grown-ups were constantly in conclave. We returned from our summer holiday, spent as usual at a remote sheep farm on the Lammermoors, on the 31st, and I remember the air of tension as we crossed the Forth at Queensferry, and the great grey naval vessels anchored upstream and below the bridge.

I was fourteen when war was declared on 3 September 1939 and I first heard the wail of air-raid sirens. In the early afternoon of 16 October, the Luftwaffe attacked those ships and, to the outrage of the local citizenry, the Forth Bridge itself – the first air-raid against mainland Britain. By the late spring of 1940 we had moved onto a total war footing. At school, blackout regulations were strictly enforced, food was rationed, the younger teachers were called up and domestic staff vanished to work in factories or on the land. At Glenalmond we were keen members of the OTC. With the very real threat of imminent German invasion we constructed tank traps, dug ditches, and buried 45-gallon oil drums in roadside banks. The intention was that, when the drum was detonated by an explosive device lodged behind it, an enemy column, hedged-in on both sides of a narrow road, would be checked by a flood of blazing oil. We also made and stockpiled Molotov cocktails and assiduously practised signals – semaphore, heliograph and rudimentary walkie-talkie.

June brought a dramatic change of circumstance for my sister Edith. Two of our girl cousins attended a Whitby convent school, which had arranged to evacuate to a sister convent in Canada. Would Edith, now happily boarding at St Bride's, join them? Our parents had thirty-six hours to decide, and a heart-wrenching decision it was. The girls boarded *Empress of Bermuda*, sailing in swift convoy for Halifax, while the parents faced the usual agonising wartime wait for news. Then a friend reported that Edith could be seen on British Movietone News, stepping down the gangway in Halifax. At the cinema father caught a glimpse of the waif, but mother was so tense that she missed the brief appearance. Eventually, after many fruitless forays, a private view was held in Lochgelly, an obscure village in Fife, where the operator stilled the reel for a moment and mother was content.

That summer holiday I went to a farm under the Ochils as paid labour. The experience was neither happy nor enlarging, and no doubt my employer begrudged having to make do with a callow youth. I joined the Home Guard, where my initiation at Path of Condie was pure 'Dad's Army'. Keen as mustard, smartly kitted-out, I held open the stout iron gate as the commanding officer drove through to inspect my first parade. I snapped to attention and my right hand sprang up in salute. The gate, no longer restrained, swung away from me, only to be neatly caught by the car's rear bumper. In those days bumpers were welded to the chassis, and an astonished CO arrived in the school yard dragging gate and fencing behind him.

I did not greatly enjoy my schooldays. I struggled academically, having been, unwisely as it turned out, jumped a year. Not until my last year did I make a breakthrough positive enough to be put forward for a scholarship at Worcester College, Oxford. The award eluded me, but I gained a place and went up in the summer term of 1942, aged seventeen and three months.

About a year earlier, family decisions which were to determine my working life had been made. Alexander Shaw, now 2nd Baron Craigmyle, assumed, reasonably, that James, the elder son, would join his father's legal practice and so proposed helping the younger son by ensuring that, when the war was over, he would have a job in India with Mackinnon Mackenzie, managing agents of the British India Steam Navigation Co. Ltd. (BI). With me thus steered towards shipping, Father, distinguished in agricultural law, must have been disappointed when James decided that he wanted to become a chemical engineer. (In fact James returned from the army to take his Llb at Edinburgh and for the next forty-five years developed the firm of J. R. Stevenson & Marshall, solicitors and notary public.) If shipping was to be my career, it seemed sensible to join the navy, and I was accepted as a 'Y' entrant, 'officer material'. The opening in Mackinnons was formalised. My course was set.

There followed an Indian summer at Worcester, declining into winter when I returned home at Christmas 1942, after failing both economics and French – the first exams I had ever flunked. My explanation that I was really just filling in time until old enough for the navy was not received enthusiastically. However, I returned to Oxford confident that I could top up in economics and French and still cultivate my new-found social life. I spoke at the Union and I rowed in the Lent bumps. My group enjoyed the fringe of OUDS, where Kenneth Tynan was making his precocious mark. We held elegant parties and mixed extraordinary drinks; explored the Cotswolds, and sampled as many pubs as possible. But below the surface of the fine, careless rapture ran a solemn undercurrent. The war we were about to enter was becoming a long haul – at times it seemed endless, and it was certain that it would prove a very hard job to finish.

In the spring of 1943 the RAF mounted their 1,000-bomber raids on Germany, targeting the Ruhr, Cologne and Hamburg. One night I was walking back to college through the precinct formed by All Souls, Brasenose and the Clarendon Building, with the dome of the Radcliffe Camera standing proud against a cloudless sky. The moon was full and, in its clear light, stone glinted and window-glass sparkled. The scene was ethereal, bathed in silver and, with no ground light, shrouded in deep, velvety shadows. Suddenly the night was filled with the noise of aircraft. Wave upon wave of bombers were passing across the sky, forming up and heading east. I was appalled by the contrast between contentment in my surroundings and the engines of destruction in the air, whose bombs were about to fall upon some great European city with its own cultural heritage. I sensed a chilling paradox which haunts me still, as does the memory of Oxford by moonlight against a backcloth of total war.

End of term examinations would soon be upon us. Two weeks beforehand, I made a determined, though sadly belated effort to make good. When I found I could absorb no more revision, I went to the cinema three times in two days. The film was *Aloha of the Seven Seas*, starring Betty Grable. I took one girl to the first show, and another to the second. I must have gone for the third time to see Betty Grable.

My friends and I had planned a night in town immediately after the last examination. In one and a half hours I wrote a brilliant essay on the Beveridge Report, the basis for the National Health Service, which the sour invigilator refused to accept until the statutory minimum of two hours had elapsed. I was just in time to catch the London train. The next morning, perhaps more independent and open-minded than before, we departed for our chosen arm of the services, assured of our places at Oxford after the war – whenever that might be.

I was astonished that the examiners failed to appreciate the eloquence of my Beveridge essay or to find its commanding argument thoughtful and perceptive. I was once more 'dipped' in economics, but passed in French. My examination record so far was not distinguished: 'Played five, won two.'

2

Wartime

The summer of 1943 saw Ordinary Seaman Marshall A.B. reporting to HMS *Ganges*, an austere shore training establishment at Ipswich. After six weeks of square-bashing, boat-handling, schoolroom instruction and 'bull', I was posted to the Sea Training Flotilla at Rosyth, where I spent three months in *Corinthian*, originally an Elder's & Fyffe's banana boat, now a training ship for 'Y' entrants.

Corinthian taught me a good deal about living, in some discomfort, at close quarters with others, about discipline, organisation, doing one's best and giving credit to others for doing the same. I recall much chipping and painting. On one occasion Ordinary Seaman Couchman and I found ourselves slung over the stern on staging, instructed to paint the hull with long-handled mops. Every so often we would hear an ominous rumble within the bowels of the ship and a warning from above to 'bear away'. We would push off with feet and mops in the hope of avoiding the discharge from the heads. 'I don't believe I joined the navy in order to paint the rectum of this ship,' said Couchman.

At the end of our course, the lieutenant-commander commented: 'You'll do all right, Marshall, if you can keep that smile on your face. Good luck!'

Next came officers' training – a further three months' 'hard' at HMS *King Alfred*, an erstwhile underground car-park in Hove. We were cadets, sometimes even called 'Gentlemen'. To my delight, and the envy of my contemporaries, I was appointed as a midshipman RNVR first to the Royal Naval College, Greenwich, and then to HMS *Oribi*, a 1941-built Fleet destroyer understood to be with the Home Fleet. Greenwich seemed little more than an entertaining interlude. We dressed for dinner, served by Wrens in the Painted Hall, and were expected to behave like officers. But once at sea, I swiftly came to realise that the history and naval lore we had imbibed there helped us to assume responsibilities hitherto undreamt-of.

I joined *Oribi* at Scapa Flow in March 1944. It was dark when her boat came to pick me up from the depot ship. Suddenly I found myself on her iron-deck amidships, alone and nervous. I saluted the first person I saw, declaring in the proper manner: 'Come aboard to join, please.' 'Not me, matey,' came the reply, 'you'd best get down aft.' Somehow I got down aft, to find myself in a packed wardroom clutching a pint of beer. There was a particularly warm welcome from Stan Jervis, a New Zealand lieutenant. I was his relief and was alarmed to learn that he was the navigator. 'I'm off,' he said. 'You're new out of school, you must know it all – you'll be all right.' Then another voice, which seemed to come from under my drinking elbow: 'I may not look like it, but I am the captain of this vessel.' Not an easy start.

Oribi, sleek, powerful and home to 247 men, functioned with two career officers plus the specialists – the engineer officer, the warrant officer gunner and the doctor – together with reserve officers of whom one was a lieutenant aged twenty-one and five others, sub-lieutenants or midshipmen of nineteen or twenty. No wonder the captain, J. C. A. ('Jesus Christ Almighty') Ingram, DSC, Lieutenant-Commander RN, was feeling the relentless strain of escort duty on the Russian convoys.

Two days after I joined, *Oribi* went north again until, in April, we became part of the D-day preparations. Going south through the Minches, Derek Laughton and I, responsible for the paperwork, catalogued a huge volume of confidential documents, which we assumed to be orders for 'Neptune', the naval side of 'Operation Overlord'. The captain had ordered that only he would open those marked 'Top Secret – Open on One', but we inadvertently broached a package and observed, before appreciating the burden of our knowledge, that the landings were to be in Normandy. What to do? Strictly, we should have reported the error to the captain. But then what would have happened? We said nothing and made the best job we could of re-sealing. When the order came through, JCA had Derek at his elbow and so never knew of the breach of security that had brought us such a heady mixture of anxiety and stimulation.

Between Channel patrols we managed to cram a hectic social life into our weeks at Spithead. At last, at dusk on 5 June, we slipped out through the Needles, moving smoothly past a long line of merchant ships bound for France – a Greek, a Norwegian and an old friend from Russian convoys, the Liberty ship *Elihu C. Root*. We exchanged waves and 'thumbs up' and would not have changed places with any of them.

The successes and losses of the landings and the subsequent weeks of hard slogging and reinforcement have been well chronicled. The navy patrolled and protected the passage of supplies to the beach-head. *Oribi* skirmished with E-boats, was shelled by shore batteries and occasionally attacked by aircraft. It was tense, boring and exciting in equal measure. I was very aware throughout that my brother James, a sapper, had already landed with 242 Field Co., 3 Div., and was in the heart of the fighting. The battles of Normandy reached their climax. The landings in the South of France came in August and the Germans began to withdraw. The temporary 'Mulberry' harbours had done their job on the beaches, and ports like Cherbourg and Le Havre began to feed the advancing allies.

Oribi and the other fleet destroyers returned to escort duty in the Arctic. In addition to the official histories, there are superb descriptions of the Murmansk run in Godfrey Winn's *PQ17* and in books by Alastair MacLean and Nicholas Monsarrat. My memories of individual convoys have blurred over the years, but certain incidents do stand out. During a lull between air attacks south of Bear Island JCA encouraged me to go below to the engineers' domain 'to see how the other half live'. Even after a brief visit to the boiler-room I was mightily relieved to be a deck officer.

Another episode was more dramatic. One forenoon watch, when I was No. 2 to Mac, an Australian 'sub', the Asdic operator's voice came through, cool as ice: 'Torpedo approaching green four-five.' He turned up the speaker and we all heard the unmistakable sound of a torpedo coming straight for us. Mac immediately and coolly ordered: 'Stop starboard, hard a-starboard, half-ahead port.' The alarm bells shrilled as *Oribi*'s head came round slowly, so very slowly. A lookout saw the tell-tale stream of bubbles approaching. The whole ship seemed to hold its breath as the torpedo passed beneath the hull. The Admiralty had warned that the Germans had introduced an acoustic torpedo which homed on the cavitation noise of the target's propellers. To counteract this device, a complex zigzag pattern was recommended, with speed under five knots, at a noise-level too low to attract the torpedo, then a change of course at a speed above 11 knots in the hope that the torpedo could not catch up. But there was precious little sea room close in to the convoy, so Mac could only reduce noise by stopping the starboard screw while simultaneously doing his best, with such power on the port screw as he could risk, to point *Oribi* on to the line of the torpedo's approach, thus reducing the size of the target. The captain of the U-boat, which we at once counter-attacked with depth-charges, had probably, with only a periscope's glimpse, mistaken us for a larger ship and set his torpedo too deep. Mac told me later that he spent the long watches rehearsing 'What if?' contingencies – a most valuable lesson.

On one convoy, we carried a group of Norwegian commandos, led by Captain Röhrholt, a much-decorated officer, whose mission was to enter occupied Norway from the Russian front west of Murmansk. They would aid the resistance fighters and also, I assume, ensure that a Norwegian military presence was established on home soil by the time the war ended.

Murmansk (in Russian, 'edge of the earth') is ice-free all year, but otherwise has nothing to commend it. The destroyers were berthed at Polyarnoe, which is even drearier. There we delivered our passengers to *Nairana*, the convoy's aircraft carrier, which had provided some reassurance on our passage. Röhrholt made a felicitous and moving farewell speech. The end of Norway's four and a half years of occupation was in sight, and he paid tribute to Britain's lone stand during the dark months of 1941, telling a story of the Blitz. He had found himself crouching in an air-raid shelter in Bayswater. During a series of shattering explosions an elderly lady next to him calmly continued her knitting. As he cringed, she remarked: 'Young man, I've often wondered how many pigeons there are in London. They must be countless, but d'you know, in all my many years, not one of them has hit me.' Röhrholt's expedition was a success, and he has had a distinguished post-war career. He may not remember a young midshipman on convoy JW62 in 1944, but he made a considerable impression on me.

We tried to make the best of grim, cold Polyarnoe. *Oribi*'s band, myself on the bagpipes supported by two drummers, played as we approached our berth and again as we left. Just before the snow fell, a sports day brought forth tug-of-war teams of enormous weight and strength from the destroyers alongside, while three-legged races mightily amused the Russian spectators. Russian submarines also lay at Polyarnoe and *Oribi* had struck up a relationship with one of these over a number of visits. The customary invitation came to join the submariners for a *prasnik* – nothing less than a monumental drinking bout. JCA led the *Oribi* team, which included Jack Wilson and me, both newcomers to this formidable version of Russian hospitality. Verbal communication was limited, but there was much laughter and, as toasts became more and more frequent, many displays of brotherly love. I was poured back on board *Oribi*, where I passed the next twenty-four hours in an unpleasant haze. To my surprise *Oribi* was the 'victor' and a plaque from the submarine's wardroom was duly delivered with their compliments. We had won thanks to the canniness of JCA and Disney Vaughan Hughes, our first lieutenant, who contrived to spill much of the vodka down their shirts and so, soaked to their socks, were among the last to remain more or less upright.

After two Russian convoys in swift succession, *Oribi* was despatched to the Clyde shortly before Christmas 1944 for escort duty with the big troopships operating across the Atlantic – 'monster running' in naval jargon. *Queen Mary, Queen Elizabeth, Île de France, Aquitania*, the Polish *Batory*, the Dutch *Nieuw Amsterdam* – the great luxury liners of their day – made the deep-sea crossing independently at full speed, but in the approaches to the Clyde they were vulnerable to lurking U-boats, so destroyers met them inwards off Northern Ireland and escorted them outwards to the same area. As we could not operate Asdic at the high speeds demanded, our role was to boost morale and to effect rescue if required.

We must have looked impressive steaming at over 30 knots with bright bow-wave and surging wake, but it was tense, nervous and uncomfortable because the sea, apparently calm from the lofty deck of a vast liner, was always bumpy for a destroyer. The US-bound monster, after passing Ailsa Craig and turning west past Rathlin Island, would work up speed and commence a zigzag pattern designated by flag and not decided until the last minute. Thereafter we were glued to the stop-watch. After ten minutes, a 20-degree turn to starboard meant that the port escort had to steam even faster to maintain position, then five minutes later the alteration could be 10 degrees to port, 10 degrees more to starboard or a nasty 30 degrees back to port. There was constant anxiety on the bridge – had we read the right pattern, had the monster followed it, were her officers concentrating? We never forgot that, in 1943, in just these circumstances, *Queen Mary* had run down the cruiser *Curaçao*. *Curaçao* was literally sliced in half, with the loss of several hundred men. *Queen Mary*, with some 20,000 troops on board, had no option but to plough on.

VE day, 8 May 1945, found *Oribi* approaching Scapa Flow after a refit at Hull. We were anticipating a low-key end to our war when orders came to join convoy JW67, for Archangel, as close escort. Then, off Iceland, we were instructed to detach and to proceed at full speed to join the cruiser *Diadem* off the Firth of Forth 'for orders'. Only when we were threading our way in line ahead across the North Sea were we told that we were bound for Copenhagen.

The weather was kind and peace within our grasp and the 'pusser' navy was resurrected. We painted ship from truck to deck – officers and ratings together. Camouflage was banished and *Oribi* was newly clad in light grey, while flotilla bands appeared on the funnel for the first time. The iron-deck amidships was stripped and polished with blacklead; the muzzles of the guns burnished; and tampions, bearing *Oribi*'s crest, were resurrected and put in place. Brasswork, hidden under dull paint since commissioning, was revealed and polished. Below deck, sailors tarted-up their 'tiddly' suits for what promised to be the run ashore of a lifetime.

At dusk on 11 May, we picked up our Swedish pilot at Paternoster buoy in the Skagerrak – the sea was glassy, the sky golden. We followed *Diadem* south through the channel, continuously swept for mines by the Swedish navy. During the first watch from 2000 to midnight I felt intensely the novel experience of peace, a feeling heightened when Jack Wilson, who had the middle watch, summoned me to the bridge, just before 0400, to share a magic dawn moment. Approaching the narrows of Elsinore, Hamlet's castle was floating like a mirage between sea and sky. It seemed natural that Jack, who was to succeed his father as Lord Moran and pursue a distinguished career in the foreign service, should call for the quartermaster to pipe as he and I saluted the Prince of Denmark and his father's ghost.

In Copenhagen we saw the dawn rise on fourteen consecutive mornings. Wonderful, wonderful! But it was not all liberation parties. Jack Wilson, Wilfred Beckerman – a new sub-lieutenant and now an Oxford academic – and I each had a particularly nerve-wracking assignment. A powerful German naval force, including *Prinz Eugen*, *Gneisenau* and *Nuremberg* (two battle cruisers and a heavy cruiser), lay captive in the Fryhavn, a series of docks which had been Copenhagen's free-port. This force had acceded in the formal surrender, but the Allies would not be able to effect its disarmament until an escort arrived in a few days' time to accompany the ships to Rosyth. Meanwhile there they lay with full complements, fully-armed and flying the Nazi ensign. *Oribi* was ordered to mount night-time security patrols through the Fryhavn.

My turn came first. I put on my boots and a pair of polished black leather gaiters borrowed from Gunner Windebank. My belt carried a revolver and a whistle. My squad, under Petty Officer Dine, was armed with .303 army rifles and bayonets. Naval boots are leather-soled, but have no steel studs, so I instructed the squad that we should plant our feet flatly and firmly, keep our eyes front and present a resolute appearance. Before we set off, bayonets were fixed – a show of bravado, perhaps? The presence of last week's enemy was overwhelming. The massive flanks of the German ships towered above us, throbbing and humming. The vessels were brightly-lit, and their crews were much in evidence. Leading my fifteen men I felt distinctly vulnerable, but it went off without a hitch. We marched all the way in and all the way out and, when it was over, one three-badge able seaman said: 'I saw more of the bloody Hun in half a watch than I've seen in six years, and I'm glad it happened this way!'

Oribi's next job, after a routine fortnight at Scapa, was as guard-ship at Travemünde, a Baltic port in north-west Germany, and a key position at the mouth of the River Trave, already agreed as the northernmost point on the line of demarcation between East and West – the future Iron Curtain.

A swift run across the North Sea was followed by a cautious passage through the Kiel Canal, undamaged, lined with prosperous-looking farms and villages, where storks nested on the red rooftops. Kiel itself was a different story. The naval base had been pounded, U-boat shelters blown apart, ships sunk in the roads. Most of the town was a heap of rubble, but the yacht club, where a bottle of champagne could be had for one Occupation mark – sixpence – had survived. Through the Baltic we hugged the coast. Navigational aids were few, there was much ignorance of German minefields and – even more hazardous – of mines scattered by the USAAF and the RAF.

It was a relief when *Oribi* moored at a jetty on Travemünde's main street. Travemünde was then a peaceful little resort with a nineteenth-century Spielhaus overlooking a long, broad beach and some shipbuilding activity on the east bank. Our role was to emphasise that, thanks to the rapid advance of 21st Army Group achieved by General Montgomery, the Trave's west bank was firmly in British hands. *Oribi*'s guns were trained eastwards.

Before the Russians arrived, the RAF Regiment was busy clearing Luftwaffe airfields east of Lübeck to ensure that nothing of importance remained. We tried to help and happily removed silk parachutes which could be transformed back home into dresses, nightgowns and shirts. I took possession of a barograph and a pair of binoculars, which are still in use.

Guard-ship duty might have been exposed and lonely had it not been for the presence of the 2nd Battalion, Argyll and Sutherland Highlanders (51st Highland Division) and a squadron of RAF Typhoons – the tankbusters – in nearby Lübeck. We were forces of occupation, ordered to keep aloof – strictly no fraternisation. But there were limits. One evening we were guests for drinks – Russian plum brandy – at the Argylls' mess. We sat on a terrace overlooking a cornfield, watching the sun go down. Suddenly one of the officers bellowed: 'Stand up that man!' Less suddenly, a number of soldiers rose up from the corn like so many dishevelled scarecrows, struggling to pull up their trousers as they came to attention. A moment's pause, then the officer barked: 'Very well, carry on', and turning to us said, 'It's difficult to enforce an order that is not understood.'

Our first encounter with the Typhoon pilots was on land, when they tried to cut out the French and Belgian girls who were part of a United Nations Relief and Rehabilitation (UNRRA) team, billeted at *our* Spielhaus. Fended off, they astutely recognised that we were only short-term visitors and invited us to their next 'thrash'. The second encounter came from the air. *Oribi* was moving up-river to Lübeck with a German pilot on board to navigate us through the Trave's narrow and winding upper reaches. Suddenly, there came a deafening roar as four Typhoons screamed low over us, it seemed beneath our aerials. Theirs was a spectacular display of close-order flying, but I had the uncomfortable feeling that these boys might have forgotten that the war in Europe was over. They had a reputation for beating up anything that moved.

The wardroom decided that it needed transport, and by deploying the argument that it was important we be self-sufficient, contrived to liberate four motor-cars to which we gave our own distinctive RN numbers. This fleet included a classic Mercedes tourer and a Horsch straight-eight. Shortly afterwards Montgomery ordered that looting of German vehicles must cease. But surely his order applied only to the army, and, in any case, we were just borrowing the cars.

We drove into Hamburg on roads of beaten dirt, flanked by

mounds of rubble. There was not a timber beam, not a pane of glass, not a fragment of cloth. All was crumbled mortar, shattered brick and splintered stone, the silence broken only by an intermittent, sighing wind, which whipped up clouds of dirt. Occasionally a ragged figure would appear, but there was never a human voice. At what may have been a crossroads a makeshift notice-board carried messages and appeals seeking news of the missing. In contrast, the Atlantic Hotel had emerged relatively unscathed and provided a comfortable officers' club. From its steps I witnessed the march past of the massed pipes and drums of the 51st Division – very much a victory parade.

To have use of a car – begged, borrowed or looted – was the key to an active social life, much of which we spent with the delightful UNRRA girls, who were always ready for a party and laughter when off duty, especially as they were doing such a demanding and harrowing job. In turn, they offered us a visit to Lübeck's hospital, where the first survivors from Belsen were being processed for onward evacuation to Sweden which was receiving them for rehabilitation. There were three categories: those who would survive; those who might survive; and those who would die. To visit the third was profoundly shocking. Lying in wards or cubicles they were skeletal. A British doctor preceded us into one room: 'Too late; he's dead.' In another he told us that when the medical staff tried to give nourishment intravenously a number of the patients simply seemed to give up. The doctors came to the horrified conclusion that this had been a reaction of fear following so many Nazi medical experiments involving needles.

We were taken below to the morgue. I was on the point of walking out, I must admit with some relief, because it seemed empty, but when the doctor threw aside what I thought was merely a crumpled sheet, there lay a jumble of skin and bones. For a twenty-year-old with no concept of the nightmare world of the death camps, to come face to face with the evidence of such inhumanity was mentally and physically sickening.

Perhaps even more disturbing was our meeting with some of the survivor group. As we entered the dormitory there was an eerie silence followed by an audible rustle of fear. 'Speak quickly, English, anything,' urged the doctor. 'In your dark uniforms, peaked caps, they think you are the Germans come back.' They did not trust any statement or any person; food, scrounged from any source, would be hidden away against future need; head down, low profile remained the order of their day.

Determined to complete our education, the UNRRA team sent us north to one of the smaller concentration camps which had not yet been evacuated. The gates were open and food was being distributed, but the inmates were still in their pyjama-like uniforms, haggard, vacant-eyed, shuffling; the ground slopping with mud, rows of wooden huts, figures slumped in the shadows. There was an almost tangible feeling of brutishness, and the UNRRA girls and the doctors were near to despair in trying to come to terms with their task. We had come through the war and for us the dying was almost done, but it was nigh impossible to believe that the prisoners' war, their private hell, would ever be over.

The evil of the concentration camps and their tragic aftermath taught us the shadow side of victory; we tended to live 'on the edge' and off duty parties were wild. After one such at the Typhoon airfield, 'Doc' Francis Blacklay was driving a group of us back to *Oribi* in the Horsch. He sped straight across a T-junction into the woods beyond, whooping with delight as he zigzagged through the trees. That night we had relived our war and won it over and over again, and for a brief moment had become invulnerable.

Having made her point at the Baltic boundary between East and West, *Oribi* picked her way back to Kiel. Off Fehmarn Island we saw further evidence of the shadow side, a capsized German ship. On passage from the east early in 1945, carrying wounded troops and, it was said, several thousand civilians fleeing the advancing Soviet forces, she had struck a mine, whether an 'own goal' or an RAF-sown mine was not known. There had been no attempt at salvage and the upturned hull was the grave of the many who had been trapped below deck. It was a relief to pass through the tranquil Kiel Canal again and head home.

A brief visit to Scapa was to be our last – the base was being run down and ships moved out. Stores marked '*Oribi* – BFP (British Fleet Pacific)' were delivered. However, orders for the Far East never came; instead, *Oribi* went back to the Clyde. We left Scapa with feelings of unexpected nostalgia – after so much foul weather, the muck and mud ashore, the cold and wet, our last memories were of pearly watered-silk skies, clear, clean air and turquoise sea. Happy summer weeks at Greenock ended with the news of the Hiroshima bomb on 6 August, then of Nagasaki on the 10th. Soon Attlee

declared VJ day. It was the signal for the lights to go on all over
the anchorage and along the shoreline, for sirens and whistles to
be whooped and screeched. Amid the cacophony, I went ashore
with my bagpipes, standing on the canopy of *Oribi*'s motor-boat.
We managed to collect our Wren girlfriends, and many more, for
celebrations which progressed during the night from ship to shore. I
recall sitting on the pavement with one of the girls as the sun
rose, quite convinced a new world was dawning. But the immediate
prospect was of parting. We were ordered to Portsmouth for refit.
Oribi had been sold to Turkey.

Our efficient, confident and happy ship's company would be
broken up. For three months *Oribi* lay in Pompey dockyard, like so
much scrap iron, with only a care-and-maintenance nucleus retained.
Now renamed *Gayret*, the heads were adapted for Muslim use and,
ironically, a modern anti-aircraft gun was fitted and new, rapid-fire
pom-poms installed.

At the end of the year, I too left. I was sorry to go twice over,
because of Dawn O'Kelly – a Wren, eighteen years old, dark-haired
and very pretty. To begin with, ours was a gentle, tentative relationship. I was entranced by her quiet reserve, so often lit up by an Irish
twinkle. She was straight from convent school, and we both trod
warily. Dawn drove a 15-cwt truck named 'Mona' for the Maltese
steward at C-in-C's residence. While shopping for him was said to
be a full-time job, we contrived to see an increasing amount of each
other, sometimes simply for coffee in between runs, more often,
as was the practice in those days, at the cinema. 'Lights out' at
the Wrennery dictated relatively early nights and it was some time
before Dawn was able to negotiate the benefit of a blind eye with her
Leading Wren. I was later to meet that L/W – authoritative, remote –
in Calcutta, where she (Bridget) was married to a friend in Macneills; we laughed when we recalled our naiveté.

Early in 1946 I was appointed to *Cygnet*, a Bird class sloop attached to *Dryad*, the Navigation School at Portsmouth. It was a
boring job, alleviated by predictable hours and the ability to plan
one's social life. Things improved when I negotiated a transfer to
Blyth, an uncomfortable little minesweeper in which I spent little
time. There was a lot of freedom and shore leave and, with Sam
Brooks the first lieutenant, I volunteered to sail reparation (looted)
German yachts back to England.

My sailing experience was, to say the least, limited, but I learned on the job and through the summer I crewed 50 and 100 sq. metre yachts from Kiel to Portsmouth. Exhilarating trips perhaps, but prolonged discomfort in bad weather convinced me that I had no wish to be an ocean racer. On one trip we rendezvoused with *Blyth* somewhere off the south coast, and for months our wardroom parties were enhanced by champagne of undisclosed origin. While at Portsmouth, we raced the 50s and made picnic crossings to the Isle of Wight. Dawn and I discovered the South Downs and the warm villages of Sussex – it was a sybaritic summer.

Suddenly the demob machine began to accelerate and it seemed that my number would be called before the end of 1946. I made an appeal to be brought forward by a few weeks so that I could go up to Oxford for the beginning of the Michaelmas term. With two days' notice, I found myself being processed on 4 October. From officer, to number, to civilian, it was strangely impersonal after three and a half years of total commitment. The most important part of the exercise was the selection of one's demob suit and overcoat. I was relatively conservative, and the raglan overcoat lasted for years, eventually finishing up on my brother-in-law's back in the South African bush.

Another parting and little time to plan how Dawn and I would arrange to see each other as much as we both wanted. I dashed north to see my parents – Edith was now at the Rachel Macmillan college in London and James was in Palestine. Having been 'in' for two years longer than me, his number was still some way off, for the army was much slower than the navy in winding down.

October 1946 saw me back at Worcester. Post-war Oxford was a strange place. The undergraduates who had gone straight into the services from school might now be twenty-five- or twenty-six-year-olds; and there were fewer nineteen-year-olds than normal. But it was the returnees like me, who had come up to complete courses started some years earlier, who lent a special character to Oxford. We had seen the pity and the waste of war, and bore the badge of victory. Now it was time to get on, first with securing our degrees and then with our peacetime careers. It was essentially work and not much play – more a comfortable settling back round the fire in Drake's Buttery and a realisation that one was so very fortunate to be there again. I was fortunate also to know that I had employment waiting for me in India.

Among those who were up again were others from my first year

– Derrick Atkinson, back from his armoured cars, Micky Palmer from his guns, John Whiskard from the navy, and Sandy Cameron from the marines. Cousins also were back, Sandy Badenoch, another ex-marine, was at Magdalen and Donald Shaw, now 3rd Baron Craigmyle, at Trinity. By extraordinary coincidence, Derek Laughton and Tim Ellis, both from *Oribi*, were up at Worcester.

My weekly history tutorial was with Asa Briggs, a newly-appointed fellow of the college, and one of whom I was in considerable awe. Only years later, when as Provost of Worcester he chose to tutor my daughter Gillian, did I realise that this towering figure of youthful memory is only three years older than I.

At Christmas 1946 I went north on my own, as Dawn, still in Portsmouth, could not get leave. It was a special reunion. James was home from Palestine and Edith was up from London. In all, there were twenty-three of us, boys and girls, who had spent the war in the services, nursing or working on the land. Three friends were missing. All had been Fleet Air Arm pilots, one of them my childhood companion David Goodall, whose absence was as real as a presence. For three weeks we got together every evening. Parties were given by each family, there were more formal gatherings, and we danced reels in a variety of village halls. Our festivities were warm and happy rather than riotous.

The winter of 1946–7 was arctic. Throughout the Lent term the quad at Worcester was ice-bound, the lake lay under twelve inches of ice and snow fell on snow. Derek Laughton and I, who shared rooms, were allowed one bucket of coal a week, and electric power was limited. I developed a survival regime. Up at 6 a.m., I dressed in almost all the clothes I had and, most important, in balaclava helmet, scarf and my demob overcoat. I placed an electric ring under the kneehole desk between my legs and sat with a rug draped around the chair to keep heat in and draughts out. I worked until 8 a.m. when the power went off. Breakfast in hall was porridge, so-called coffee, bread and, once a week, an egg. The loos were in the basement under staircase 7 and the cold was so severe one frequently just missed out on that part of one's routine. Then off as quickly as possible to the Radcliffe Camera, which was heated to an almost tolerable temperature. There may not have been a seat at a table, but it was essential to be there in time to secure at least a perch on the stairs.

A game of squash in the afternoon kept the circulation going, and occasionally there was hot water for a shower. In the evening we might huddle round our electric ring, or find someone who was using his coal ration, or attempt to work in the college library (a facility not readily granted by Dean Wilkinson) and after dinner perhaps a cinema, where body rather than artificial heat prevailed.

All things considered, it rather surprised me that I was able to add a fourth section to the pass I had achieved in the Michaelmas term, for there had to be a compromise in the interests of completing the course in two terms. In the end I believe I got a wartime degree in history rather than the PPE on which I had embarked in 1942. The actual qualification does not appear to have been of much importance in later life, but the relative rigour of mental discipline, the need to question rather than assume, and the self-confidence which Oxford life affords are invaluable assets. I have never ceased to recognise the privilege of having been up, if only as a wartime undergraduate.

The Worcester College Commem. ball was revived that summer and provided the opportunity for an *Oribi* reunion with Derek Laughton and his sister, Tim Ellis and Diana, myself and Dawn. It was an occasion the like of which none of us had ever experienced. I went up to the Charing Cross Road to hire my first evening tails, but they fitted so well that I purchased them there and then for £11 and they are still in use today. We had a base in our old rooms on the terraces, and held open house for a host of friends. At daybreak we took punts from Magdalen Bridge. Derek managed to fall in – fully rigged in white tie and tails; by June 1947, Oxford had resumed normal service.

3
India

The last six months of 1947 helped to bridge the gulf between the past and the future. In some ways they were an astonishing comedown after officer status in the navy, but then that had been a wartime aberration.

My business life began at 122, Leadenhall Street, the London headquarters of P&O and British India and the offices of Gray Dawes & Co. In India my employers, Mackinnon Mackenzie, were managing agents of BI and agents for P&O. In London P&O handled its own ships, while BI used Gray Dawes as agents. Both Mackinnons and Gray Dawes were largely owned by Inchcape family interests and, until his death in 1932, the 1st Earl of Inchcape was chairman of both P&O and BI. To outsiders it seemed a complex relationship – as indeed it was (see page 296).

Routine shipping work – customs entry, bills of lading, accounts – was dealt with on the ground floor. Above the noise and bustle was the quiet, exclusive world of the rulers of this great shipping empire – the P&O chairman and managing directors and the 'partners', the owners of Gray Dawes, most of whom had served in the Inchcape companies in the east. Young men like me awaiting dispatch to India occupied a kind of limbo in between. We were expected to work like clerks and behave like crown princes.

After an unpleasant fortnight in digs in Earls Court, I moved out of London to lodgings in Woldingham, high on the North Downs, where, apart from my thirteen India years, I have lived ever since. My salary was £4.18.6d per week plus 6d per day luncheon vouchers. My weekly expenditure of three guineas on bed, board and laundry and £2.10s on train fares left me drawing on my modest demob bonus to make ends meet, but I relished the fresh mornings as I sprinted to the station to catch the steam train to London Bridge.

In the autumn, I embarked at Liverpool in *Empire Brent*, an ex-Nordeutscher Lloyd troopship operated by P&O as a civilian transport on the Indian run. The passenger list was typical of its time:

koi hais returning to Calcutta, tea planters bound for Ceylon, Assam
and the Nilgiris, and bankers for Bombay. A number of chokras like
me were off to their first jobs with Burmah-Shell, ICI, Lever Bros,
James Finlay . . . the range of British companies was vast.

Dawn had spent most weekends with me at Woldingham during
that golden summer and we had become very close. But Mackinnons
assistants on their first tour were not permitted to marry and she and
I faced the traditional parting, intense and filled with pledges of
commitment. But we cannot have been ready for the final step. After
she met Charlie, I received the classic 'Dear John' letter. But her
words – 'You first taught me what love is' – remained for years as a
warm reminder of those days.

The voyage to Bombay via Suez, Aden and Colombo took twenty-
seven days. Once into the Red Sea, we would leave our double-
tiered, six-berth cabin above the boiler-room to sleep on deck and in
the heat of the day to cool off under a salt-water hose. We grumbled
a little but, after six years of war, were no strangers to discomfort.
When *Empire Brent* called at Colombo I first recognised Mackinnons
authority and prestige. Stanley Osborne, in charge of the office
there, paid his respects to the captain and then took time out to give
me a whirlwind tour. At least I saw the golden beach and swaying
palms of Mount Lavinia in its heyday.

Sadly there was not time (and I was probably too shy to insist) to
visit the Commonwealth Cemetery in Colombo. I sought it out
years later to find the headstone: 'David Goodall, Sub-Lieutenant
(A) RNVR, 1925–45, Killed on Active Service'. His DC3 had shied
into a narrow lane of palm trees as a thunder-squall struck on its
final approach. All thirty-six on board were killed, mostly Wrens. I
wrote to his mother, who had no prospect of visiting, that it was a
remarkably warm, scented, calm place and he was in good company.

In Bombay I was 'processed' down the line from the Mackinnons
partners to the Goanese travel clerk, who guided me to my compart-
ment on the Calcutta Mail – one of the great trains of India. The
journey was thirty-six hours of heat and dust, and of impressions
that endure for a lifetime. The comforting noise of the steam train in
motion, the clamour of the stations, and, after a meal in the station
restaurant, the charwallah running beside the carriage dispensing
tea. The full moon over the plain; blue hills on the horizon; sandy
river beds bereft of water in the dry season; a solitary camel, a line
of women carrying lotis of water and bundles of firewood, paddy

fields and mango trees; the evening scent of dung fires and the flicker of the chula; the warm, soft, musty smell of morning and the rising sun a ball of red flame in the sky.

Some hours behind schedule, we pulled into Howrah Station. It was bedlam as hordes of coolies fought to lay hands on any piece of baggage. To my relief a travel babu emerged from the chaos, identified me and calmly assembled my gear: tin trunk, kitbag, picnic basket and bagpipes. He led a file of porters to a waiting car and advised me that we were on our way to the house of Mackinnons senior partner, L. P. S. Bourne, where I would stay for a few days.

On arrival at a brightly-lit No. 3, Alipore Road, I was dismayed to be faced by an army of servants and the sounds of a party. It was 10 o'clock at night; fortunately dinner was over. My host, Bill Bourne, greeted me: 'You'd best have a quick wash and then a bite to eat in the morning room.' I was black from head to foot so it was indeed a quick wash – as far as possible above my cuffs and below my collar. As I ate I was joined by the burra sahib. 'Rrmphh, d'ye play tennis?' 'Not well, sir, just as a kid really.' 'Rrmphh, d'ye play golf?' 'As boys we all played a bit, but not well.' 'Rrrmphhhh, d'ye ride?' 'Well, we used to have a pony – I was not much good.' 'Good God, what do ye do?' It was not a very auspicious start. But I was reminded of my introduction to *Oribi*, and cheered up at the thought of how well that had turned out.

I did three tours in India, all at Mackinnons Calcutta headquarters. The first lasted four and a half years, the second three years, and my final spell was two and a half years. In between were long leaves – nine months in the first case, then six months – to which was added a year's secondment to one of the Group companies in London.

Subject to the demands of the job, we could take a month's local leave each year. But even when air travel became possible I recall only one of us having the financial resources to visit the UK. We bachelors tended to save little of our salaries. In any case the reward pattern in those days could be called 'back-end loaded'; only the most senior people enjoyed high earnings.

By the end of 1947, India had been independent for just three months and in Calcutta, the second city of the Empire, the privileged lifestyle of the Raj was slow to disappear. Although I came later to realise the artificiality of many aspects of that life, and was not unhappy to come home, I thoroughly enjoyed my India years.

I shared a chummery at 10, Lord Sinha Road with three other new

assistants. The spacious house had a large garden, bright with can-
nas, marigolds and garish zinnias, and carnations for our button-
holes. We each had our personal bearer and shared a staff of cooks,
gardeners and sweepers. Sometimes one or two of us would house-
sit in Alipore Road when the burra sahib was on leave. Luxurious
maybe, but it brought frustrating responsibility. There were twenty-
one servants in that compound. Like 'request men' in the navy, the
morning could bring forth a delegation: a dispute over water between the cook and the dhobi; a complaint about the bearer's wife.

Sport occupied a large part of the weekends and the frequent
religious festivals. I rowed on Dhakuria lake. I played hockey on the
left wing, much to my alarm when a turbaned Sikh stormed down
bouncing the ball on his stick (not yet disallowed). I turned out for
Mackinnons soccer team. There was rugby and cricket, and every-
body played tennis. It was from the grass courts of Lord Sinha Road
that a swift romance took us into the international press. Tony
Davenport, a member of the chummery and a competent tennis
player, was asked to provide practice for Gussie Moran and Pat
Todd, Americans on a ladies tour. He and Gussie played well together; I 'looked after' her colleague and, to the great excitement of
the *Daily Mirror*, 'Gorgeous Gussie', of frilly pants fame, and Tony
announced their engagement. Sadly the commitment did not survive
the demands of the professional circuit.

My good friend Tony Murray and I jointly owned horses, first
Duke and then Rob Roy. We rode either on the Maidan or the
racecourse every day and on holiday mornings there was little to
compare with meeting horse and syce at the ten-mile mark on the
Gariahat road. In the cold weather there would be a paper chase
across country – paddy fields, mud walls, ditches, between bamboo
clumps and under peepul trees – followed by a picnic breakfast,
well-earned, at least by those who had remained in the saddle.

Golf at Tollygunge was a Sunday fixture for years. Mike Vlasto,
Tony Trevor, Tony Dalton and I would tee off at 9.08 a.m.; none of
us was much good, but we made an impressive sight as we marched
down the fairway – four sahibs, four caddies, four boys with as-
sorted dogs, and two age-wallahs to spot the fall of shot.

From late October, after the monsoon, until February social life
was at its peak. 'Visiting firemen' from the UK prompted a round of
drinks parties, invariably followed by nightspots ranging from the
300 Club, through the Park Street bars, to the less salubrious haunts

of Dahrumtulla Street and Acre Lane. It was the season, too, for numbers of girls to visit from home – the fishing fleet as it was traditionally known; competition was fierce.

I was launched into that world soon after I arrived with an invitation to Calcutta's Burns supper in January 1948. At 22, Camac Street Hammy Shedden, No. 1 of Macneills, presided over a large party where the haggis took second place to the whisky. Towards the end of a long evening I found myself standing next to a fellow guest in the splendid marble cloakroom. He had celebrated well, but I was surprised to find him in sombre mood as he leaned towards me: 'Laddie, ye'll have heard that Gandhi has been shot dead. Let me tell ye that they Indians are at this very minute at the gates o' Camac Street waitin' for us. They ken we're here and they think we're celebratin' the death o' the Mahatma.' We dispersed quickly and quietly. There was no demonstration outside, the streets were eerily deserted – a most unusual situation. It was not then known who the assassin was – Muslim or Hindu or Sikh – but the likelihood of violent repercussions hung in the air. Since severe communal troubles in 1946, the tension in Calcutta, whose population was almost 50% Muslim, had been palpable. The assassination was, however, so shocking that, to our immense relief, it was met with a stunned silence and the nation seemed united in mourning.

But over the years we were alert for trouble. We might be gheraoed – imprisoned in the office by staff squatting outside the door or even, inside, on one's desk. We shuddered at an appalling incident at Jessop's steel plant where a mob savaged three Europeans and stuffed them into the furnaces. Yet despite these and other disturbances, my memories are not of violence or threat, more of a vanishing way of life.

The job of a Mackinnons assistant played a great part in one's appreciation of life in Calcutta. In the head office at No. 16, Strand Road, three or four partners had reached the top. Approaching retirement from India aged fifty-five, they were by now wealthy and looking forward to continuing involvement at one of the London offices, or perhaps to a large house in the English countryside, even a castle in Scotland. Thirty covenanted assistants, almost all British and many of us Scots, provided the key management. A very few Indian assistants were covenanted – Oxbridge to a man. A degree was not considered necessary, even I suspect desirable, for us Europeans. I was one of a handful of graduates. Under a layer of locally-engaged managers, mostly Anglo-Indian, were several hundred babus, the eponymous Bengali clerks, meticulous, bureaucratic, rigid, but each knowledge-able within his defined field.

As it had been for a hundred years, the newly-arrived assistant, however wet behind the ears, was quickly in a departmental role relying greatly on his clerical staff, but knowing that decisions and responsibility were his – a classic case of sink or swim. Starting in the Asian crew department, I moved on to the Rangoon Mail, steamers carrying up to 2,000 deck (unberthed) passengers, cargo, livestock and the Royal Mail thrice weekly from Calcutta to Burma. I was attached to the department which managed coal mines in Bihar. I learned something of the jute mills on the Hooghly, of tea gardens in Assam and the engineering works at Garden Reach. After this in-doctrination, I became No. 2 to W. J. Campbell on the Australian Desk, responsible for twenty-five ships trading from India and the Persian Gulf to Australia and New Zealand. More exotic was my additional responsibility for the Nourse Line ships which loaded each month for Caribbean islands. When James Nourse, a sailing ship master from St Ives, pioneered the route in the nineteenth century it was the coolie trade – Indian indentured labourers for the sugar plantations in the West Indies with rice from Burma and Siam to sustain them. The movement of labour ceased during the Second World War and the ships now carried gunny bags for the sugar crop and, still, rice.

Ships were at the core of my work. Every day, after riding for an hour, I handed over my horse to his syce and at 7 a.m. went off by dinghy from Prinseps Ghat to the ships of the day which lay at buoys in the stream. Over coffee laced with rum I checked stowage with the Nourse master. Then more coffee (and gossip, for this was his home port) with a BI captain while I ascertained if there was enough customs-cleared cargo ready in barges alongside to keep the ship working day and night. In a P&O ship my business was with the chief officer, although the captain might deign to receive a courtesy call – a Mackinnons assistant being merely the agent.

In the majority of trades we were monopoly carriers and there was little in the way of selling a service. The ship would arrive, load, and sail, and woe betide shippers if cargo was late; it would just have to wait for a month. Gradually we became more customer-oriented, but it was not until 1953 that the 'desk' went to Australia to study the trade in jute goods. The importers, with whom, belatedly, we were to establish friendly relations, were a tight-knit group of largely family-owned firms – the Freemans, Colquhouns and Hemphills. I sailed, went up country and partied with them. I enjoyed Australia; it was a young man's country.

Northbound cargo was of great variety: prefab houses, frozen food and equipment for the oil-producing kingdoms of the Gulf, milk powder for India and sheep for Iran. The sheep were relatively easy, but we were glad to lose one trade to specialist carriers: goats from Geraldton in West Australia to Singapore were strong stuff, both in muscle and in smell.

Romance touched the century-old supply of horses for the Indian army. In the outback they were 'brumbies' and in India 'walers' from New South Wales. When *Pemba*, carrying about 200 horses, berthed in Calcutta, the intention was to run them ashore in small numbers to be held in corrals until accepted by the army. The first brumbies off, having been cooped up for three weeks, made matchwood of the fencing, and before unloading was half over a group broke out, thundered up the road and got lost in the back streets of the Kidderpore bazaar. As the Irish would say, it was Donnybrook, and an Irish horse-coper might well have relished the outcome for, despite all apparent efforts, two or three horses mysteriously disappeared, never to be heard of again. Or were they? It was rumoured that some of the new blood seen on the racecourse over the next two seasons had an Australian connection. Billy McGrath, wily old king of the brumby business, had a good eye for a thoroughbred.

Although the seasons moved from the cold to the hot weather in March, our work pattern remained unchanged. The morning ride might be curtailed, but ship visits never. To preserve crisply-starched shirt and trousers we sat on the edge of the car seat while the driver took a route to the office which avoided traffic lights. It was a relief to reach the comparative coolness of lofty office and ceiling punkah.

The social scene did change, however. There were fewer formal parties; instead perhaps bridge evenings, with luck in an air-conditioned room. Sunday evening cinema at six followed by a supper party was popular and there was always dinner to be had at the 300 Club under the flamboyant trees. Most years it seemed that only seven or eight European girls stayed on and the bachelors went to considerable lengths to keep a girl 'attached'. Sometimes the effort required was too great, but there were often airline stewardesses in town for a few days. Always in the hot weather there was a tendency to see more of the Anglo-Indian girls, often strikingly beautiful and sweet and very much in limbo. Relationships could be intense, but almost inevitably time-barred. And there were, to later dismay, sad compromises when excuses were made in the interests of convention; discrimination was never far away.

The build-up to the south-east monsoon was a fractious time, with temperatures over 100 degrees Fahrenheit, high humidity and a heavy, brooding atmosphere. Forward thrusts in the way of spectacular thunderstorms might relieve the pressure, but the oppressive, steamy heat would only redouble, to be followed in turn by prickly heat, lethargy, bursts of activity to 'sweat it out' and the bliss of someone's air-conditioned room for a evening. We kept an eye on the *Statesman* weather column to see the advance of the rains and sometimes to share in the real threat to the villages of Bengal, Orissa and Bihar if the breaking of the rains was delayed or, worse, if it seemed the monsoon might fail. But usually the drama reached its climax in Calcutta in early June with a towering black sky and a monumental storm of thunder, lightning and torrential rain. The rain could continue for days, and when it stopped a miasma would hang over the city. The roads steamed, the earth sprang green and the dust was settled. The rain was much needed for the whole agriculture sector, but July, August and September were uncomfortable months for everyone.

Few of us took an interest in Indian culture. We learned Hindi and were reasonably fluent in 'kitchen bat', but there were many missed opportunities that I have regretted in later years. Our priority was physical experience rather than intellectual pursuit, hence river expeditions in the marine superintendent's launch *Ronachan* which took us to Chandernagore and Bandol, forlorn relics of French and Portuguese colonialism; to the Botanical Gardens; or to one of the jute mills for picnics, tennis or swimming. I spent my annual local leave trekking and climbing in the Himalayas rather than studying temples and ruins.

Sandakphu and Phalut are names which still give me a shiver of anticipation as I recall my first trek in 1948, the complete exhaustion at the end of each day and, next morning, the glory of the mountains spread out before us from Everest to Kanchenjunga. Tony Murray and I were so excited by our initiation that we mounted a more ambitious expedition the following year. This time we had with us Tony Davenport and Marie Millington-Drake, a very independent girl, a cousin of Kenneth Inchcape and a frequent visitor to Calcutta, and Bob 'Baldy' Waller of Bird & Co.

From the roadhead at Gangtok, the capital of Sikhim, we trekked with porters and pack ponies by stages of 10-15 miles up the Teesta Valley to Lachen, at over 8,000 feet, through jungle, crossing and recrossing the river, scrambling over landslips. We saw the sun rise on the peak of Kanchenjunga and within half an hour its rays flood the east face and the valley below – 27,500 feet of illuminated mountain – a breathtaking sight.

At Lachen we paid off the mules, recruited local porters and visited the monastery where lamas blessed our expedition and danced for us wearing their formidable animal masks. We bought fresh-picked apples in the village and potatoes from Tibetan traders. We redeployed loads to give each porter 60 lb, leaving me, at least, with nothing more than a camera to carry.

Our equipment was rudimentary. I had leather 'army' boots with heavily tacketted soles made by a Calcutta Chinaman; we had, allegedly, waterproof tops. For warmth we relied on layers of clothing. One of my sweaters had been purchased in the Faeroes in 1944 and, drawing on *Oribi* experience, I wore pyjamas as a foundation when the temperature dropped. Cooking and eating utensils were basic and food was straightforward – rice, potatoes and tins of stew, plus a long-suffering sheep which was led to its end at base camp.

As was proper, a mountain tent was hired for Marie while we men made do with an army surplus canvas tent. We camped at 12,000 feet on the tongue of the Zemu Glacier. About midnight came a crack of doom and the tent collapsed about us. For a moment or two there was silence – no one knew whether we had been flattened by a rockfall, an avalanche or, indeed, whether anyone else had survived. I was pinned to the ground. Then, to our relief and later amusement, there was a plaintive cry of 'Koi hai' – Is anyone there? – the typical Calcutta call when summoning the bearer to bring another drink. The porters, sensibly sleeping under a rock overhang, extricated us without damage other than to our dignity, although it was sobering to find that when the wooden tent-pole snapped under the weight of a heavy fall of wet snow, the top half had been driven like a stake into the ground only inches from Bob Waller's head.

The Green Lake, the camp site for Paul Bauer's Austrian expedition some fifteen years earlier, provided an excellent base for exhilarating and exhausting scrambles up the glacier into the basin

behind Kanchenjunga. Tony Murray and I also climbed on the north
side of the valley, only to some 18,000 feet, but even so an introduction to four breaths to a step, and we were rewarded with glorious
panoramic views of the twin Siniolchu peaks, one of the most sublime groups in the eastern Himalaya.

Back at Lachen at the halfway point of the trek we were told by
the chowkidar in charge of the dak bungalow that there was no
room at the inn because a high official, the new Dewan of Sikhim,
was arriving on tour.

There had been political rumblings in the independent state of
Sikhim for some months. Rumours of discontent with the autocratic
rule of the hereditary Maharaja were rife. But more important to the
Indian government was any hint of instability in the border region
adjoining Tibet, which it seemed probable would, in short order, be
absorbed by China. With some justification in the broad strategic
sense, but perhaps little enough in local terms, India effectively took
over Sikhim in 1949 and installed a Dewan whose rule over the
next few years was to be quite as beneficently autocratic as any
Maharaja's.

Early in the afternoon the sound of horns echoed up the valley. A
welcoming party of village elders and priests – lamas from the
gompa – made a colourful sight as the procession skirted the mani
wall, the prayer wall at the entrance to Lachen. Drums and cymbals
were followed by Tibetan horns sounding their resonant, discordant
and lugubrious tones. So long and heavy were they that the bell was
carried in a sling by one lama while the mouthpiece was supported
on the shoulders of a second and the lung power was supplied by a
third.

The sound rolled round the hills as though announcing the arrival
of a pantheon of gods and there, astride a small pony, was the slight
figure of the Dewan dressed not in splendid ceremonial garb to befit
the occasion but in grey flannels and a blazer. He raised his hat:
'How simply splendid to see you – I am John Lall, ICS. Can we dine
together this evening?' He was, and is, a great character – a government servant of immense distinction, an erudite historian, and altogether a most civilised person.

Back at Gangtok we were bidden to dine at the royal palace with
the Maharaja and two of his beautiful, enchanting daughters. A fellow guest was Hugh Richardson, formerly British representative in
Lhasa who had come down over the Natu La ahead of the Chinese

'army of liberation'. He had sobering views on the march of Communism, but believed that his beloved Tibetans would somehow protect their way of life.

The Sikhim princesses brought out a version of planchette after dinner – it was played on an occasional table, the legs of which were of bone formed into miniature skeletons. Among the questions posed was 'Will Tibet go Red?' The answer, as the cup slid round the board, was 'Pink.' Was it steered by a hopeful Richardson?

Tony Murray and I went again to the Himalayas in 1950, up to the Tibetan border and to over 20,000 feet on the flank of the Jonsong Peak, beyond Kanchenjunga. It was a hard trek, initially successful, but ultimately disastrous when we lost two porters. I wrote an account of this expedition in an article, published in July 1951, in *Blackwood's Magazine*.

A postscript to these Himalayan adventures came in 1954. A year after the successful ascent of Everest, Edmund Hillary led a New Zealand team to Makalu, the world's fourth highest peak. In May information came that their attempt on the summit had been abandoned following a serious accident to Macfarlane, who had fallen into a deep crevasse. The rescue had been long and difficult; and during it Hillary had fractured some ribs. The party was withdrawing to Dharan, carrying Macfarlane in a backpack.

There was no immediate cause for concern but, as the days passed, porters who had been paid off and were coming down ahead reported slow progress on a difficult route and worries that the monsoon might break, raising the river levels and washing away tracks and bridges. The officers of the Himalayan Club consulted the UK Assistant High Commissioner. If, having heard of the problem, the UK community took no action, what criticism might be attracted if something went wrong and the lord of Everest was abandoned? On such a craven basis it was decided to send a support team into Nepal to meet Hillary as he came down from the mountains. Don Mackenzie, an ICI doctor, and I were nominated. Permits were secured, medical supplies and equipment assembled and within forty-eight hours we were on our way. We were aware that we might be brushed aside by the professionals, but Mackenzie was able to offer considerable medical assistance and I was, after all, simply the trekking support.

We planned on going north into the valleys for five days and, as the train-boat-train journey proceeded across the scorching Ganges plain, we rehearsed the 'Dr Livingstone, I presume' scenario. At Jogbani porters grabbed our baggage and led us towards the PWD bungalow. 'Dusre sahib log abbhi aye heyn – bungla ek dum pura hai.' 'Other sahibs have just arrived – the bungalow is full up,' they said. The penny did not immediately drop, but it was soon all too clear that we had been cut off before we had even started. 'Who are you then, mate?' asked one. 'Hey, cobber [or the NZ equivalent], look what's turned up to rescue us,' and much of a more ribald nature.

The first hours were uncomfortable, but gradually we were accepted. We assisted with transport and fixed welcome calls to New Zealand and the UK. We contributed sulfa drugs for Macfarlane whose frost-bitten feet and hands were in bad shape – black, crusty and oozing pus – and expert advice on other lesser injuries.

The rains had not broken so the heat was fierce, but Macfarlane was philosophical and cheerful. He even joked when his legs were put into a gunny sack and tins of talcum powder shaken in to moderate the smell of his rotting feet. In Calcutta we faced more ribbing about our 'pretentious rescue expedition', but we knew we had been of real help.

Although there was always a shifting population as friends came and went on long leave or transfer or, indeed, left for good, there was a basic continuity to life in Calcutta. I was absent for extended periods between my tours, but I was usually greeted on return as though I had only been away for the weekend. As I prepared for home at the end of 1951, I was asked to undertake a lengthy trip to the Caribbean and New York to study the receiving end of the Nourse Line service. I went first to East Africa, sailing from Bombay via the Seychelles on the once-monthly steamer. From Nairobi to the Cape and from the Victoria Falls to Portuguese East Africa, I met traders and producers and arranged that Nourse ships would call at Durban and Cape Town every month to pick up 1,000 or more tons of wattle extract, wine, canned fish and bottles. It was a useful supplementary trade until the British West Indies became the first to boycott South Africa.

The Nourse *Megna* of 10,000 tons dwt, making 10 knots on 10 tons of diesel fuel took twenty-one days from Cape Town to Trinidad, calling afterwards at the sometimes remote, even primitive ports of the Caribbean from Barbados to Haiti, San Domingo to

Jamaica. While *Megna* was berthed in Nuevitas, Cuba, in February 1952, King George VI died and the authoritarian President Batista declared three days of national mourning.

In New York I met the sugar barons who controlled the purchase of Indian gunny bags and secured an understanding of their methods. I was dazzled and excited by this first visit. It was a major business success and I got credit for it. Heading at last for home I sailed from New York to Southampton in *Queen Mary*, last encountered as a troopship on the Clyde. For the first hour I regretted having been bold enough to book first class; cabin class looked likely to be more fun. But I soon came to my senses and enjoyed an appropriately romantic voyage. I am glad to have had the opportunity to make one of the great ocean passages in a ship of such style.

My remaining leave, nine months, seemed to flash by: time at home in Scotland, crewing in a Dragon during Clyde Week, a hectic continental trip with Tony Davenport and soon I was returning to India, via southern Africa, to review what progress we had made in the year since I was there.

In Calcutta I now took full charge of the Australian desk. We had to deal with surging nationalism. BI had met competition before and had seen it off, but times had changed and we accepted our fate with as good a grace as we could muster. Indeed, I took C. P. Srivastava, the new managing director of the government shipping company, the Indian Shipping Corporation, to Australia to show him the ropes – he was an ex-civil servant and later, for many years, secretary general of the International Maritime Consultative Organisation (IMCO).

In 1956 I planned six months' leave, flying first to Istanbul in PanAm Flight One, hoping to find *Oribi* in her new colours. I had no luck there, but found Marie Millington-Drake at her exotic home at Bellapaese near Kyrenia, then a glorious part of undivided Cyprus.

After a short visit to Scotland I skied at Kitzbühl with friends from India. They were polished exponents while I struggled with the beginners. There was nothing for it but to settle for catching up during the après-ski. Compensation, however, came with one of many tangles at the foot of the nursery slopes, when I managed to collide with a striking girl. Wendy Notten from Johannesburg was tall, pretty and full of laughter. She had a sense of the ridiculous combined with an apparent innocence, and at the presentation of awards that evening was quite delighted to receive a medal, blissfully unaware that everyone got some recognition. What I did not know until we returned to England was that in Wendy's party was another South African, Mona Kirk, whom I would marry some years later.

In London, I received an offer to spend a year attached to the Nourse company. I accepted with alacrity and rented a bed-sitter in Chesham Street, round the corner from the Antelope, a very popular pub in Eaton Terrace. The South African girls lived in a basement flat in Eaton Terrace, even closer to the Antelope.

In many ways life at '122' did not live up to expectations. My office was in an attic room. I missed the Calcutta infrastructure – no peons to fetch and carry, no bearers bringing cold drinks and coffee, no Chinese shoemaker or tailor on hand, no lunch-room. Above all, no office car. I was fortunate though to escape one of the most common complaints, that of resistance, perhaps unconscious, from the 'home' team. There was frequently a sort of inverse snobbery, or just plain envy: 'These people who have come home think they know it all, while in fact it is we who have slaved away here who have made it all possible.' It is tricky to get the balance right and to ensure that all the talents are used productively. But I was in a small management structure and L. C. Williams, the managing director, was enlightened. He was also imaginative in evolving a role for Nourse in a rapidly changing environment, so that my work was stimulating and rewarding.

With an expanding group – still friends today more than forty years later – I did many of the things I had missed while in India: the Grand National (where we saw the Queen Mother's Devon Loch, with Dick Francis up, spreadeagled before the winning post), Wimbledon, Test Matches and Henley. Then all too soon the girls returned to South Africa, some of the boys went overseas, and a number of the group were close to marriage. I was not too unhappy to be going back to my familiar life in Calcutta, although I had recognised at home in Scotland, where my parents revelled in their growing band of grandchildren, that to my siblings I was, at thirty-one and unmarried, a bit of a curiosity. There might be something to be said for a lifestyle less exotic than mine.

That final spell in India was, however, an important stage in my development. I was 'E', the senior assistant, next in line to the partners, with considerable authority. 'E' was responsible for fleet planning – matching ships to demand – a complex task given the ramifications of the BI network. E's direction and influence touched every aspect of the company's business.

In 1947 there were 100 BI ships based in India, operating on the coast, to the Far East, to Africa, the Persian Gulf and Australia. Other ships traded from the UK to the East and to Africa. When I left Calcutta at the end of 1959, BI had withdrawn from many of the old trades, squeezed out by legislation and subsidised competition. The managing agency system – day-to-day operations controlled in India, purse strings held in London – which had served British industry and commerce so well was ended by Government decree. The Inchcape family had anticipated the demise of the structure and had already sold the Mackinnon Mackenzie network to their principals, P&O.

I parted with feelings of nostalgia for an old friend. The sixties, a decade of personal happiness and achievement, opened with a new phase in my career as Manager of BI Eastern Services, based in the City at One Aldgate.

For years, too many years after 1947, the British seemed to nurture a guilt complex about India. Perhaps the shattering events of partition, the slaughter in the Punjab, the crude separation of the country, left a feeling that we had washed our hands of a problem too difficult to solve; that we had abandoned our responsibilities too precipitately. As others – the French, Germans and Japanese in trade and the Russians in military matters – filled the gap, British political and commercial relationships were hesitant, tentative and relatively unproductive. In the 1950s India was, in its own way, taking back what it regarded as having been expropriated.

I too went through many years of withdrawal from the sub-continent until in 1983, my daughter Gillian spent some happy months there in her 'year off', and Mona and I joined her for a visit to Kashmir and Rajasthan. After that I kept telling the young that they should trek in the Himalayas before it's too late. One of them responded, taking a different viewpoint: 'Perhaps it's you who should go again before it's too late.' The thought took hold. I planned the expedition and in October 1990 a group of seven self-styled geriatrics assembled in Delhi for a 'low level' trek from Outer to Inner Suraj.

Only Edward Studd and I had done any trekking before, forty years ago. I was apprehensive about everything; might the trek be too easy, too trippery, the discomfort too great, the people 'spoilt', might one of us break down? It was tougher than I anticipated – yet I don't think there was a day on which any one of us failed to make a comment along the lines of 'Isn't this wonderful?' or 'I wouldn't have missed this for anything.'

I made the 'bundobast' thanks to Christina Noble of Manali, whose book *A Home in the Himalayas* covers much of the area and the people. We did not see another trekking party. We walked for up to eight hours a day, we sweated and froze and went to bed, seldom after 8 p.m., in tents or dak bungalows, wearing every stitch of clothing we could muster. After tea and porridge we were on the move, every day, by 7 a.m. Our cavalcade of fifteen pack ponies, nine porters including Karma, the sirdar, two cooks and two syces with riding ponies was impressive.

Dick Bristow and Edward Studd were our ornithologists, Wiz Bristow and Patricia Blundell Brown knew much about plants, Prue Studd wrote a journal. Mona collected wild flowers and produced an exquisite watercolour every evening. I was just very glad to be there and revelled in almost every minute and it was satisfying that Edward and I, more than thirty years after leaving India, found that our Hindustani came back, halting but useful as we exchanged greetings with those we met along the way.

So, full circle, and I am happy to have rediscovered India – warm, vital, frustrating, dirty and difficult – and ever-absorbing.

4

London

I took the long road home from India – via Australia, to assure my business contacts there that in London I would continue to watch over their interests, and then Johannesburg, where I caught up with Mona. I visited The Fountains, her family's farm in the Eastern Transvaal, for the first time and have loved it ever since. As I set off north through East Africa perhaps I began to dream dreams.

Mona followed my tracks later in a much more adventurous style. With three companions, she drove a 'combi' north through the Rhodesias, Nyasaland and Tanganyika to Kenya, climbed Kilimanjaro and camped with the Leakeys at Olduvai. She arrived in London in the late summer, protesting that she had really only come to collect her baggage which had been sent ahead.

By that time I had settled into my new responsibilities and was beginning to strike a balance between office routine and social life. I became a foredeck hand in Donald Craigmyle's *Norsaga*, a 12 metre yacht with which his Red Duster syndicate was attempting to mount a high-tech challenge for the America's Cup. My weekly schedule was a busy five days' work at One Aldgate, a dash to Cowes on Friday evening followed by a weekend of hard, competitive racing; back to London on Sunday evening; Monday an early night, with an active social round in the evenings on Tuesday, Wednesday and Thursday.

Working life promised a conventional and predictable future. As senior people moved up the BI ladder or retired, I would follow. While I enjoyed those summer months, I began to feel that my life had become somewhat frenetic, with every moment filled to overflowing with work and play, and when Mona arrived it was not long before I realised that I was ready for a stable and lasting relationship. By the end of the year we were engaged and, after a quick Christmas trip together to Scotland to meet the family, Mona went home to prepare for an April wedding.

I was responsible for one of BI's most historic runs. The D class vessels, in the Express Mail Service from Bombay to Basra, followed the route established in the nineteenth century, when BI first located navigational aids from Muscat to Bander Shahpur and from Khorram-shahr to Bahrein. The trade was as exotic as it was varied: bazaar goods for the souks, materials for the new oil fields, supplies for expatriates, personal effects for the huge workforce drawn from Pakistan and India, pilgrims according to the season, or a Gulf sheikh with his harem on a hunting trip or a courtesy visit. This last could put the ship's captain under some strain, and heavily tax his diplomacy. But the chore had its compensations; many a Gulf service officer sported a gold watch.

On 7 April 1961 *Dara*, southbound, was returning to Dubai from her overnight anchorage some ten miles off shore when a sudden heavy explosion amidships shook the entire ship, started a series of fires and caused severe structural damage. Bad weather the previous day had delayed her departure for Muscat, and she had been forced to spend the night well clear of the congested port. On board were upwards of 1,000 souls including a full crew, several hundred deck and about sixty saloon passengers, coolies from the cargo gangs working when she cleared for sea and numerous merchants who peddled trinkets – everything from sweetmeats to gold.

I received advice in London within the hour: 'Unknown explosion severely damaged *Dara*, rescue operations underway, casualties likely.'

The next forty-eight hours were hectic. Marine, engineer and electrical superintendents and a medical support team were despatched to Dubai. An experienced technical team was formed to investigate the cause of the explosion and Lloyds Register, the P&I Club, the underwriters and the Foreign Office were kept posted. Our agents at all Gulf ports and at Karachi and Bombay set up the then equivalent of a 'help line' for relatives and we tried hard to ensure that only factual information was communicated.

Ships in the vicinity came to *Dara*'s aid with commendable courage and skill. As the official Board of Trade report later made clear, the ship's company performed magnificently, but over 200 lives were lost. It was hinted at the Inquiry that a number were drowned by the weight of gold bars hung around them.

Initially the cause of the explosion was a mystery; was it a burst boiler, flailing machinery in the engine room, volatile cargo, a collision even? Gradually the master, Captain Charles Elson, and the chief engineer became convinced that some external agency had been responsible. In London, the navy and the Foreign Office began to produce a picture of a terrorist attack – something relatively unknown in 1961. The Ruler of Oman was facing sporadic and at times violent opposition in the south, and had *Dara* sailed on schedule she would have been anchoring at Muscat when the explosion occurred.

Although the Inquiry could not formally identify the cause of the explosion, the circumstantial evidence seemed to confirm an explosive device – a particularly shocking event at the time when *Dara* and her sister ships were part of the fabric of life in the Gulf.

Today *Dara* lies on the bottom off Dubai, a reminder of the mindless waste caused by the evil of terrorism, but now a popular resort for scuba divers, few of whom will ever give a thought to the distress and loss suffered by so many families of her crew and passengers in India, Pakistan and the Gulf States.

Sadly, because of Father's illness, none of my immediate family could attend our wedding in April, but, to a great extent, that was compensated for by the warmth of the welcome from the White River community, which held Mona's family in such high regard, and by the large number of friends who came down from Johannesburg. The tiny church itself might have been plucked from an English village. The guests overflowed and I remember, through the windows, the blue sky, the bamboos and the bougainvillea. The Fountains looked its best. Edna, Mona's mother, had done wonders with the garden, the Swazi hills were blue on the southern horizon and the farm children sang, unselfconsciously and hauntingly, 'Nkosi Sikelele iAfrika' – long before it became a political anthem. Mona's brother Howard was my best man and her father, Leslie, presided benignly and proudly. It was a marvellous day.

We drove off across the border into Portuguese East Africa, to the splendid Polana Hotel in Lourenço Marques. We followed with ten days in the Greek islands, finding Mykonos unspoilt, quiet, almost primitive, and finally spent a few days with Jo and Gordon Bisset in Milan.

Immediately on our return we went up to Scotland to see my father. He was dying of cancer – diagnosed six months earlier. He and my mother bore this burden with astonishing fortitude and dignity. They had insisted that our wedding plans should not be affected and now rejoiced at how lovely Mona looked in her wedding dress. They greatly enjoyed our cine-film of the day and it was deeply moving to sense their pleasure at having another end timeously knotted.

We house-hunted, it seemed to me all over the south-east, and started to learn the realities of domestic life. In 1962 we moved into our first house a few days before Alastair was born on 7 August. When, three children later, it became too small, we moved to our present home, which has given us space, a lovely outlook and an adventurous garden for children and grandchildren.

But there was a sameness about my work and the horizon offered no excitement. I began to feel somewhat undervalued and certainly under-occupied. As I prepared to follow Mona and Alastair (aged four months) to South Africa at Christmas, I wondered whether I should look seriously at the possibility of working there. I was ready for a move and Mona had no affection for the English climate.

Out of the blue came a summons to '122', P&O's seat of power in Leadenhall Street, to see Sir Frederic Harmer, the deputy chairman, and Lord (Ross) Geddes, a director of P&O and Group tanker adviser. They came straight to the point:

> We propose to form a new company to put together the management, and possibly later the ownership, of all the tankers in the P&O Group. If you were to be offered a senior role in such a company what would you bring to it in the way of management experience and skill, and what would you regard as important in terms of structure?

I immediately assumed the role would be in commercial management. I replied that my Mackinnons experience showed that having been thrown in at the deep end I had survived; had undertaken considerable responsibility; was not afraid to take decisions provided I had the facts; had shown leadership in the navy and in BI and was a self-starter. As to structure, I would consider it essential that to be profitable the enterprise must be run by management which must not be overborne by technical people. This last shot was a direct result of my BI experience, where time and again technical superintendents, greatly skilled and widely experienced, dominated general management to a degree which, while maintaining fine ships, lost commercial advantage. Today one might put it that the company must be customer- and not product-oriented.

A few hours later Lord G, as he became generally known, telephoned: 'We would like you to be managing director of Trident

Tankers. You will have a pretty free hand. I will be your chairman to help all I can. The salary will be £5,000 per year.'

I did not hesitate. I cut my South African holiday short. Mona, despite initial disappointment, was enthusiastic. In England the winter of 1962–3 turned out to be the most severe since 1946–7, when we froze at Oxford. With Mona and Alastair warm at White River, I buckled down to the nuts and bolts, as well as the strategic issues, of forming a company from scratch.

A catalyst in the decision to form Trident was an unprecedented contract with Texaco for four supertankers of 60–90,000 dwt to be built in British yards. Texaco was expanding its Milford Haven refinery and increasing its penetration of the UK market. To employ ships under the red ensign would do no harm, but there was another influence; Gus Long, the Texaco chairman, had a warm regard for Britain stemming from his wartime experiences.

It was an extraordinary opportunity, and my term as managing director of Trident Tankers was to be stimulating, rewarding and great fun. Lord G was an ideal chairman. He was a big man in all ways. One of his friends said of him: 'The world was his china shop' and he had little enough time for the demands of management – 'That's your job.' But he was unfailingly supportive, knowledgeable in the ways of the industry, and dedicated to tanker safety. Freddie Harmer was a senior wrangler. His quiet, cerebral, diplomatic style complemented Lord G's more robust approach. He did a great deal to help us in the early days when we encountered resistance from the traditionalists in the Group. The logic that underpinned Trident was inescapable, but many Group companies, mindful of their long history, were reluctant to accept a reduced role. The argument against duplicating effort and diluting experience coupled with the case for rationalising resources and for emphasising specialisation was compelling, and Trident rapidly took over the management of all Group tankers, going on to increase the fleet with new and larger vessels. Trident was soon, and by a margin, the largest independent British tanker company.

A highlight of the early years came in June 1964, when Mona launched her first ship, Trident's flagship *Ottawa*, the biggest vessel yet built in England. Mona looked stunning and performed the traditional ceremony with grace and charm. As managing director I was proud both of the ship and of her sponsor.

For fifteen years *Ottawa* performed well for Trident and for

Texaco, and that might have been the end of her story, but for a strange twist. Our younger son James, having joined John Swire & Sons straight from Cambridge, was posted to Dubai in 1990. On one of his visits to the UK, I realised, as we were talking shop, that the large tanker providing lengthy and profitable employment for one of his offshore supply boats as stand-by vessel, while she was gas freed and cleaned prior to demolition on the west coast of India, was the *Udang Natuna*, ex-*Ottawa*. After twenty-seven years she had come full circle – and her bell now hangs at our front door.

Building such pioneering vessels on the Tyne and the Clyde did not blind us to the attractions of contracting in Japan. In those years I saw arguably the best and worst of shipbuilding practice and, unhappily, the worst was in the UK. The 1960s and 1970s were dark days for British shipbuilders who believed that theirs was still a seller's market. They had enjoyed unprecedented order books in the 1950s when wartime losses were being made good. But work and management practices were outmoded. Industrial relations were essentially adversarial and attempts to secure a minor concession could escalate into a major stand-off. The walk-out and sometimes the shut-out were all too frequent.

By 1966 I was conducting concurrent negotiations with BP and Shell as charterers and with Mitsui Zosen as the builder of a series of 200,000 ton dwt VLCCs (very large crude carriers). Trident needed the assurance of the ten- or fifteen-year timecharter. Shell and BP needed the assurance of firm delivery dates as the tankers were scheduled to fit into their world-wide transportation systems. Mitsui needed the assurance of firm orders before committing to the construction of a new shipyard at Chiba. The pieces of the deal were put together and the first sod was cut on a green-field site in Japan. Mitsui undertook to deliver the first VLCC, *Ardtaraig*, on 31 March 1969 and they did so with flair and ceremony and with the ship in mint condition.

Impressed with the fierce efficiency of the Japanese yards, I suggested to two British shipbuilders that they might consider 'lending' Trident one of their managers to go out to the Mitsui yard as a building superintendent. It seemed to me this would afford a useful opportunity to study developments at first hand and, provided the man did a good job for us, I did not mind if he was a foreman or the managing director. Ross Belch, of Lithgow's, welcomed the opportunity and made very good use of it. But Len Redshaw of Vickers responded: 'What on earth could we learn from them? After all, we taught them how to build ships in the first place.' Not surprisingly, Vickers's yard was one of the early casualties in the increasingly competitive shipbuilding world.

In 1964, the year *Ottawa* was commissioned, what might seem at first blush an unlikely alliance had been formed between P&O and the Anglo Norness Company. The latter, Bermuda-based, was experienced in the major bulk trades, in contracts of affreightment, in relationships with, for example, the principal Japanese and European steel mills and the ore producers in Brazil. The P&O Group had access to funds and a desire to spread its shipping investment into new areas to balance the loss of its traditional liner trades. The logic of taking a potentially powerful competitor out of the market may seem evident now, but the match would not have been made had not a spirit of warmth and trust matured quickly between the patrician Sir Donald Anderson of P&O and Erling Maess, the free-wheeling Norwegian entrepreneur.

Associated Bulk Carriers (ABC), the name of the new joint venture, took into commercial operation the bulk carriers operated by Anglo Norness and the new ships being introduced by the Hain-Nourse company for P&O. Trident was initially on the fringe of ABC, but when we found ourselves on the same track as Anglo Norness in our interest in a revolutionary design for a type of vessel able to carry coal or oil or ore, even grain, we progressively became more closely involved. The commercial synergy was evident, as too was the value of pooling our technical resources. So started for me a long, constructive and happy relationship with the Anglo Norness people. Corporately the venture was subject to some stormy episodes, but I think the players always held each other in warm regard. Erling Naess has claimed credit for naming the new design of ship, but I cling to the belief that during a late session in the nightclub of the Princess Hotel in Bermuda it was I who suggested OBO – oil-bulk-ore carrier.

As the OBOs were developed, the overlap between Trident and Hain-Nourse led to strained relations. I sat on the H-N board and knew how strongly the management felt about holding onto some of the new shipping opportunities. I sympathised, but was adamant in insisting that if a ship was even a part-time oil carrier she must be treated with the respect and attention that only the experienced tanker operator could give. Also, we placed special emphasis on

Trident's early development of inert gas systems in motor ships. This had not been a straightforward exercise and we, who had struggled through it, knew well how vital it was to have engineers and deck officers afloat, and technical staff ashore, who had a feel for the system – who 'lived' inert gas. We took a firm – perhaps to Hain-Nourse an intransigent – stand, and the OBOs came to Trident.

The principal hazard of the crude oil transportation cycle occurs when the vessel is in ballast with empty cargo tanks. Unless cleaned, the tanks fill with a hazardous gas mixture. During cleaning, the introduction of washing equipment can provide a probe, causing a discharge of static electricity which triggers an explosion. The consequences of an explosion, particularly in older tankers with accommodation amidships, can be catastrophic.

Different ideas emerged to counter this hazard. Shell tended to favour strictly controlled and sophisticated operating procedures. BP, Texaco and Trident added to these operational safeguards the introduction of a blanket of inert (non-explosive) gas in the air space (ullage). The inert gas progressively filled the tank as the crude was discharged. The washing would then take place in an inert atmosphere.

While it is relatively simple to draw adequate supplies of inert gas from the flue discharge of a steamship, the waste gases of a diesel engine are more complex and require specialised 'scrubbing'. There is an additional commercial pressure in motor ships, in that there is a requirement for waste gas to fuel the auxiliary boiler.

Explosions during tank cleaning, including the emerging VLCC class, focused attention on the hazards to the crews, to the ships and to the environment. Tanker safety was, and still is, high profile. The technicalities and the politics of inert gas were an important feature of international and domestic discussion throughout the 1960s when there was a quantum leap in the understanding of the problems, both operational and technical. Pollution of the seas was also demanding increasing attention. The name *Torrey Canyon*, whose dramatic stranding on the Scillies and whose fiery end at the hands of the RAF made headline news in 1967, still reverberates.

I followed Lord G in contributing to the development of a proactive response by the industry to the issues of safety and pollution. He was always a champion of research and action: 'The ocean is not the world's dustbin.' In 1967 he chaired the first International Tanker Safety Conference at Brighton and, although I had moved on from Trident, I was chairman of the second conference in Bergen in 1976. Trident's, and later P&O Bulk Shipping's, standing in this field was well recognised. We had been among the first to implement the safety and operating audit of ship's practice and to follow up with onboard training. Captain Harry Long, RNR, a useful recruit from P&O, set up Marine Safety Services and, to demonstrate that he and his colleagues were not hired whitewashers, we gave his company independence and enabled it to sell its services to third parties.

Our safety record was good, but we were not immune. It was with dismay that we heard in November 1971 that *Heythrop*, one of the OBOs, had suffered an explosion while tank-cleaning off South Africa. Fortunately the emergency drills worked well, the weather was kind and the ship was saved without loss of life or serious injury. The hazard is ever-present and there is never margin for error.

And there were casualties, not many, but unnecessary and therefore all the more distressing. A junior officer is overcome by gas when inspecting a tank. Safety lines are rigged, lighting is adequate and a senior officer is standing by at the tank top. Yet instead of donning breathing-apparatus and going down with the appropriate rescue gear, the chief officer believes no time can be spared and that he can get down and up again quickly enough. A tragic decision. A much more complex rescue has to be mounted to recover two casualties and the outcome is that the first man is saved but his would-be rescuer dies.

Noel Mostert published an absorbing account of life on board a Trident VLCC, with extensive comment on the industry itself and on the type of men who crewed and managed these first-generation Leviathans (*Supership*, Knopf 1974). He sailed in *Ardshiel* under Captain Basil Thomson in 1973 and his book gives a penetrating account of a round trip from Europe to the Persian Gulf. Mostert made a number of challenging points. He emphasised the threat of pollution, which he believed was heightened by the risks associated with the startlingly rapid development of the supertanker, the new and untested dimension in which it operated, and the proliferation of new flags and untried crews. One of his most interesting assertions was the danger inherent in insulating the seaman from the surrounding elements within a more technical and less sensitively aware and 'respectful' atmosphere. Size in itself seemed to Mostert to imply domination.

Safety was paramount, but there were other important demands.

We had drawn personnel from across the Group and had thus gathered invaluable experience. There was, too, continuing stimulus as new technical and operational frontiers were challenged. At all levels we used best practice and built upon it. Modern management practice was to the fore (I was impressed by the American Management Association courses I attended for 'young presidents') and we were early in the field of job descriptions, definition of corporate objectives and performance reviews. This applied as much at sea as ashore, and Trident led the way in introducing flexible manning arrangements which improved efficiency and interest in the job, and saved in crew numbers.

The operation of the OBOs took me onto the Associated Bulk Carriers Executive Committee which oversaw the commercial side but did not interfere in the day-to-day management. The Executive Committee was involved with policy and also with the relationship between the ship management companies. We learned much from each other.

I was fascinated by the ABC operation. ABC were always interested in good quality period charters, but of more importance were the contracts of affreightment under which shipping would be provided to carry, for example, 500,000 tons of ore from Brazil to Japan, or from West Australia to Japan, over a twelve-month period. The Japanese steel industry needed ore and coking coal to support its steel production, then rising to some 120m tons per annum. The concept and challenge of the OBOs was to match ore and oil movements – to eliminate the long ballast hauls from Japan to the ore loading areas by using OBOs to carry oil from South East Asia or the Persian Gulf to Europe and the USA. But that was not always, even often, possible and so there was a lively pattern of chartering in other ships and chartering out our own for short periods.

ABC was a Bermudan, mid-Atlantic, company and it was important for tax reasons that neither mind nor management be manifestly located in the USA or the UK. Board meetings were held in Bermuda and the frequent Executive Committee meetings at a more convenient point – if possible where the working members, Bo Madsen and Henning Petersen, representing Anglo Norness, and Jim Bayley with Steve Carter, P&O, could also visit customers. At first I found Bermuda a considerable strain and surprisingly disappointing. We would fly direct, arriving at the Princess Hotel in Hamilton in the afternoon. There would be a meeting in the office in the afternoon and a drink afterwards in the gazebo overlooking the harbour, followed, for those with the stamina, by dinner and the night club. More meetings in the forenoon and lunch at the Yacht Club before heading back (at 25 mph) to the airport. It seemed to me that there must be something more to Bermuda and I began to explore – moving to Newstead across the harbour where at least one had some feeling of being on a resort island. Things began to look up when we held meetings at Elbow Beach Club and the Southampton Princess in a more relaxed environment, with scope, occasionally, to get to the beach or on to a golf course.

The Plaza Athénée in Paris, Vier Jahrezeiten in Hamburg, the Angleterre in Copenhagen and the Amstel in Amsterdam were all regular ports of call for the Executive Committee until, feeling virtuous or simply under pressure, I suggested that perhaps there might be somewhere as efficient but somewhat cheaper in respect of travel costs and time. After much investigation, Bo Madsen and Jim Bayley proposed Reykjavik in Iceland or, failing that, Drumoland Castle on the West Coast of Ireland. We, although I received most of the credit or opprobrium for it, chose the latter. It became known as 'the end of the runway at Shannon'. There were no communications to speak of – our priority telegrams arrived by cleft stick; our meeting room was only ready late in the morning when last night's bar had been packed up; and we smelled of smoke and Guinness for days. Splendid in its way and with some attractive fishing, it was no business hotel and after that experiment we reverted, with relief, to our more familiar venues.

In 1968 we were concerned when, after much internal wrangling, Anglo Norness agreed to a takeover bid by Zapata, a Houston-based oil conglomerate ('Not proper shipowners,' said Erling Naess). Our friends were renamed Zapata Norness and, fortunately, the executives remained so that our cooperation continued undisturbed.

In October that year Donald Anderson summoned me:

> P&O is changing – we've made the big move into containerisation, we have done the right thing in getting our tankers under one control, we may or may not succeed in turning our passenger liners into cruise ships; but we have an awful ragbag of other interests and inherited baggage. We must get our plans for the future more orderly and co-ordinated. You, in Trident, have shown that there were good opportunities and I want to exploit

that talent and enthusiasm – I, we, would like you to become an executive director of P&O with responsibility to me for all marine activities and developments other than passenger, container and liner services – it will mean your handing over Trident to someone else. I've consulted Ross Geddes of course and he is fully in support – in fact he takes it as a compliment to himself.

There was no doubt about my answer, but it was nevertheless somewhat difficult to absorb. At the age of forty-three to become the first executive director of P&O was as unexpected as it was unprecedented. Hitherto the senior executives of P&O had been the managing directors – at the time Donald Anderson, Freddie Harmer, Michael Thwaites, Ford Geddes and Andrew Crichton – with John Mitchell being Finance Director.

P&O itself was a strange beast – part operator of passenger and cargo services (P&O Orient Lines), part holding company with a huge array of subsidiaries, but a holding company now showing considerable interest in influencing management. I would have a responsible and stimulating role, covering the bulk trades, offshore, gas, chemicals, deep-sea fishing and all manner of new developments.

First I had to share the news with Mona and then with my Trident colleagues. Perhaps Mona was becoming accustomed to my upheavals; she was surprised and excited. One thing we needed to make abundantly clear was that our Christmas family holiday in South Africa must go ahead. With the Suez Canal closed by the Arab-Israeli war, P&O's Far East ships, *Cathay*, *Chitral*, and *Chusan* were being routed via the Cape, and we were delighted to have the chance of going out by sea.

The holiday confirmed, I got on with the change. In 1962 the opportunity to 'cross the road' had come at a time when I was predisposed to move on. In 1968 the situation was quite different. I was immersed in Trident and enjoying my chief executive job enormously. I now realised that Trident had been an experiment in rationalising Group resources, and it later became clear that it was the success of that experiment which encouraged Donald Anderson to take the next step. Had we failed in creating a successful working model in Trident, who knows how the Group would have developed? But thanks to a most capable, imaginative and dedicated team, Trident was a success and, in due course, provided the paradigm for further development. I was happy to see Frank

Murphy, who had been with me from the start, take over as managing director.

My new appointment would demand diplomacy as I brought the subsidiaries into closer communion. I had to learn the ropes as a director of a public company, one with an illustrious history, immense prestige and some degree of formality. My life-style changed apace: a welcome increase in salary; an office car to meet me at the station and ferry me round during the day; a considerable programme of corporate social activities. I had no staff apart from my secretary, Betty Fairclough. She had joined Trident in 1965 bringing with her experience in ship agency in Las Palmas, a qualification as a chartered shipbroker and a talent not only for administration but for editing and rephrasing manuscripts and speeches. The secretary's job demanded much application and patience. Betty was to make herself indispensable for fifteen years.

One tends to forget that as little as twenty-five years ago there was no memory typewriter, let alone the word-processor or fax. While the mechanics of secretarial work may seem laborious to us now, the constraint of going direct to hard copy exercised a discipline on author and secretary alike which resulted in a higher quality than is general today. The written word was the record, and every level of the organisation took pride in its standards of expression and presentation. The 'quick fix' and relative ease of communication today have, I feel, led to a decline in standards: 'Oh, what do grammar and syntax matter? The meaning is obvious.' Obvious at the time to those most closely involved, perhaps; but what of their successors?

When I returned from our family Christmas in South Africa at the beginning of 1969, it was to a newly-built head office at 122, Leadenhall Street that I went to work. This splendid building had been developed on P&O's original site in conjunction with Commercial Union, whose tower block stands across the piazza. The development is one of the 1960s' more successful architectural schemes. Strangely, the P&O and CU buildings, the Baltic Exchange, the Chamber of Shipping and the Royal Bank of Canada in Bishopsgate, which between them covered most of my business activities over some twenty years, were among the buildings most severely damaged by the IRA bombs of 1992 and 1995. I had a sumptuous room on the top floor, the tenth, with a fine view of St

Paul's to the west. Yet I have to say that, as an office, the layout was not altogether efficient. Too much time was spent walking up and down stairs, and on the tenth floor there was a feeling of ivory tower remoteness. My activities were themselves somewhat detached from those of the managing directors. Thwaites and Crichton, in particular, were deeply involved with the liner business and the politics of ports and shipping. I had closer contact with Donald Anderson and Freddie Harmer, both of whom were looking above and beyond the day-to-day concerns. They were intensely interested in the dynamics of the bulk trades and in my attempt to establish P&O's entry into LPG transportation.

Through John Maccoy, the Group's in-house broker, we made contact with Mundo Gas, a trading company operating from Bermuda and jointly owned by Mobil, the Lorentzens of Norway and Pery Igel of Brazil. Mundo Gas had a number of its own ships and chartered many more. Association with us would enable them to spread their shareholders' risk and to join hands with a financially-strong provider of ships. Our interest was, again, to link with well-respected, strong partners who controlled a significant share of the world LPG trade and who would have a continuing use for ships which we, P&O, would build.

As we got down to detailed discussions, I came to know the first top-flight commercial lawyer I had met thus far – Peter Peddie of Freshfields. We were not interested in a minority position and insisted on a holding at least equal with the other shareholders, and in 1970 P&O bought into Mundo Gas as equal shareholders with Mobil and Lorentzen at 30% each, and with Pery Igel of Brazil holding the balance of 10%. We had already placed orders for two 30,000 cbm gas tankers at Cammell Laird's yard on the Mersey. The contract delivery date was later that year, but the order was running way behind schedule, plagued by strikes on apparently inconsequential grounds but of daunting ferocity, and our initial contribution to Mundo Gas was of little note. But we were learning.

More exotic than gas was P&O's developing interest in the energy business as a whole. Our dependence on shipping was bringing some uncomfortable exposure in its wake. Political threats were increasing. Cargo reservation, third world preferences, UNCTAD intervention, regulation, ready availability of credit which permitted, indeed encouraged, easy and widespread entry into the business, all suggested that it would be prudent to diversify (the 'in' word) and ideally to establish additional interests, counter-cyclical to shipping, which would bring the Group into better balance. When an opportunity arose in 1969 we moved quickly.

Natomas, primarily a Californian oil 'independent' but also the parent company of American President Lines (APL), was, through the high development costs of an Indonesian offshore oil concession, suffering severe cash-flow problems and they needed to sell a share of the oil venture. Shell were said to be in the wings. Our merchant bankers, Lazards, asked if P&O wished to express interest.

We immediately set up a task-force and retained Lazards to advise. Through their parent company, they had long experience of the industry in Mexico, the USA and, more recently, in the North Sea. They introduced Brian Downward of Pearson's Whitehall Petroleum, a colourful and powerful character. We retained DeGolyer, Mac-Naughton as assessors, and we had a team from Lazard Frères in New York and the Houston lawyers, Bakers. For two months I commuted between London and San Francisco. Frequent meetings involved Donald Anderson, Freddie Harmer and John Mitchell and a large cast from Lazards headed by Lord Poole, their chairman.

Gradually the picture took shape and, given that our objective was to secure entry into the oil and gas world at a meaningful level, this purchase seemed increasingly attractive with its combination of production, offshore interests and, perhaps, an edge on transportation of Indonesian oil as back-haul cargo for our OBOs. There was much technical appraisal, legal proof and political assessment to be put together. The timetable was tight. The most sensible and convenient arrangement was to bring all our consultants and advisers together, armed with their reports and recommendations, for a round-up session. This I fixed at San Francisco's Fairmont Hotel, all red and purple plushness, and the group assembled in Donald Anderson's vast suite. Freddie Harmer flew in from Prudhoe Bay, Alaska, where, as one of the government-nominated directors of BP, he had been attending a board meeting. Others came from London, New York, Oklahoma and Texas. The suite buzzed with activity.

Natomas invited us to an early dinner in their glittering offices and expressed themselves delighted with the way negotiations had gone. They assumed that we would return the following day for the closing ceremony and that, at some $150m, their cash squeeze would be relieved.

Unfortunately, when we continued our assessment that same

evening, it became clear that there was a very high risk factor in the appraisal of oil reserves, and that our consultants' view of likely drilling success was very different from that of the vendors'. Also, there was a significant degree of uncertainty over likely oil prices (how very conservative were our assumptions!). These concerns began to coalesce and we realised that it would be difficult to justify the price even if the risks were acceptable. I do not believe any of us had come to the meeting other than with the expectation that we would conclude the purchase, but equally, when all the individual assessments were married up, the case against was compelling.

After an all-night session, I had the rather unhappy task of advising the Natomas team that P&O would not be joining them and that we had decided to withdraw. There was great anguish at Natomas – they needed quick action and were now faced with starting again.

The cost of this 'circus' was not small, but there was value to P&O in that the investigations had confirmed our decision to pursue this new area of business. In mid-1970, Lazards secured for us an invitation to join a group bidding for exploration licences in the British sector of the North Sea. This was the fourth round of such licensing and our partners included Kerr McGhee of Oklahoma, Stuart Bennett, an independent, and Mesa Petroleum of Amarillo, Texas.

This was a risky route, but we decided that we should test the water, and even if the application was unsuccessful, we could establish what value we, P&O, had to the group – apart from the necessary Britishness. Again we retained various experts, as did all the partners unless they were experts themselves – and there were not many such around then.

The procedure was to make preliminary application for the right to drill on one or more, or indeed part of, the eight blocks to be allocated. If successful in getting onto the short list, the group would then be invited to submit a plan to the Department of Trade and Industry, setting out what drilling the group would commit to, timescale, type of well, etc. The DTI would grill the group on technical competence, management structure, financial strength, and so on. I attended one of these meetings to emphasise the true-blue character of our group.

Our first applications were for the 'hot' blocks in the central North Sea, for which we had acquired some seismic. It was clear that Beckett of the DTI had heard similar presentations and that a number had, unsurprisingly, targeted the same areas.

However, when our team made an application for Block 11/30, which lay close inshore in the Moray Firth, the DTI showed interest; or was it amusement that newcomers had the temerity to play such a wild card? The background to our choice was rather delightful. George C. Pendleton III, an Oklahoma geologist and a member of Stuart Bennett's subgroup, was a large, close-cropped egg of a man with a generous heart and a simple appreciation of values. He and Professor Cliff Potter, a geophysicist at Imperial College, struck up a happy, if at first sight unlikely association born of mutual respect. One weekend shortly before the applications were to be submitted, they went off together to Inverness and Speyside 'to sample the single malts', as George said. What part the malts had to play I'm not sure, but the lore is that, as George and Cliff gazed north to Ben Wyvis and over to the Black Isle, they speculated on the fall of the land to the east, into the Moray Firth. They teased each other a bit, looked at such data as there was and recommended that the group should have a go for block 11/30.

Ours was the only application for block 11/30 and in due course, together with participation in part-licences in the middle North Sea, we were granted sole rights with an obligation to drill one well. In 1976 the operators, Mesa Petroleum, struck oil at 3,600 feet. The Beatrice field, named after the wife of Mesa's Boone Pickens (later notorious as corporate promoter and raider) was estimated to hold 150,000 barrels of oil only some eleven miles offshore.

George Pendleton remains a close friend and we see him once or twice a year when, en route to Vienna for the music, he visits London for his tailor to construct his ample suits, and for good food and comfort at the Connaught. I once enabled George to cruise in the eastern Mediterranean on board *Uganda* – a small thank you from P&O. He has never forgotten the experience.

P&O continued to search for new shipping business in which higher and hopefully consistent margins were obtainable. By now we had good working experience of pooling resources in joint venture operations: ABC covered bulk shipping in association with Zapata Norness; and Overseas Containers Ltd (OCL) had been formed in 1965, when P&O, Ocean, Furness Withy and British & Commonwealth agreed progressively to merge their conventional liner trades into specialised container services. When we discovered that Ocean, like us, was well forward with a study of multi-purpose chemical carriers, it made good sense to co-operate in this field and to share the substantial investment required to ensure significant market 'clout'. The outcome was Panocean Shipping & Trading, which became a leading player in this complex business.

The launch of Panocean was beset by the same problems as had bedevilled P&O's gas carriers – troubles at Cammell Laird. Shipbuilding contracts had been placed with Cammells as both P&O and Ocean believed it would be safer to build this very sophisticated tonnage at home rather than in Japan. How wrong we were.

Labour relations at the Birkenhead yard continued to be abysmal and there were disputes over quality, over organisation, over correspondence, over conditions for our staff, indeed over every single issue. Other owners were facing the same problems, in particular Canadian Pacific, whose lawyer, Graham Day, became a partner in adversity. Eventually, and apparently inevitably, there was one strike too many and a cash crisis hit the yard. The management seemed helpless and the minister of technology, with his whizz kids of the Industrial Reorganisation Corporation, came on the scene, effectively negotiating on behalf of the yard. It was a strange form of negotiation – it almost seemed as if we, the customers, were in the dock. It was as if we were responsible for the yard's imminent collapse: we were too demanding, we had driven too hard a bargain, we had imposed unrealistic conditions, and so on. It would have been ludicrous had it not been all too serious.

We were conscious that Panocean's future was at stake; whatever the outcome of this crisis there would be a prolonged delay before the vessels could be completed and replacements elsewhere would not be easy to secure. We were not, however, prepared to let the yard walk away from the contract and the confrontation was fraught. In the end Harold Lever, the minister, put it bluntly: 'Either you cancel the four Panocean vessels without compensation and we (Cammell Laird) undertake to complete your two gas carriers (two years late) or I will let the yard go into liquidation and you can scrabble in the dust with everyone else for your halfcrown.' Canadian Pacific received much the same treatment. Graham Day, however, so impressed the officials and politicians that he was offered the job of running Cammell Laird and restoring it to the reasonably competent naval yard it had once been. Graham went on to head the nationalised British Shipbuilders and became one of the UK's leading industrialists – chairman of Rover, Cadbury Schweppes, British Aerospace, *et al.* But thereafter almost all P&O's orders went abroad.

By 1970 I was getting the hang of my new role in P&O and, to my surprise, a most interesting and useful string was added to my bow during the year. Through Denny Marris, a non-executive director of P&O and a managing director of Lazards, I was introduced to Ronnie Brooks, chairman of Commercial Union, where Marris was a deputy chairman. Shortly thereafter, Brooks invited me to join the CU board. Thus began a twenty-year association which immediately opened an invaluable window onto the workings and attitudes of another major public company.

I was now stepping into the years of intensely hard work, long hours in consequence, and greater stimulus. The political climate made managing difficult – far too much time was spent embroiled in trades union matters, and also in seeking ways to circumvent the effects of rising inflation, a punishing top rate of income tax at 83% and a further impost on so-called unearned income. My Presbyterian background made me uneasy about the complicated devices employed to offset tax and about the proliferation of 'perks'. Artificial activity of this kind breeds deviousness and inequity. The end result was a softening of management, coupled with an increasing atmosphere of envy in our society which persisted for a decade until, in the 1980s under Margaret Thatcher, we began to see effort and enterprise rewarded fairly and the right to manage upheld.

During that difficult period, 'Corporate Britain' reacted in different ways. Some companies turned defensive and introspective and withered away. The shipbuilding and motor industries were enmeshed in seeking subsidy and 'bail-out' from government. P&O took a different tack. We had begun to recognise that there had to be a marked change in approach to business and in organisational structure if the company was to survive and grow. Yet I felt there were some within the Group who, in lamenting external pressures on their business, seized upon diversification as their salvation.

While need for change was becoming accepted, it should be acknowledged that, for its time, the structure of P&O had been remarkably successful. It was by far the largest shipping group in the world and a number of its constituent companies were leaders in their own right. BI had run an enormous and adaptable complex of services based on India; New Zealand Steamship and Federal dominated the NZ meat trade; there were coastal operations in Europe, Africa and New Zealand; there were flourishing tramp companies; and there were the huge passenger trades to the Far East and Australia. There was practically no part of the shipping world in which P&O was not engaged. But technical advances, political restrictions on earlier trading patterns, and the imperatives of the economy of scale presaged and demanded a new approach. By 1970 certain foundations for a new P&O had been laid – Overseas Containers, Trident, Associated Bulk Carriers, and the essential shift towards cruising demanded by the decline in passenger traffic – but the building had scarcely begun. Donald Anderson, having declared his intention to retire the following year, called in McKinsey. Under the leadership of Roger Morrison, one of the London partners, they undertook a classic analysis (DFA was said to have assumed that 'about ten or twelve people' reported to him; McKinsey identified twenty-seven who each maintained that his reporting line was direct to the chairman – a motley crew). Their recommendations as to structure and practice would have come as no surprise to any student of management.

McKinsey's report was adopted, and P&O was reformed with five operating divisions backed by specialist staff service divisions. This entailed the relatively rapid demise of some 127 subsidiary companies. I was nominated head of Bulk Shipping Division which, in August 1971, was the first to be up and running. Colleagues – Dick Adams head of General Cargo, Peter Parry of Passenger, MacNaughten Sidey of European and Air Transport and Harry Beazley of General Holdings – were all by this time directors. In January 1972 Clifford Nancarrow was recruited as head of Corporate Planning, a key new appointment, while Denys Brown, after joining in 1971 from the diplomatic service, was head of International Affairs and Government Relations.

We now had the structure in place to become a professionally-managed company. Clear lines of communication, authority and accountability were laid down and, apart from some understandable regrets at the passing of long-established loyalties, the Group as a whole began to tick encouragingly. It was indeed fortunate, in the light of events less than a year into the future, that a part of Sir Donald Anderson's legacy was an effective structure.

Less effective was his choice of successor. Michael Thwaites, a powerful and intellectual figure, had died unexpectedly and in 1971, by a process of nods, winks, assumptions and acceptance, Ford Geddes emerged as chairman. When Freddie Harmer retired at the same time, his successor from the New Zealand stable, Bill Dawes, became deputy chairman in much the same way. Having long family connections in constituent parts of the Group, Geddes and Dawes were of the old school and had functioned reasonably well within it. Geddes in particular embraced the theory of new management techniques and structures with enthusiasm, but I was never entirely convinced that he and Dawes would be able, within themselves, to adapt. They assumed too readily that staff would understand the need for change and would continue to serve the company as before. But reorganisation had brought many upsets. Little empires had gone, and at every level there was a demand for more professionalism and greater awareness. There had been an influx of new recruits, particularly in the important areas of finance and personnel services. The culture shock was immense.

In these delicate circumstances I do not believe that there was adequate leadership from the chairman and from the board. The executive directors enjoyed challenging, interesting jobs and understood the purpose of the restructuring. Some divisions were more coherent than others, and I was fortunate that the McKinsey change had no great significance for Bulk Shipping – already a success story like Trident. But the message had to be spread far and wide. It was going to take time and understanding for the new style to bed down; but we were not to be afforded the time.

PART TWO
P&O 1972–1979

5
Takeover

The year 1972 opened quietly with no inkling of the dramatic events in store that would mark a turning-point in our lives. I was forty-seven, married to Mona, then thirty-eight, for eleven years. Our children were flourishing, thanks to Mona's devoted care. Alastair would be ten in August and in September would go to Streete Court as a boarder. Gillian, eight in March, was at Laverock, a popular girls' school in Oxted, and James, shortly to be five, was already attending the pre-prep at Hazelwood School in Limpsfield. All of us were happy, contented as a family, and looking forward to the coming months.

I had been a director of P&O for just over three years, and my strong base in Bulk Shipping Division had given me confidence. But in the boardroom there were worries about overall performance: in particular, the 1971 results were not good. The relative cosiness of the business world had already been given a severe jolt by asset strippers. Slater Walker, arch-exponents of the break-up principle, were on the prowl and although their activities seemed to bring immediately beneficial results, many of these proved unproductive in the long-term. It was a decidedly uncomfortable time for any company which might be perceived as resting on its laurels.

In its article 'P&O for the Asking', the *Economist* of 12 February put the chairman's anxieties in a nutshell: 'There are after all many ways of making assets of over £200 million turn in a better than 2 per cent profit.' The recent takeover of Cunard by Trafalgar House, the construction and property group, had disconcerted Geddes and such press comment did little to steady his nerve.

The new divisional structure was beginning to work, despite the inevitable strains between those in charge of day-to-day operations and the central staff divisions. I knew that Bulk Shipping was set to perform well. Our morale was high; our markets were showing an upward trend; we had the management and technical skills to operate our fleet profitably and to contribute an increasingly larger share to Group returns.

If prepared, I believed P&O could see off any predator, and in a note dated 16 February I submitted my views to the chairman: 'It would be surprising if we were not to receive a takeover approach within the next few weeks.' I urged contingency planning. We should set up study teams for each part of the Group (as had already been done for Property) to establish facts and to identify possible courses of action; identify and research our major stockholders and 'get them on side'; recognise the importance of our public image and retain Peter Thomas, our PR man who was about to leave (this last was to rebound later with odd results). One of my most important points was: 'Select your merchant bank.' Many of us were by then very critical of the contribution, or lack of it, made by Lazards, our entrenched financial advisers. From my direct involvement with them over our oil and gas developments I had a high regard for certain individuals, but it was perhaps the failings of Daniel Meinertzhagen, their senior adviser, which left us dissatisfied. He may have been under some inhibition due to the powerful presence, as a non-executive director on the P&O board, of Denny Marris, one of his most senior colleagues at Lazards.

In a brave attempt to win over the head poacher to the cause of the gamekeepers, Lord G, on 3 March, introduced Jim Slater of Slater Walker to Ford Geddes and Bill Dawes to discuss ways in which P&O's property interests might be better managed. It may have seemed an unlikely alliance, and one cannot think that Geddes and Dawes felt entirely comfortable at the prospect, but it was a typically bold and imaginative move by Lord G. Slater recommended that we proceed over a period in association with a number of different developers, so as to make a recurring impact on the market. Each development would be the result of an auction approach, and the evolution of such schemes would be put in the hands of someone well-regarded in the property development world. While Slater did not push himself forward, he left them in no doubt that he believed he could deliver.

A few days later, Ford Geddes and Lord G discussed Slater's recommendations with Lazards and Jones Lang Wootton, our property advisers. Lazards had rolled out a big gun, Lord (Oliver) Poole, to support Meinertzhagen. Poole was generally in accord with Slater's advice and it was agreed, subject to board approval, that P&O would proceed along the lines proposed. But in hindsight, this probably amounted to no more than window-dressing.

At the AGM on 15 March, Ford Geddes opened his first chairman's address to stockholders by repeating Sir Donald Anderson's words when taking the chair in 1960: 'It would have been nice for me if this had coincided with a smart upswing in the fortunes of shipping.' Sadly he lacked Sir Donald's charisma. When Geddes reported that property values exceeded book by some £50m and that 'it is impossible at this stage to forecast how the current year may turn out', a number of those present must have sensed the first chill wind of the gathering storm.

Ford Geddes too often played the role without comprehending the script. In an April circular to staff he included a blunt warning that P&O was not immune to takeover. Having failed to appreciate the crushing effect his words would have on ears already unsettled, he was badly rattled by staff reactions and did not seem able to respond firmly. He had failed to consult widely among his directors beforehand, although I must admit that had he done so I think I would not have objected – it was after all only the truth. But then I would have been making the mistake of judging its impact on Bulk Shipping, not on the Group as a whole, and I am sure my colleagues, particularly in Passenger and General Cargo Divisions, would have advised a spoonful of sugar with the medicine. Today such a sentiment would not need to be expressed, but in 1972 the average P&O staff member would have assumed (a) that P&O was 'too big to take over' and (b) that, as a unique company incorporated under Royal Charter in 1840, a takeover 'would not be allowed'.

On 17 May Oliver Poole was appointed to the P&O Board. His credentials included Eton, Cambridge, a distinguished war record, and a peerage awarded for services to the Tory party – as party chairman he had stage-managed its 1959 landslide victory. He attended his first board meeting on 31 May and was given a welcome which touched on the obsequious. Ford Geddes was obviously proud of having secured him for P&O. Poole was urbane and articulate. Geddes hung on his every word, displaying an eager willingness to defer without question to his judgement.

Poole certainly added a new dimension to our meetings. One had the impression that he moved in important circles and that he regarded P&O as an interesting sub-plot, the directors as ingenuous (he had a point), and the company as merely one of many building blocks to be deployed as part of a grand plan, the extent and complexity of which it was not necessary for us to know.

There is no doubt that Poole dominated Ford Geddes. He was soon to spend much time in the office, behind closed doors. I was busy running Bulk Shipping and saw nothing of him except at board meetings, but I was always aware of his august presence flitting in and out. He wielded immense influence. Both Ford and Bill Dawes would refer, somewhat awe-struck, to 'Oliver's views' or say 'We should put that to Oliver.' I had some regard for him on account of his role in introducing us to the oil world, but could not, as some did, see him as our saviour. He was clever but mortal.

At the 14 June board Poole expressed certain views on the long term strategy for the Group. He now considered that it would be unwise to make any commitments which might conflict with the development of 'future plans' and the board accordingly agreed that negotiations on property, which had already been initiated, should be suspended.

It was probably at this meeting that Poole suggested we might merge with a company having complementary characteristics – high earnings, property expertise, proven management skills, and a market exposure different from ours. A merger of this kind would effectively remove P&O from any possibility of takeover. His candidate was relatively unknown to most of us except as a high-flying name. I remember that, when first mentioned, his candidate was referred to as 'Company X, one of whose major interests is as builders to Marks & Spencer'. Unfortunately for the cloak and dagger department, the Bovis name and humming-bird logo were plastered all over the giant hoardings protecting the Marble Arch site of the flagship store that they were then building for M&S.

Bovis was a modestly-capitalised housebuilder (some 1,000 houses a year) with a struggling civil engineering business, mostly in motorway work, and a small but successful specialised management construction division. Its high-performing share price was based on property speculation and on a Brighton-based enterprise rejoicing in the name of 20th Century Banking Corporation, primarily engaged in the second mortgage field. Frank Sanderson, the chairman, was said to have visions of floating off this 'bank'. But when the secondary banking crisis of 1973 developed it became obvious that, in reality, 20th Century could only, and then if lucky, be classed as tertiary. But this was for the future – in mid-1972 the question would be 'P&O and who?'

With much coming and going around the chairman's suite, I for one began to feel, and resent, the emergence of a cabal within the board. Ford Geddes, Dawes, Poole and Marris held lengthy sessions to which the executive directors were not privy. Indeed there seemed to be an assumption that we were merely management and our corporate responsibilities for the wider interests of the company as a whole went unrecognised.

Poole introduced Geddes to Sanderson at his Knightsbridge flat, ostensibly neutral ground, and exploratory talks began. What the majority of us did not then know was that Lazards, with Poole in a leading role, were advisers to both companies and that they were working with Bovis on a possible merger with MEPC, another property company, to whom, according to the *Investors Chronicle*, three approaches had been made between May and the end of June. Poole was brilliant in some aspects, but the devastating health problems which struck him down in the 1980s may have been beginning to affect him, so it is sad now to have to criticise his conduct. But the fact was that his keenness to do a deal put him in a position of appalling conflict. He primarily, and of course Geddes too, should have recognised this. I believe that attitudes to corporate governance today would probably ensure that such a conflict would not be countenanced even if the chairman himself were to be so star-struck.

To minimise the risk of a security breach, the board accepted a proposal on 26 June that, should the company be interested in taking over or merging with another company, the chairman be authorised to form a sub-committee of not less than three members of the board to investigate the possibility up to the stage before the company would be committed. The Finance Committee would, of course, review any proposition recommended by this sub-committee in the normal way before it was brought to the board for decision. Given the activity one could sense 'below the surface' I was, as a member of the Finance Committee, reassured that the checks and balances built into the system would be heeded.

The same day – 26 June – was a busy one for Lazards. They delivered a seventeen-page document, 'Report on a merger, P&O/Bovis', which, it transpired, they handed to both companies. This suggested that a 50/50 merger would be appropriate (I was not to see this document until late in August). They identified the benefits of the merger as greater financial muscle, with any surplus funds from P&O activities to be channelled to the Bovis side, where

Lazards suggested they would attract an 18% return. The unlocking of P&O's tax allowances would give an immediate and substantial increase in attributable earnings and, due to anticipated fiscal changes, a rather higher benefit in 1973.

Two days later, the chairman's sub-committee requested Williams & Glyn's Bank Ltd to act as independent financial advisers on the merger proposals. R. E. B. Lloyd, chief executive of the bank had been a non-executive director of P&O for the last two years. The game plan was for Wms Glyn first to assess the proposal independently and then to act jointly with Lazards as advisers to P&O. The Lazards report of 26 June provided the basis for the review, although by this time it was already in the hands of both parties and had thus set the scene. Only now did Lazards resign as advisers to Bovis who, at some time during the next three or four weeks, turned to Warburgs. The timing of this transfer of loyalty was a grey area which was to prove a costly hostage to fortune for Oliver Poole.

The Wms Glyn merchant banking arm was a relatively new venture. David Horne, the leader of the team, worked throughout July with his colleagues evaluating the proposal, and they must surely have had a deal of quiet satisfaction when they found the Lazards outline suggestions deficient. They could not accept Lazards' balance sheet value of the assets. Inadequate value had been attributed to a better use of P&O's assets, and too much weight had been given to the immediate benefit of the tax allowances at the expense of the future. Wms Glyn concluded that the equity split should be 60% P&O/40% Bovis, and on this basis an acquisition of Bovis by P&O rather than a merger should be explored. The new financial advisers impressed on Geddes the critical importance to the success of a merger of management compatibility and the establishment of an acceptable line of management control. Horne was to put his findings to Geddes officially in a letter dated 25 July.

In parallel with all this activity, but quite independent of it, Clifford Nancarrow was producing the first, McKinsey-type, Group Five-Year Plan for submission to the Finance Committee on 18 July. At this meeting, enlarged for the occasion by the addition of Poole, Parry, Sidey, Beazley and Brown, the plan was approved for submission to the board, while, as a separate item of business, a brief verbal report on the possibility of a merger with Bovis was made by the chairman.

The following day, 19 July, Ford Geddes circulated a paper on

Bovis to the executive directors 'to help in focussing discussion' at the board meeting arranged for 26 July. He concentrated solely on the management structure while omitting all reference to the financial aspects. I had no argument with the principle – Bovis's business could, in theory, balance the shipping cycle and certainly they had the expertise to exploit our property. The formation of an executive management committee under a small supervisory board, guiding two operating boards – one P&O, one Bovis – was suggested: a complicated structure to say the least, particularly when putting together two different businesses with distinct cultures. Before I could get to grips with assessing the merger's true merits, I needed to know both how the structure would work and what it would cost P&O. The devil was to turn up in the detail.

On 20 July Lord Geddes retired from the P&O Board. Since the formation of Bulk Shipping Division in August 1971 he had continued to play a valuable role in the tanker field. He also had wide contacts in the property business and contributed positively in that area. However, although he was a first cousin of Ford Geddes, he was by background and inclination far more a Donald Anderson and Freddie Harmer man. It was perhaps not altogether a surprise that he decided to go, but the manner of his going was. I wonder now if I missed an important pointer. He had been very much a part of the Slater Walker discussions. His sub-committee made the recommendations on the strategy for property which the board accepted and subsequently, on Poole's intervention, put on hold. From his very active and influential participation Lord G moved quickly to sever his long and productive membership of the board. Was it that he realised he would find himself in fundamental disagreement with the plans now evolving? It would not have been in his nature to compromise, and perhaps he felt unwilling to confront his cousin so recently installed in the P&O chair. Such a situation could explain the unusually swift transition. It would not, of course, have been Lord G's style to disclose such conclusions, but only a modest cocktail party was to signal the end of his colourful and powerful period in shipping, during which he made a formidable mark on P&O's development and played a role of the highest importance in tanker safety and design and in industry co-operation. As president of the Chamber of Shipping he had been a persuasive spokesman for international consultation and regulation.

On 24 July Ford Geddes gave a lunch in the office for the executives to meet the Bovis chairman, Frank Sanderson. (I did not then know that he had a phobia about lifts and had walked up the thirteen floors.) Apart from Nancarrow and Mitchell, we were largely ignorant of the financial package. This probably explains why the lunch was neither very constructive nor, indeed, informative. Geddes was totally committed to the imperative of capturing Sanderson for P&O and I believe, for him, the exercise was simply one of presenting this management wizard to us as a *fait accompli*.

Undoubtedly Geddes's unease with most, if not all, aspects of financial criteria ('Leave it to the experts' was to become his battle cry) had blinded him to the necessity of considering Wms Glyn's report before presenting the management structure to his executives and introducing Frank Sanderson as a colleague. We were effectively being told by Geddes: 'This is what you will buy on behalf of the shareholders, but how much you will pay for it is not your concern.' Over the coming months Geddes was to repeat this error – of saying what the end result would be without setting out how it could be achieved.

In Corporate Planning, Clifford Nancarrow had a bright and competent group. On 25 July he produced a seminal paper on the Bovis deal which argued that, as formulated, it amounted to a reverse takeover by Bovis of P&O. Although Lazards had suggested a 50/50 financial split, it was becoming clear that Bovis would secure the key management jobs. The paper concluded with the recommendation that we terminate discussions with Bovis; develop our property interests through other channels; intensify profit improvement plans; and dispose of fringe activities. This perceptive analysis was never fully considered – I think on the superficial assumption that it was suggesting the same objectives but by other means.

It is ironic that the Wms Glyn's report recommending going ahead with a bid on the basis of a 60/40 split in favour of P&O and *subject to detailed examination* of Bovis was also submitted on 25 July.

At the board meeting the following day it was agreed that Geddes should take the talks a stage further by exploring the terms on which P&O might acquire Bovis, and then report back. During the discussions, reference was made to papers which had been prepared by Lazards (on 26 June) and by Wms Glyn (on 25 July) setting out possible parameters for a deal. But these papers were withheld from directors as they were not considered to be in their final form.

Warburgs, now acting for Bovis (and themselves David Horne's former employers), had boldly countered his proposed 60/40 split in favour of P&O with 60/40 in favour of Bovis. Against the background of the Lazards 50/50 paper given to both sides, and with Lazards nominally in the lead, Horne was having an extremely difficult task negotiating a deal on the 'independent' terms he recommended. The further they moved away from 50/50, the more difficult it was going to be to carry Lazards. It looked like being a long haul.

We were now coming into the holiday season. The Marshall family was to join P&O's *Oriana* for a cruise to the Eastern Mediterranean on 2 August. As I would be absent from the next board meeting on 9 August, I talked at length to John Mitchell, and we both agreed that nothing much was likely to mature for some weeks – there was so much detail to be worked out by the bankers. However, John undertook to keep me posted in the event of unexpected developments and, encouraged by Geddes, I went off to board *Oriana*.

But I remained concerned. I told my secretary, Betty Fairclough, that I needed to take with me an open-dated air ticket to cover a return to London from Naples or Athens, but that I did not want it purchased through P&O channels. The impassive way this instruction was received and carried out told me that the events of the past few weeks had not entirely escaped her attention.

For a week Mona and I enjoyed the comfort and freedom of *Oriana*. I was not wholly relaxed, but as the days passed I began to accept that, yes, developments were going to take time to mature. In London, however, Geddes was blundering his way onto a course which would leave his career on the rocks.

The bankers were making slow progress. Even with the P&O share price at a record high of 240p and compromises on the equity split, the arithmetic still left P&O with only a fraction over 50%. To his credit Geddes said that this was unacceptable. On 7 August Frank Sanderson apparently offered to take some 75p less than the price offered for Bovis – on his personal holding this would mean his forgoing over £1m.

The next day, 8 August, Geddes circulated to directors 'known to be in London' a paper detailing organisational proposals for a merger or acquisition which he 'hoped would meet with the board's approval after the financial terms, being dealt with by the merchant bankers, are agreed'. The proposals preserved theoretical control for the P&O board while handing over far-reaching powers of initiative and day-to-day management to Frank Sanderson and Malcolm Paris, the Bovis finance director who was to become joint group finance director. Geddes had asked the Lazards and Wms Glyn representatives to attend the board the next day and report the position reached in the negotiations. Whether this would allow the board to take a decision one way or the other Geddes believed 'is as yet too early to say'. (Since I was known not to be in London I was not to see this paper until I officially returned on 21 August.)

Oriana lay peacefully berthed in Naples. It was steaming hot and we were 'doing the sights': Pompeii, where, in the forum, I photographed a very heated, very grumpy Gillian, transformed moments later by a *pistachio gelato*; then off to Capri for a lovely afternoon of swimming, fresh lemons and visits to the Blue Grotto and San Michele. When we returned to *Oriana* at 6 p.m. I was surprised to be confronted by our agent, Gilbert Harrison, a colourful character, widely respected in Naples. He was in a state of high excitement. John Mitchell had telephoned asking him to track me down – if I was not able to return the call then I should know that John felt I might wish to attend the board meeting in London the following day. While Harrison made the travel arrangements, I telephoned John, who told me that it seemed possible, following the outcome of meetings now taking place, that the chairman *would* put to the board a firm proposal for a merger. Throughout the day David Horne had been endeavouring to negotiate a compromise and it seemed to John that he might succeed. Horne had proposed an equity package which, together with some cash, would give Bovis 42.5% of the new company.

Warburgs had countered that the Bovis profits were likely to exceed P&O's for the foreseeable future, thus the equity gearing was too favourable to P&O's stockholders. Late in the evening, after Mitchell had alerted me, it became clear that the bankers had reached deadlock. The principals agreed to terminate discussions. David Horne, assured that there was nothing more he could do, departed for a family holiday in Dorset.

Unaware of the emerging situation, I gathered myself. I advised John Wacher, *Oriana*'s captain, of my departure; encouraged Mona and the children to expect me back 'some time'; and off I went by car to Rome. I was too late to leave that evening, but fortunately there was a room at the Grand before an early flight next morning.

En route to London I quickly shed my holiday mood. I needed to focus my mind on Bovis. I gave up, as a fruitless exercise, trying to figure out how, in such a short time, the detail leading to a firm proposal could have been finalised, and why it had apparently bypassed the Finance Committee. Handicapped by a dearth of financial data and not understanding exactly how the new management structure would work, it was impossible to prepare a reasoned case for or against. All I could do was to identify and define my areas of concern just in case – what? – just in case I, a junior director with only three years' public company board experience in P&O and two in Commercial Union, happened to disagree with my chairman and with two merchant banks. I concentrated on my notes:

> We have *just* got ourselves into the position of being able, with reasonable knowledge, to consider action and we risk picking the first mayfly to be floated past us.
>
> 'No alternative' is not an answer. We haven't seriously tried to find an alternative because we haven't sufficiently focused.
>
> Tax considerations should not dictate.
>
> 'Feel?' Could we work with them? I don't know them.
>
> Forecast – we *can* forecast our results to end September.
>
> The deal feels artificial – what is really intended?
>
> What about our staff? We, Bulk Shipping, have done all that has been asked of us and a lot more. Why are we so defensive?
>
> Staff already critical of leadership – if we chuck in the towel we may not bring much to the party.
>
> Ford seems to be saying: 'There go my ships – quick, I must follow, for I am their leader.'
>
> I have particular concern too about our joint venture partners. What would one think if one were Ocean, Zapata, Møller, etc.?
>
> I do not suggest inaction – I simply don't feel this is the right one.

This exercise was of some help in clearing my mind, and in the light of later developments it was probably just as well that I didn't know that negotiations had been broken off.

On the evening of 8 August it must have seemed to Frank Sanderson that from having two birds in the hand, he now had none in the bush. After a sleepless night he called Ford Geddes early on the morning of the 9th to propose one further attempt to salvage the deal. They met at P&O with Barnes of Lazards leading for the bankers, while David Horne gave his input over the telephone from Dorset. In this bizarre situation a formula was agreed and, as the board began to assemble, Barnes and Sanderson were apparently working on figures to prove its viability.

I arrived, somewhat breathless, ten minutes before the board convened. I bumped into Ford in the corridor: 'What on earth are you doing here?' Either he thought it unhelpful of me to return or, more likely, he thought it unnecessary.

A buzz went round the room at my appearance – why was I there and did I know more than the others? Some directors had heard nothing since being told the previous evening that everything was off; some had heard rumours of an eleventh-hour deal. The opening proceedings were chaotic. The chairman was absent and Bill Dawes, as deputy chairman, explained that there had been some 'late developments with Bovis'.

There was tension and expectancy in the air as we moved through the routine business. Geddes and Poole entered with Barnes, who had the task of explaining the principal points of an agreement that had been reached between Geddes and Sanderson within the last hour, then recommended by Lazards and Wms Glyn and was now to be approved by the board.

We had no papers. Lazards appeared to be reading from handwritten notes. Two, three, four directors spoke at once, and the chairman found it difficult to control the meeting. Board members and advisers would appear and disappear. It was surreal.

I was struggling to understand and evaluate the implications of the financial details and the proposed management structure. It was only after Kenneth Inchcape, almost spluttering with indignation, had protested 'This is a circus', that, about noon, a typewritten memorandum of salient points was tabled. This document could well have been labelled 'e&oe'. Even with the assistance of the memorandum, I still found the deal unclear and the arguments specious. No balance sheet for Bovis or pro-forma combined balance sheet was available. Against the pro faction it was proving increasingly difficult to make any form of constructive contribution, but I think I managed to make all the points I had jotted down on my morning flight.

The proposed management structure gave rise to a great deal of disquiet. Denys Brown in particular asked for clarification of the roles of chairman, executive deputy chairman, chairman of the Executive Committee and of the bland assertion that 'we will each go on running our own businesses'. What authority would be vested in the Executive Committee and how would the chief executives of P&O divisions relate to it? Geddes's response was on the lines of 'Frank and I understand what is meant and that is the important thing.'

Geddes pushed questions on the financial detail to one side, saying repeatedly: 'The bankers have looked at that and are satisfied.' Sir Andrew Maitland-Makgill-Crichton, the most vocal of the non-executives, exploded with enthusiasm for the deal. I shall never forget his arrogance, and my thinking at the time that his approach would achieve the worst of all possible worlds for P&O. He was not remotely concerned about the figures, which he declared were a matter for the bankers to work out. He ranted on: 'What we need Bovis for is to get some proven management into this company – look at their record – you lot will have to look to your laurels.' The proposal was away above our heads – we couldn't be expected to understand corporate finance – Crichton and the other senior City people would look after that. He came to the end of his outburst with a patronising 'Just thank your stars you are being rescued by joining with a dynamic company led by a paragon like Sanderson.'

After four hours of confused wrangling the chairman took the sense of the meeting as in favour, authorised Lazards to go ahead and closed the proceedings.

Had he taken a formal vote he would have noted opposition from: Kenneth Inchcape, Harry Beazley, Peter Parry, Denys Brown, Clifford Nancarrow, Sandy Marshall and John Mitchell.

He would have noted support from: Andrew Crichton, Mac Sidey, Dick Adams and, of course, Bill Dawes, Angus Mackinnon, Dick Lloyd of Wms Glyn, and Poole of Lazards. Although Marris, also of Lazards, was not present to hear the arguments, Geddes 'knew' he would be in favour and obligingly counted him in.

Adding the chairman's vote, Geddes arrived at a consensus of nine to seven in favour. Three directors associated with the company's merchant banks, which were recommending the bid, had assented, but apparently this was not considered out of order. No vote was actually taken.

With hindsight one can say of Ford's performance on 9 August that when the warning bells rang he didn't hear them.

As we grabbed our sandwiches in the lunch-room afterwards, I spoke to Geddes. It seems surprising to me now, but I must have said something along the lines of 'Well, that's it then.' I suppose we were all a bit dazed. I said that if there was no objection I intended to rejoin the family on board *Oriana*. 'Absolutely no reason to stay here – off you go – I am going myself tonight, and' – significantly – 'so is Oliver.'

I arranged with Jim Bayley and others in Bulk Shipping to communicate the bald announcement of an 'agreed' bid to our fleet and to our associates as soon as the press release had been issued the following day.

I caught a Lufthansa flight via Frankfurt to Athens. As I flew through the night I made notes of the meeting, covering page after page with questions for Ford Geddes and John Mitchell. Back on board *Oriana* I found that the family, and particularly Mona, had been befriended by two couples who had ensured she was looked after at dinner and had fussed over her in a very kindly way. I told John Wacher that he would be getting an interesting cable later in the day and that I would be available, if he wished, to talk about it to his senior officers. Then I changed gear and we took the family off to visit the Acropolis.

As Gillian well remembers it was again a very hot day, but we walked the Parthenon, Lykabettou and the Agora before, to everyone's relief, deserting culture in favour of the sea at Vougliameni. That afternoon on the beach is one of my focal points of the Bovis saga. While the children played happily around us, Mona and I sat in quiet companionship on somewhat uncomfortable white plastic chairs watching the movement of the sea. It was the best therapy in the world.

I explained that the merger was a major step for P&O and that there would be opportunities as well as problems. My personal opportunity was that I was likely to become a member of the Executive Committee. But I was concerned. I had responsibility for a part of P&O which had been transforming the potential for its shipping activities – as Donald Anderson, Freddie Harmer and Lord G well knew. But since their departure there was no one at the top with the same appreciation of the new dynamics of the Group. There was still a basic inwardness in the P&O culture. Before I had had time to show what Bulk Shipping could do for P&O, before we had had time to set our hands to the five-year plan, before we had had time to establish the ground rules for such a major diversification, we risked giving ourselves away. I knew so little of Bovis; I really had no idea if they would make a good fit or a good partner; we were surely chalk and cheese: P&O, a charter company with a great and international history; Bovis new, brash and, yes, down-market, but above all unknown. Sanderson was the magnet.

As I fielded Mona's relentless 'Why? I don't quite understand', I knew that I, too, didn't quite understand. I needed to know more about objectives, about valuations, about structure, about implementation, before I could be convinced that this proposal answered P&O's needs. The Bovis deal was being presented as an opportunity 'not to be missed'; 'to be grasped before it disappears', etc. But Bovis appeared to be the sole candidate on offer.

The children, sensing the seriousness of our conversation, had left us undisturbed. I can't remember which of us noticed it first, but from sitting by the sea we were now sitting *in* the sea. It was wonderfully ridiculous and broke our sombre mood, but I knew now that I would need to be given the arguments with which to be convinced and, at that point, I believe I wanted to be convinced.

Oriana sailed that night for Beirut, in 1972 a jewel of a city – colourful, elegant, mysterious and teeming with life. The next day, the 11th, a Fleet message arrived announcing the board's decision to 'acquire' Bovis. I spoke to John Wacher and his senior officers in Deputy Captain Mike Bradford's cabin. They were keenly interested if somewhat confused. Passenger Division was in the process of changing from ocean route passenger services to cruising. The concept was not fully developed, the market not yet established, the hardware a compromise and the officers' main worry was whether resources might be directed to the glamour businesses of Bovis. I gave the party line and did my best to explain the safeguards and controls built into the management structure, but I could not answer many of their questions. Hard as I tried to take a positive approach, I suspect my audience, for more traditional reasons, was as sceptical as Mona. Later, I was greatly heartened to receive a cable of support from *Oriana*, a significant and bold action by senior officers whose loyalties were being challenged.

On Monday 21 August it was back to the office, after a very rough passage through the Bay of Biscay. I recall being much stimulated by the storm, by the turbulent power of the sea and by the magnificence of *Oriana* in facing such weather. On the way into London, I studied the press reactions to the bid. Initially they were largely uncritical: some defensive action had been anticipated and interest seemed to be less in the detail and more in what was thought to lie behind the merger. Then, within a few days, speculation about a mystery buyer waiting in the wings had become widespread and the share price had leapt ahead. On the bid announcement P&O stood at 260p, making Bovis worth 475p; when P&O advanced to 373p Bovis would have been valued at 725p, but the market seemed uncertain that the bid would fly and Bovis rose to only 500p. Some sections of the press were valuing P&O at 400p.

The *Sunday Telegraph* of 13 August had focused on Inchcape: 'Counter-bidders biding time? . . . The P&O arrangement is not to everyone's liking. Lord Inchcape is believed to be less than enthusiastic and although it looks an outside shot, a bid from Inchcape should not be ruled out.' The press, particularly a broadsheet of the standing of the *Sunday Telegraph*, would not have speculated about such an established City figure without being reasonably comfortable with the veracity of its report.

I found to my surprise that John Mitchell had evolved into an ardent supporter of the bid. On 16 August he had tried his hand at a spot of damage control. Interviewed by the *Standard*, under the headline 'Why P&O has been booming', Mitchell said: 'If I thought the shares were climbing to a false level I would feel obliged, as would our merchant bankers, to advise the chairman to make a statement.' He detailed P&O assets as 'property more than £100m, near-cash of around £45m, more than £50m for the ships just as scrap and since September 1971 we have purchased nearly £50m of new ships'. The City Editor's comment included two items John had left out: the benefit to a shipping company of tax allowances, and 'The cream on the top of this very rich cake is the 15% stake in two oil blocks in the North Sea close to the Forties and Montrose fields.'

Two days later, the management editor of the *Financial Times* wrote perceptively about the management structure: 'Do Sanderson and P&O understand just what the terms of reference of the two groups of managers will be? . . . If P&O and Bovis have not talked out and thoroughly satisfied themselves that they have the same answers to these questions then there is some danger of rows to come.' Our shares reached 390p, but some analysts were now valuing P&O at 500p. On 20 August Nigel Broackes of Trafalgar House, one of the front-runners in the mystery buyer stakes, indicated no interest in P&O – Trafalgar House put P&O's true net worth at 400p.

There was also press comment generated by some of the unions, in particular ASTMS, P&O's white-collar union, and the Bovis unions – the former being worried about job losses. A nasty dock strike had just ended, but it had shown that liner and cruise shipping were still vulnerable to union pressures.

Ford Geddes's letter of 8 August, together with an organisational chart, was awaiting my return. Although there was a great deal of divisional work on my desk I welcomed the opportunity to plunge straight into Bovis. This was my first opportunity to study the chairman's thoughts. I found the chart and the narrative incompatible. Unusually for a Monday, there was a Finance Committee meeting, to be followed by a board on Wednesday the 23rd. As Geddes was still on holiday, Dawes took the chair.

On the agenda of both the Finance Committee and the board was the proposed wording of, and information to be disclosed in, the offer documents. Under rule 14 of the City Takeover Code (the Yellow Book) all essential elements of the deal must be included in the offer documents. In discussing the management structure the same points of concern emerged at both meetings. My understanding that the offer did not commit us to the structure outlined on 9 August, but simply set out preliminary ideas on how the company might be organised, was confirmed at the Finance Committee, but, at the board on the 23rd, fears were expressed as to whether, after all, we might find ourselves committed in some way. Under pressure, Bill Dawes made it clear that these proposals represented ideas only and were in no way crystallised. There was, therefore, support for the suggestion that the offer documents should emphasise that the powers to be delegated by the board remained to be defined. Concern was expressed that some agreement already existed between Geddes and Sanderson in respect of the managing directorship, and the question of whether this too should be included was raised. All points were noted; none were resolved.

It appeared that we had neglected formally to advise our auditors, Deloittes, that the half-year figures to March 1972, which they were required to confirm, were needed for bid purposes and must conform to the Takeover Code. It was surprising that Deloittes had not appreciated this point themselves, but fortunate for those of us who needed more time. On the 23rd they had to recommence their work to ensure that figures from around the world were properly signed off. Having railroaded the deal through the board, it was obviously imperative for its success that momentum was not lost. John Mitchell was responsible for the figures. Was he sidetracked by the need to secure his future under the new management structure? As for the merchant bankers guiding P&O through the takeover maze, where was their advice? This further proof of the pro faction's readiness to play the role without comprehending the script did little to dispel my concerns.

Friday 25 August proved a watershed; nothing would be quite the same again for the P&O board. The day began with publication of an article by Douglas Moffitt in the *Investors Review* strongly recommending stockholders to frustrate the bid, which the *Review* concluded was financially unsound: P&O proposed to pay a huge price for management; no allowance had been made for the long-term sacrifice; Sanderson's management expertise was still relatively untested; ethically, the deal was questionable (the role of Lord Poole and P&O's purchase of seven million Bovis shares needed more public investigation); politically, the deal was an affront to stockholders. The *Investors Review* being a fortnightly magazine, Douglas Moffitt had had the luxury of time to evaluate and present his case. His words no doubt hurt Ford Geddes, but the real damage was done at the end of the day when George Pulay, Inchcape's PR man, let it be known publicly for the first time that Inchcape opposed the bid and had arranged for the *Sunday Times* to run an exclusive interview.

The discussion about what Inchcape was up to and how far he would go made the *Sunday Times* required reading. Graham Searjeant reported:

> 'This deal is in the worst interests of P&O shareholders,' Inchcape told me late last week. 'Shareholders must know what the facts really are. We are giving away control to Frank Sanderson on grounds that are not justified. It would be much better for P&O to go on as it is. Our results are going to be much better. We have a capable young management on the shipping side and we need to recruit an able man to develop our properties.' He let it be known that seven members of the Board opposed it and claimed that the issue had only been swayed by Poole and Marris. He went on 'Of the seven, six

were executive directors, a majority of P&O management . . .
One must make sure that shareholders have a chance to decide.
If it is agreed by shareholders, fair enough, then we'll all want
to make it work.'

Searjeant interpreted Inchcape's lone public stand as meaning that
'the six executive directors are hesitating to oppose the board in
public as they are worried about their jobs'. A reasonable assumption, but far from the truth. Inchcape had approached none of the
opposing directors. In taking his grievances to the press, Inchcape
had transgressed one of the City's unwritten rules. That such a
private man could behave in this manner stunned us all. Geddes
responded by returning immediately from holiday and calling an
emergency board meeting for Monday the 28th – the August bank
holiday – and a full board for Tuesday the 29th.

Geddes had persuaded himself that by 'summoning the troops' he
was paving the way to a coming together. The reality was that, by
riding roughshod over Inchcape's objections, he had alienated, even
outraged him. I suspect also that Inchcape resented the implied
criticism of a company with which his family had been closely
associated for the best part of 100 years. Inchcape did not seek
support in his move to opposition, because he did not need it. He
was, in this, his own man. When he inherited the stagnating family
business, he promptly shook it up, turning a £1m per annum profit
in 1966 to £10m in 1970. He was in control, and when the *Investors
Review* threw down the gauntlet he didn't hesitate to pick it up.
Whatever the outcome, he would now be perceived as the man with
the moral courage to speak out. The question which disturbed me at
the time, and even with hindsight I have difficulty in reasoning
through to an answer, is why he chose a public row as the first
resort? He was not an articulate man, so moving the board with
words was probably not a likely course. But he could have written to
Geddes, to Poole, to Marris, to the board; his standing in the City,
his long association with P&O – in many lay quarters actually
regarded as a controlling interest – his directorships of BP, Burmah,
Guardian Royal, Standard & Chartered Bank, would certainly have
ensured that he would be taken seriously.

Absent from the board on the 28th were Poole, Marris, Lloyd,
Mackinnon and Nancarrow – some quite important figures. First the
board took points arising from the meeting of the 23rd:

If Sanderson's appointment as managing director was to be absolute this must appear in the offer documents. A compromise, now to be discussed with Sanderson, was proposed: if, after a year, Geddes and Dawes were satisfied, then the appointment would be confirmed. (At first blush this may have seemed reasonable, but, of course it would effectively remove the decision from the board.)

Organisation chart. The defects would be addressed (after the merger) by the Executive, Planning & Finance Committee.

Finance directors. John Mitchell and Malcolm Paris (Bovis) would be joint for twelve months, after which Mitchell would become non-executive until his normal retirement on terms agreed. Advice would be sought on whether these points should be included in the offer documents.

Inchcape made a personal statement on his comments to the press.

Although Geddes maintained his satisfaction with the independence of our financial advice, a proposal that a further firm of merchant bankers be brought in would be put to the full board (by implication, when support for the chairman was available), as too would a proposal either to withdraw the offer or issue a statement of unity.

I found the proceedings no more satisfactory than the first time round; none of my fundamental dilemmas had been resolved. However, one question had been answered: the price of John Mitchell's now warm support for the bid – employment until retirement. What I did not know then, although it emerged later in the offer document, was that Mitchell had been given a three-year contract dated 9 August. Malcolm Paris had been given a five-year contract by Bovis on the same date. One may surmise that Mitchell's contract was settled after the board meeting on the 9th and that its terms governed his change of stance, although I am sure he would have maintained that he simply fell into line following the board's decision to bid. The minutes of the meeting had carefully avoided labelling individual directors as pro or anti.

Only Lloyd and Marris were absent from the board on 29 August, but Ian Fraser and Tom Wyner, of Lazards Corporate Finance department, came armed with a five-page document. I remember this meeting as being virtually a re-run of the 9th, even to Geddes stubbornly refusing to see what was in his own best interests. Simply by accepting the resolution to appoint another firm of merchant bankers he could have redeemed his position. But with ringmaster Poole directing the circus it was inevitable that Geddes would follow his leader. Finally it was agreed to issue a statement of 'unity of intent' to go ahead with the bid on the terms published and to await the stockholders' decision. 'Unity' in this context meant all directors apart from Inchcape, for none of the waverers, myself included, had yet summoned up the courage of our convictions.

The next day's newspapers enjoyed themselves with headlines such as 'Lord Lonely' and 'Not a Split but a Splinter'. The market, however, reacted positively to the 'unity' statement, with Bovis rising 18p to 502p and P&O falling 4p to 322p, making Bovis worth about 549p. Lazards added their mite, explaining that, for security reasons, the announcement of the bid on 10 August had been made before the full P&O Board had been informed (Marris being absent), but after hearing the full explanation of terms on the 29th, there was complete unanimity with the exception of Inchcape (yet Marris was again absent).

Inchcape moved fast. He published his position in the *Standard*, expanding on the views he had already expressed, but adding that 'if the merger did go through he would have to reconsider his position as a P&O board member'. He sent a note to Geddes to say that he was sorry he could not first clear the press release with him, but it had to be issued 'within the next half hour'. This was tough on Geddes; Inchcape could have made time. He was proving a doughty (even, perhaps, a dirty) fighter. Poole, with his experience of the political fast lane, might have recognised Geddes's weakness in this area, but until this broadside the City establishment had not fought its battles through the columns of the press and he too missed the sea-change which Inchcape's public stance heralded. Despite Inchcape's protestations that he was not seeking to lead opposition, his was not the action of someone seeking a diplomatic solution.

The *Daily Telegraph* had managed to get through to Sanderson who, by a curious coincidence, was enjoying a cruise on board *Oriana*. He told the newspaper that he hadn't known of Inchcape's objections 'until fairly recently', but he was confident everything would go through as planned. But Inchcape scooped the press pool with his resignation hint.

It was anticipated that the offer documents would be issued on 7

September, when Geddes and Sanderson would meet the press. The directors were advised of, and began to appreciate, the implications of the responsibility statement which, under the rules of the Yellow Book, the Stock Exchange publication governing the conduct of takeovers, had to accompany any company document, statement or press release. This would confirm each individual director's acceptance of the content of such publication and any dissent had to be specifically recorded.

The weekend press continued its attack on the board. The *Economist* questioned the way the majority of takeovers were engineered:

> Shareholders do not have a legal right to be consulted. . . . Far too many takeovers are cosily agreed and go through on a nod and a wink, thus the independent thinking director has a special duty to make up his mind and speak out and warn shareholders that there is an alternative way of looking at things . . . The long-serving executive director can tend to see things the way of his chairman and of his pension rights . . . At present it looks as if P&O is making the right decision but at the wrong price and possibly with the wrong partner.

Bovis came swiftly to its own defence, indicating in Saturday's *Daily Telegraph* that their Barry Abbot would take responsibility for P&O property if the merger went through. Under the headline 'Bovis poised to exploit £100m P&O properties', Abbot commented that our portfolio was a 'mixed bag which included many good properties in first class locations' and that 'the organisation to deal with them is already in place.'

The heavyweights on Sunday had their opportunity to pick over the Inchcape interview. Graham Searjeant commented in the *Sunday Times*: 'Lord Inchcape has withdrawn into his shell, still opposed to the bid, but he has no intention, he told me last week, of organising opposition from shareholders.' The *Sunday Telegraph* was curiously muted, reiterating Inchcape's position but adding: 'The odd thing is that it did not mention the vital point on which the takeover proposals are most open to attack – the price being paid for Bovis.' The *Sunday Express* urged stockholders to agitate for more information.

The monthly *Director* magazine had, coincidentally, carried an interview with Inchcape on his family company, the Inchcape

Group, making no mention of P&O. On Monday morning Kenneth Fleet, the perceptive City Editor of the *Daily Telegraph* commented: 'The brilliant accident of timing of the Inchcape interview is excelled only by the third Earl's claim that "after all, we are simple traders".' The article can have given Geddes little comfort. A number of companies must have been running an eye over the possibility of making a bid and it would have been surprising if the Inchcape Group had not been one.

My own position was becoming increasingly untenable and I decided that I must try to clear the decks with Geddes. First thing Monday morning I sought a meeting.

Our discussion was primarily about my problem with the management structure. I maintained that a company can have only one chief executive and if Sanderson were to be appointed chief executive in January 1973 that meant, to me, that he, Geddes, would *cease* to be chief executive.

'Oh yes, but I will remain executive chairman.'

I tried again. I questioned whether Sanderson would accept this, as I felt he saw his position of group managing director as reporting to the board, of which Geddes would simply be chairman, thus his interpretation was fundamentally different. Geddes disagreed, so I moved on.

Apart from possible sources of discontent further down the line, I foresaw potential strain at top level operating a structure which retained existing P&O divisional chief executives under a P&O management board with, superimposed, an Executive, Planning & Finance Committee.

Geddes maintained that a triumvirate of himself, Dawes and Sanderson would run the company. 'What then', I asked, 'is the Executive Committee and does this not devalue the jobs of divisional chief executives?'

Geddes ducked this by suggesting I should have a talk with Sanderson, but I emphasised that we, P&O, should work out what *we* wanted. Geddes found this a somewhat novel concept and one he seemed unable, or unwilling, to grasp.

We would not get out of this mess without frankness, brutal as that might be. I told Geddes that I had been shocked and bruised at his handling of the board on 9 August. I had found it almost inconceivable that he should go against six executives; this had been very difficult to assimilate, and my response had perhaps not been as considered as it should have been because his action was so unexpected. When our views, experience and commitment led us to question his actions on our behalf, he disregarded them and created, certainly in my case, a serious crisis of confidence in his style and judgement. He had to re-establish that confidence. He could never 'manage' in that way again.

Geddes was taken aback, but offered no comment except: 'It was very difficult for me. I had to decide one way or the other and if I'd accepted your views I would have ignored those of the majority.'

I believed the situation was precarious in the extreme, and that the cracks papered over on 9 August could split wide-open unless real progress was made in resolving our problems. I told him that it could well be that other equally serious issues and divisions would arise as we got further into the detail. Urgent action was required if I was to be genuinely convinced before the offer documents were issued. I assured him that this was in no way a threat; simply, and regrettably, my reaction to the haste of the original decision.

I left the meeting with the distinct feeling that I had been talking to a brick wall, so little impression had I made on Geddes, but I clung to the belief that the rising swell of reasoned argument against the terms of the bid would shift him.

Shortly after I returned to my office, Geddes's secretary telephoned to make an appointment for Sanderson to meet me. This was my second and last meeting with him and I let it happen in my office, again obliging Sanderson to climb the thirteen floors. He appeared full of relaxed good cheer: 'Glad things are going along so well.' He had come to assure me that he would be relying to a great extent on me; that he knew of my record in Trident, with P&O's new developments and in Bulk Shipping and that 'he and I together . . .' It was a bravura performance, although it was quite clear he had scant knowledge of the P&O Group. I said little – I didn't want to commit myself. He hinted that some of the old brigade in P&O would not survive for long – 'you know who I mean.' With that he departed to trudge down the stairs to Leadenhall Street, with no assurances from me. He left behind him the faint air of a deal which might have been done had I risen to such bait as was dangled. And this was the man whom Geddes naively thought he would control.

Negative reactions were now surfacing. Andrew Alexander of Belisha, a highly respected investment analyst, produced a 'Draft letter to P&O stockholders', cogently reasoning against the bid and arguing for it to be dropped. The *Daily Telegraph*, following the Belisha line, asserted that if the deal went through it would demonstrate a board with 'more buoyancy than brains'. John Ormond of Surinvest (holders of some 140,000 P&O ordinary shares) announced he would be seeking stockholder support in opposing the resolution.

Because this was theoretically a bid by P&O for Bovis, it would be necessary for P&O stockholders to approve an increase in P&O's authorised capital. This was to be the saving grace.

When the board met on 6 September, we faced the market opening with Bovis down to 486p and P&O down to 308p. Absent were Beazley, Nancarrow and Poole. A new draft of the chairman's letter to stockholders and the sixth draft of the offer document were to be discussed and the usual phalanx of advisers was in attendance. At Denys Brown's request, it was agreed that he and Fraser should seek a ruling from the Takeover Panel on the necessity of making reference in the offer document to the board's intention to consider, in twelve months' time, the appointment of Sanderson as managing director subject to recommendation by Geddes and Dawes.

It was agreed that if it were impracticable to summon a board meeting, and in order to avoid delay, a committee of the board consisting of the chairman, deputy chairman and any two other directors be empowered to authorise the issue of statements and documents in connection with the bid. Here David Stebbings, the meticulous senior partner of Freshfields, the company's solicitors, pointed out that it would be necessary for all directors, whether present at such a meeting or not, to sign the final offer document.

I raised the point that when the bankers had been asked at the 30 August board to display the logic of their valuations, much emphasis had been placed on the short-term aspects – indeed on the 1972 results. Horne said he had given weight to 1972–3 by accepting the figure of £12m to £15m produced by Nancarrow and Mitchell, but dismissing later years as 'realms of uncertainty'. I described this as the 'Crichton line' which, although loudly asserted, had been neither proven nor challenged in detail. The facts were that on 14 August Bulk Shipping had produced a final 1972–3 budget; General Cargo's had not yet been produced; and Passenger Division's was expected on 11 September. None of the divisional heads had been questioned on his figures, far less on forecasts for the years 1974–6. How then could a reasonably informed view have been taken by the bankers, or, indeed, by the non-executive directors?

I submitted that the reference to tax allowances in the draft offer document was misleading, to say the least, and that Lazards were confused. In 1972 allowances enabled shipping companies to invest in new ships and to set off the cost against taxable profits at an accelerated rate, thus deferring payment of tax and improving cash flow. Lazards seemed to believe that the enlarged company would be able to use these allowances by September 1975, but this assumed we would build no more ships – an immediate benefit – but was it sound to gobble up tax allowances at that rate and was it reasonable to assume that P&O would not be ordering new ships?

I considered that the draft letter to stockholders undervalued P&O and exaggerated the disadvantages to P&O of remaining on its own – the inherent danger in this view being, if the market valuation is right and the bid fails, what does one then say to an unwelcome bidder?

So ended another board meeting, with Geddes steadfastly adhering to his course, vociferously supported by the various vested interests. Despite the board's much vaunted unanimity (Inchcape now always excepted), the market's perception was still that the deal might well not go through and Bovis plunged 42p to 445p before closing at 458p – down 29p. In sharp contrast P&O attracted solid support and finished with a net rise of 10p to 324p, at which level the bid valued Bovis at about 553p a share.

The next day's press confirmed that the flight out of Bovis had, to a great extent, been on the back of the criticisms voiced. Ian Fraser, the leader of the Lazards team, publicly dismissed Belisha's open letter as 'full of inaccuracies'. Fraser was fast becoming a source of immense irritation to me. He came across as arrogantly dismissive of those who disagreed with him, and I understand that in his memoirs he concedes that this episode was not his finest hour. I scribbled a pencil note for Beazley and Nancarrow on proceedings during their absence on holiday. After covering the board's deliberations, I warned them that the executive directors had had a lot of lousy press over the last ten days and that I had concluded that it was in the best interests of the company to try to improve the terms and ensure there was no ambiguity, but that I was not optimistic.

The *Standard* of 8 September reported on Deloittes' activities. They had produced figures for the deal, suggesting that the year-end result would be some £13m compared with £11.5m – the current general consensus – against only £5.2m the previous year. This was viewed as a shot in the arm for Inchcape who, the paper stated, 'is at work preparing a minority report on the bid which will go out to the shareholders'. As such a letter could be regarded as a logical next step for Inchcape, no one bothered to question just what he was 'preparing' for P&O.

I spent many hours with David Horne at this time, but apart from Denys Brown always and Harry Beazley sometimes, I cannot remember any other executives being present. Denys's incisive mind, coupled with his extensive experience in preparing briefs and in negotiation, left him appalled at the sloppiness of the whole proposal. He tended to see skulduggery in the undergrowth and took his responsibilities to stockholders to biblical dimensions. David Horne did his best, but the further we probed the more dismayed I became. We were putting together an asset-rich P&O with a low capital, high profit Bovis at valuations related solely to historic profit, and were ignoring developments already underway in P&O which would bring increased profits in the current year and substantial improvement in the next. The potential was not being rated at all. I could see morale being knocked, management discouraged and investment put at risk. We did not have details of Bovis and did not see it as our concern to attempt to analyse them at that point – our main objective was to persuade ourselves that we could support the concept. Despite David Horne's valiant efforts, this we were patently failing to do.

I also saw Dick Lloyd, for whom I had a great regard. It was difficult for him, yet he gave me good advice and real moral support: 'I am in the position of believing that this is a good deal for P&O, but if you are not in that position you should not compromise – you must do what you believe to be right.' I said that I felt David Horne had been very honest and helpful, recognising that he had been largely responsible for producing the arguments which improved the split to P&O's benefit, but that in my view it still did not look good enough.

I went to see Inchcape and told him that I, and I thought one or two others, were finding it difficult to support the proposal. At that first exploratory talk he would not be drawn, simply confirming that he would not lead the opposition – he had discharged his responsibility by making his views known and was content to leave a decision to the stockholders.

It must have been the second Sunday in September that Peter Thomas, head of Public Relations, asked if he could come to see me at home. As we talked on the terrace that warm morning, I was astonished to find that he was an emissary from Geddes carrying some sort of garbled plea for solidarity – how important I was, how valued I was. I gave him short shrift. Perhaps he should not have been put in the position of arguing a case about which he knew so little – he should certainly have been man enough to recognise that I was not going to take that sort of preaching from the monkey when I was doing battle with the organ-grinder.

On 11 September the board met to discuss the profit forecast for the year ending 30 September 1972 together with the bases used and the assumptions made in arriving at the figures. Adams and Poole were absent, so too was Crichton, granting us a temporary respite from his vitriolic language and specious arguments. With the interim statement also on the agenda, our advisers were present in force, including Ian Fraser who seemed to me to be exhibiting a tendency to brush Geddes aside if he could field a question which, in his opinion, fell within his expertise.

The drafting of the offer document was more difficult than anticipated. It was acknowledged that the board might be forced to produce a forecast to end-September and, as this involved operations around the world, it was becoming evident that we were not likely to achieve the required standards of accuracy in the time available. There were difficulties in explaining the management structure, in explaining the comparative values of P&O and Bovis assets and, of course, the directors were beginning to seek more disclosure about Bovis and some were asking questions, particularly about the quality of its high-flying house-building and banking profits.

The date for issuing the offer document was deferred from the 7th to the 14th then again to 19 September. Throughout, it was business as usual in Bulk Shipping, but I had an increasingly hard time fielding queries about Bovis from colleagues around the world. I trod a delicate balance between loyalty to the board's position, from which I had not yet dissented, and conveying my concerns. Bo Madsen of Zapata Norness was typically robust in asking what the hell we were doing. Russ Madigan of Hammersley in Australia took a more careful line, but was interested in respect of our joint venture. The Lorentzens, Mobil Oil, our Japanese clients and BP all made cautious enquiries. At the Chamber of Shipping, Johnnie Wood, the director-general, would like to have heard more, and

Maersk Møller in Copenhagen conveyed that he was sure we had everything under control and would take the right decision etc., but left me in no doubt that he was sceptical about the whole proposition. I supposed that all my colleagues were receiving the same vibes; would they able to respond with conviction and so dispel concern?

I talked incessantly with Mona, more in anguish than in anger. Meanwhile Denys Brown and I, from our different perspectives, drew closer to a shared position. I considered P&O was being sold short because I knew we could secure future benefits for the P&O stockholders and need not give away a substantial element to the Bovis shareholders (including Frank Sanderson who stood to gain some millions of pounds). Denys found it a disreputable deal, put together on the one hand by a crafty entrepreneur and on the other by a bunch of frightened men who did not have the courage or the confidence to lead their troops.

At an extra board meeting on 12 September, a redraft of an interim statement and the bases of assumptions made in arriving at the figures were considered. The now customary pattern was followed. Nothing one could say – and much was said – dented Geddes's belief in the viability of the deal as presented by the bankers. I felt like the invisible man. This board was my Rubicon.

On the afternoon of the 13th I went back to Geddes and said that, with regret, I had decided I could not support the bid. I wanted him to know before the board the following day.

He was shaken. He begged me to join with my colleagues; he invoked history and loyalty and trust and hinted at the prospect of my becoming chairman in due course. He said my support was crucial, and that if I failed to support the bid he would feel compelled to resign, 'and you, Sandy, will have to bear the responsibility for the chaos into which that will throw the company.' I responded sharply that his suggestion was not only surprising, but wholly irrational. I was not demanding his resignation and had at no time sought it. That would be entirely his decision. If he thought his resignation would throw the company into chaos then that would be his responsibility – he could not put that burden on me. Anyhow, I maintained, it was not in any way an issue which could not be resolved. The more facts that had emerged as the due diligence studies developed, the clearer it had become that the proposal was not in the best interests of P&O stockholders. I proposed that the bid should be withdrawn – a perfectly respectable conclusion to the past weeks of study and negotiation, and one for which Geddes himself could take the credit.

He was by now very emotional: 'Decisions have been taken – we would look fools.' I remember feeling sorry for him – he was very nearly in tears but, through weakness, becoming ever more entrenched. He pleaded that I should reconsider my position overnight. But it was too late.

Looking back, he may have seen my dissent as a more potent threat than Inchcape's. He may have been concerned that my success in Trident and Bulk Shipping would be a strong card for the opposition to play. Also, Inchcape was not an insider and he had stated firmly that, having declared his position, he would not attempt to lead a campaign, but would leave stockholders to decide the issue. I had given no such undertaking and, as he must have known, I had canvassed the waverers on the board.

Early in the evening I went to see Inchcape and told him of my interview. In the event of Geddes resigning, I needed a fallback position: 'Would you be prepared to take the chair?' Inchcape said he neither sought it nor would he in any way want this to be his initiative. I said I would make up my own mind. I thought I would not be alone, but I had to weigh the consequences threatened by Geddes. Inchcape then confirmed that he would be prepared to become chairman.

I had a word with Harry Beazley, who was still undecided but tending to fall in line – he had a long career of working with Dawes, but did not have a very strong base within the Group. Each of us was under individual pressures, although I believe that for Denys Brown and me there was a genuine primary recognition of duty to the company and stockholders. Had this not been so, I very much doubt if we could have taken the strain of the coming months.

Denys and I drafted a press statement for the next day and he arranged to inform Geddes of his decision in the morning, before the board meeting. I believed this was the proper course to take, but as events unfolded there was so little 'proper' conduct that I wonder if it would not have been better – it would certainly have been more entertaining – if Denys and I had kept the denouement until the meeting itself.

On the morning of our 'outing', the press was most encouraging as it carried the news that the merchant bank, Morgan Grenfell, had announced its dissatisfaction with the terms of the bid. Although the

Governor of the Bank of England had been urging City institutions with substantial investments to play a more active role in corporate affairs, few showed any inclination to stick their heads above the parapet. Bold as this unprecedented initiative by Morgans was, I believe that even they would have been reluctant to take issue had someone of Inchcape's standing not created the opening.

As the board assembled we could sense a withdrawal – there was a distancing, a space around us. Inchcape sat next to Geddes, but the barrier between them was almost visible. This was no simple difference of opinion – there were weighty issues of loyalty, proper behaviour, respect, awe, and the rest of the code. Inchcape was never forgiven for having breached it by revealing the discord on the board to a 'Sunday rag'.

Fraser presented the draft offer document, ostensibly as an adviser submitting it for discussion and approval by the directors. In reality he was speaking for the chairman. There was more than ever a sense of this being someone else's deal being explained to a bunch of schoolboys who could not be expected fully to comprehend it. Fraser took himself very seriously, to the point of becoming an almost passionate advocate. He was, as usual, aggressively dismissive, which caused Denys to draw the chairman's attention to the fact that 'Mr Fraser appears to have forgotten that he is present to offer advice'.

There was the inevitable claque of enthusiasm from the gang of four – couched in Crichton's case with contempt for those who were crass enough to have a different view, but I was surprised that Denny Marris had apparently 'given up on P&O' and seemed so warmly in support.

I voiced my dissent. It was greeted by a pained silence. This confirmed the feeling I had had on entering the room: that Geddes had already informed colleagues of my decision and secured their support. Except for Inchcape's mumbled, 'As you know, Chairman, I am against it too', there was no reaction to my statement. Denys presented his case – well-constructed although, one has to admit, somewhat pedantic in style.

The chairman pointed out the seriousness of dissent, the damage we would do to the company and his personal disappointment at our decision. He made no reference to resignation. He was applauded by Crichton, who offered his opinion that we would live to rue the day and that our careers in P&O must be regarded as in jeopardy. It was a bombastic, vicious and unnecessary intervention.

I looked round the table in an attempt to judge my colleagues' true reactions. I saw little interest, and certainly no willingness to hear what Denys and I had to say. Yet here we were at a defining point in P&O's history. I felt – as Denys must have felt – like the protagonist in a Greek tragedy, surrounded by a shadowy chorus intoning the repeated chant 'Boring, boring, boring . . .'

The proposed bid was approved by a majority and the responsibility statement agreed, 'with the exception of Lord Inchcape, Mr D. D. Brown and Mr A. B. Marshall'.

6

Going It Alone

During the remainder of the board's business my thoughts leapt ahead to what we had to do and how we would do it. We already knew that we would get no co-operation from colleagues in making our views known – we would have to put them across ourselves. At least a week would go by before the offer document was despatched to stockholders – we had to be ready. We had the current draft to work on, but precious little time to consider any last-minute adjustments.

The board agreed that P&O would make our dissent public and announced:

> No member of, or spokesman for, the P&O Board proposes to comment further on the situation, or to add anything to the present statement, before the issue of the offer documents.

It was probably just as well that Denys and I accepted this embargo, however reluctantly. The build-up to the point of decision had been enough to cope with. Unwittingly, the board had given us time to prepare our case. Had I been granted a higher profile, having to formulate an opposition policy off the top of my head, we might never have reached the starting line.

The *Daily Telegraph* was later to write of me as 'the man whose choice of sides really determined the issue'. But that was by no means evident on 14 September. Geddes was in the limelight; I was not. The public was in the dark. Only when we had prepared our case, established reasons for our confidence and put on record the strengths and potential of Bulk Shipping, did it become clear that there was a viable alternative to Bovis, that of independence. Yet the fact that a credible alternative management was emerging not only supported independence, but also offered a potentially attractive target for a bidder from outside the shipping industry.

There was no respite. Immediately after the meeting we had to prepare our case. While Morgan Grenfell could provide a focus for opposition, we decided that, as directors, we must demonstrate our independence and keep our distance from those who might have their own agenda. Inchcape too preferred to keep his distance, but he did offer us a room in his headquarters (just across the road at 40, St Mary Axe) with telephone and telex and some secretarial help. With relief we accepted this secure base outside the P&O hothouse.

Not surprisingly, Denys was swiftly informed that he was relieved of his responsibility for Public Relations. This was a bonus: he was now able to devote most of his time to research and to essential staff work, and we gained time for reflection and planning.

Our first week was one of high excitement and even higher tension. *The Times* neatly summed up our position: 'The dissenting directors are in a worse spot than the rest of the board; equally responsible for past failures, but opposing the only solution yet offered.' One newspaper headline rejoiced in pointing the finger at 'Three Men in a Boat'.

I knew my job was on the line. If the bid went through I would get my comeuppance. Denys Brown was equally realistic. To an extent, therefore, we could put that aspect to one side. But we were concerned about others who offered support. Jim Lindars of Corporate Planning, Euan Geddes in General Holdings, Andrew Robb and Jim Bayley in Bulk Shipping, and, of great importance, David Greenslade. David, who had only recently joined P&O as group financial controller reporting directly to John Mitchell, was in a particularly difficult position. His immediate grasp of the figures, an immense capacity for detail and for analysis and a complete, almost biblical, conviction that the structure of the bid was wrong in concept coupled with his readiness to say so, articulately, to the board, gave us a considerable boost. John Maccoy of Birt Potter & Hughes was a powerful supporter as his broking operations not only spanned the whole Group but also reached out into the market; while John Maltby in Panocean Shipping and Trading contributed quiet, authoritative encouragement based on his wide experience.

It was imperative that I keep abreast at Bulk Shipping. I must give the board no grounds for criticism nor any excuse to suspend me from executive responsibilities – I had to perform and I must keep my seat at the board. This added enormously to the strain of the ensuing months, but from the outset, and indeed throughout the campaign, I had every possible support within Bulk Shipping and, as we shall see, increasing support from other parts of the Group. My core infrastructure, Betty Fairclough and Powell, my driver, did wonders to ease the administrative juggling which was required, to provide communication and cover-up and increasingly to anticipate issues. Betty was carpeted by Frank Thomassen, head of Personnel: her contract was with P&O, and if she stayed loyal to me 'when I lost' she, too, would go. She should therefore think carefully about her position. Her response to this threat was akin to 'Publish and be damned'.

We were of course tyros in the takeover game. We knew nothing about the Takeover Panel, which was to play such an important part; we were not yet clear to whom we should address our concerns or how to go about it. Were we entitled to try to attract support within the company, ashore and afloat? Was that fair or even ethical, given that, formally, the board had a clear policy? How could we find out more about Bovis and would this be an appropriate use of resources? I felt, recognising that to date Bovis had apparently been successful, that we would probably be ill-advised to attack them; better to concentrate on producing the evidence to support our argument that P&O was being undervalued and, by developing its own strengths, that P&O could do better for its stockholders on its own.

I was not opposed to diversification nor to the acquisition of Bovis *per se*, but I could not countenance the reverse takeover which the majority of the board seemed prepared to accept – the precipitate surrender of everything that the 30,000 members of staff had been building up.

There was a strained atmosphere in the office. Denys Brown and I had the distinct impression that our executive colleagues, having made their decision, were content to sit back and let the 'experts' follow through – we were regarded as disloyal and, I can only assume, misguided. It was perhaps easy to dismiss Denys, who could not be expected to know about these things; but I was a different animal and I made them uncomfortable. Nancarrow gave every impression of anguish at the conflict between his conscience and his career prospects. Harry Beazley remained civilised and friendly. Mac Sidey, who had a black-and-white view of the world (and who was later to prove a most loyal and spirited supporter), was at this point severe in his condemnation of those who refused to march to the regimental drum; Dick Adams, an intelligent Wykehamist with a strong base from his time in Mackinnons and British India, was an enigma: he might perhaps find himself a fish out of water in a new Bovis/P&O. Yet somehow he could not address the issue and seemed simply to echo Ford Geddes: a decision had been taken and that was the end of the matter. Etonian Peter Parry, another intelligent man, made, as I recall, little impression.

There were some amusing anomalies. As CEO of Bulk Shipping I was responsible for producing our estimated results for the half-year to March 1972. John Mitchell, who was co-ordinating Group figures, tried to work directly with my management team. He maintained that I should not be bothered with this routine chore. In fact he was hoping to deprive me of useful ammunition, but I insisted that the Bulk Shipping figures were my responsibility and that everything must go through me. Actually I was already fully informed on all such calculations, and early on this gave us much confidence in our case.

I spoke to Lord G, who took a broadbrush approach. He was anxious about the implicit loss of P&O leadership in the world shipping industry. It was a sad time for him. After all, Ford Geddes was his cousin, but having been so closely involved in recent developments, he knew we were being sold short.

On 19 September I agreed with Stephen Catto of Morgan Grenfell that, while all opposition was welcome, it was important that Denys Brown and I should not, at any rate at this early stage, be other than independent. On the same day Dick Adams wrote to General Cargo staff: 'Unfortunately the Takeover Panel of the Stock Exchange does not recognise board decisions by a majority and it insists on the responsibility of individual directors for all statements of facts and opinions.' By implication he was saying that it was a nuisance that three directors had refused to accept the majority decision, particularly as the dissident view now had to be made public. On the 19th also, Denys and I consulted Stuart Menzies of the City solicitors Allen & Overy, putting him on notice that we might have to seek his advice urgently if, for example, there were attempts to suspend or dismiss us.

Denys, based 100 yards away in St Mary Axe, would scurry across to the P&O building when Geddes or Dawes found a reason to summon him. Betty Fairclough was imaginative and effective in defence and never failed to point out to others that both Denys and I had our jobs to run and therefore our own priorities.

Our priority, not to be communicated to Geddes, was to be ready, within the week, to give reasons for not supporting the bid and to go public immediately after the offer document was issued. At this stage I am sure we did not contemplate being able to defeat the bid. We were simply intent on making it clear that our objections were responsible and realistic. We were not against change; indeed I had been leading change.

Now, in drafting our first rebuttal statement, we began to be persuaded that we also had a viable alternative policy to propose – a heady mixture. While I was to an extent known to the shipping world and to the press, Denys was not and certainly neither of us was widely known in the City. It was important, therefore, to persuade Inchcape to join us so that our protest would gain his muscle and credibility.

It was a strange process of persuasion. Inchcape wanted no part in the preparation and offered no contribution to the thinking. He would stick his head into the room in St Mary Axe from time to time, but was not really part of the team, far less its leader. He remained aloof and most reluctant to commit himself. But I remember with appreciation the friendliness of Mackay Tallack, John Sim, Jim Millington-Drake and others whom I had known in India and Africa, and who were now in Inchcape HQ. Oliver Brooks, Inchcape's finance director, was helpful with his 'detached' comments.

When it was pointed out that we could fall foul of the Takeover Panel, we had to modify our initial intention to show up the board by including definitive forecasts in our statement. We had to learn quickly how to deal with the Panel. Denys Brown and I, particularly Denys, spent time with its executives and gradually persuaded them that we were not only honourable but practical. We sought, and got, approval to use published data, whether generated by the company or by external sources and to use data for which we had personal responsibility.

The original announcement of the bid had been made on 10 August but it was 19 September before the formal offer document was issued. This included a revaluation of P&O properties showing them to be worth £108.47m – some £85m over book value and an increase of £35m over the board's February estimate. With the document showing total assets of some £300m this represented about 500p a share. But still no attempt had been made to value the fleet of 170 ships.

The offer was launched at a press conference which became notorious for the hostages to fortune offered by the chairman and by Lazards, and for Frank Sanderson's comments on the proposed management structure:

Ford Geddes: 'If this merger goes through there is no doubt about who is the executive chief; I am.'

Frank Sanderson: 'I have a long record of back-seat driving. I didn't go into Bovis at the top.'

Ford Geddes believed that only some £28m of properties could be redeveloped.

Frank Sanderson thought the figure on the low side: 'In the end there is more than £28m of development property over a period of time.'

Ford Geddes: 'Too much is made of the property angle. It was not the basis of the deal but a bonus.'

But it was Ian Fraser of Lazards who made the most outrageous statement:

We have taken the view that it is quite impossible to say anything meaningful about the value of the ships .. you cannot realise a fleet of 170 ships just like that, which is tantamount to saying that there is no market for fleets of P&O size, which goes on to say that it is tantamount to saying that it is impossible to put a market value on P&O's fleet.

In the market, ships do have value. As John Mitchell knew perfectly well and, indeed, had acknowledged in his statement in August: 'Even for scrap the ships would fetch £50m, and since 1971 we have purchased £50m of new ships.' Also, as P&O's financial director, he knew that in the international shipping market the standard method of financing is to take a mortgage on the ship, thus confirming its value.

The transcript of this conference became a key document for all parties – to the benefit of the opposition and the dismay of the proponents of the bid.

An Extraordinary General Meeting was fixed for 12 October, three weeks after the issue of the offer documents. This EGM was necessary to secure P&O stockholders' approval for an increase in capital to provide capacity for the acquisition of Bovis. At the same time, it was proposed to remove the limitation on voting rights which, for over 100 years, had restricted each stockholder, however large his holding, to a maximum of twenty votes. This was an important issue for Geddes. Although such restrictions were perhaps becoming less common in 1972, they were still in place in a number of major companies. At the time, P&O stock was held approximately 40% by institutions and 60% by individual stockholders. The board sensed that the small stockholder, more emotionally attached to the company, might be persuaded to vote against. It was important to get voting power into the more 'sophisticated' hands of the institutions. We dissidents concluded that, however much in tactical terms we might have wished to maintain the status quo, the abolition of limited voting rights was equitable.

P&O's financial year would come to an end on 30 September, but even now, in late September, the board was unwilling to produce a forecast of earnings. This seemed unacceptable to many City commentators and, indeed, to many executives. In Bulk Shipping we were able, in fact felt duty-bound, to estimate for a number of years ahead to justify investment proposals. John Mitchell sheltered behind the Yellow Book, according to whose terms the Takeover Panel required that forecasts, in this type of situation, be validated by independent auditors. Thus it was easy, if it suited a company, to make the auditors' task difficult, if not impossible, by introducing a myriad of uncertainties. This hit us hard, because our estimates of the Group's potential profits for 1972 could not be firmed up without the company's co-operation. That co-operation was withheld.

So, while awaiting approval by the Panel, we had to bypass the constraint by using such comments as 'Informed observers estimate that . . .' We used figures published in the press to illustrate 'What if?', until Geddes, oblivious to the implications, released his estimate of anticipated unutilised tax allowances. Our financial team pounced on them with glee, as they enabled us to deduce the profits needed to support such tax allowances. It was a coup which did much to lift our morale.

On 21 September, the Panel gave us the green light and we issued our statement on the 22nd, embargoed for Saturday 23rd so as to give time for journalists and analysts to produce a studied comment. We were pleased that Inchcape had finally agreed to let the statement go out above his name, but the content was pure Marshall and Brown.

Our principal points were:

– The share of P&O equity to be issued to Bovis shareholders was biased unfairly in Bovis's favour.

– The whole tenor and timing of the offer failed to reflect P&O's potential.

– Bovis's profit trend reflected a recent and unprecedented rise in land values.

– The merger was proposed at a time when P&O and Bovis were at opposite ends of their respective trading cycles.

In short, we put forward a very positive go-it-alone stance.

In spite of Geddes' attempt to scupper us by issuing an immediate denial of our points, press coverage was good.

Having won a high public profile, we needed to maintain it. My personal statement was issued on Sunday 24th and was prominently featured in the press next day:

> 24 September 1972
> Press Release
> PERSONAL STATEMENT ISSUED BY MR A. B. MARSHALL, EXECUTIVE DIRECTOR OF P&O:
>
> I have been asked how I reached my decision to oppose P&O's offer for Bovis. I opposed the outline terms as advised to the board on 9 August and thereafter as opportunity arose I explained my views to Mr Geddes and urged that the terms be re-negotiated in favour of P&O stockholders or that the offer be withdrawn.
>
> The more information I secured over the ensuing weeks both on the financial terms and on the proposed management structure, the more concerned I became.
>
> I have been with P&O for 25 years and it was not easy to go against the judgement of the company's financial advisers and of my chairman. However, I have been closely involved in recent years in most of the changes in P&O attitudes and policies. From my detailed knowledge of the company, its immediate past, its present situation and the possibilities open to it in the future I came, with admitted reluctance, but with complete conviction, to the conclusion that I could not recommend to the stockholders a proposal based on what seemed to be a grave under-valuation of both assets and future prospects.
> END

Issued for Mr A. B. Marshall through Charles Barker City Limited

Two institutions went public: Eagle Star found the terms 'hard to accept', and the Pru said that 'if the accounts we read are true, it looks as if the bid was put together with unreasonable haste' and felt that 'Lord Inchcape would not dissent from this sort of thing lightly'. It was a heartening moment, but we still had a mountain to climb.

During the week after the issue of the offer document, Clifford Nancarrow came to terms with his wobbly conscience, came off the fence and joined the dissenting directors. His disaffection was dismissed as irrelevant by Geddes as he had only been in P&O for nine months, but to the outside world it was more significant – here was an independent mind at work. Since his job at Corporate Planning was effectively in limbo, the addition to our resources was useful, although I always felt he suffered somewhat as a 'Johnny-come-lately'.

With Nancarrow under the spotlight and Morgan Grenfell organising a meeting of no less than thirty-five institutions representing a total of 25% of P&O stock, Ford Geddes staged a riposte. This took the form of an interview with Crichton in the *Standard*. Such exposure may have been good for Crichton's ego, but his views did little to further the board's cause.

On 25 September Morgan Grenfell wrote formally to the chairman asking some fifteen important questions about valuations, profits and future plans. At first Geddes simply ignored this request on the grounds that Morgans had no standing in this affair. However, they put it to the Takeover Panel that answers to their questions were vital to stockholders and that, if they were not forthcoming, stockholders would not be able adequately to consider the issues before the coming EGM. Although the appeal did not succeed, it raised our profile and emphasised that a wider range of objectors was seeking a voice. The *Daily Telegraph* carried a delightfully ironic observation on the workings of the City:

> Will the full Panel (of which Morgan chairman Lord Harcourt is a member, though he would not sit) waive the rule book, re-written earlier this year under the chairmanship of Morgan director Mr Ken Barrington, and tell Morgan to be a good boy and pipe down? Or will Lord Shawcross tell his old friend and trusted lieutenant of many years, Mr Ian Fraser, that in this instance the Code cannot protect him and he should tell all to his opponents? There's a moral here somewhere about the wearing of hats.

The last week of September was hectic. With David Greenslade's support, I tackled Trevor Spittle of Deloittes. Why were they willing to endorse Geddes's negative approach to the valuation of the fleet? Surely the auditors' responsibility was to value the business as ongoing – perhaps, if they considered it necessary, giving alternative bases for valuation. I protested vociferously at what I regarded as a weakness on the part of independent auditors who seemed ready to be swayed by their client's wishes.

There were occasional comic incidents which were good for our morale. One morning I arrived to find Betty Fairclough unusually subdued. Our filing cabinets had been tampered with. Two CID officers had asked her who she thought might be the culprit. Impulsively she had replied 'Frank Sanderson, of course' – and then had some difficulty in extricating herself. There was nothing vital in the cabinets, but, to indicate that there might be, we changed the locks and took the keys home at night.

There were no formal office hours during this period. Willing hands in Bulk Shipping assumed all the responsibility I could delegate and the senior people worked with me when I was available. It was a tough routine for the Bulk Shipping team and for the bid team, with working days starting at 7 a.m. and rarely ending before 10 p.m. sometimes not until midnight.

A particular strain on my diary was a requirement to make time every Monday morning, en route to the office, for a visit to St Mary's Hospital, Paddington. In 1971 a prolonged investigation into some abnormality in my metabolism had culminated in a diagnosis of pre-symptomatic haemochromatosis, a blood condition which, if untreated, could ultimately lead to diabetes and organ failure. Professor Victor Wynn, who discovered this during examination under the P&O executive health scheme, was delighted to have made the earliest diagnosis of the condition on record. More important for me, it had been identified in time to allow successful treatment. Until the diagnosis it had been a bad time for Mona; there was an unspoken assumption in some quarters that, inevitably, I would be found to have a cancer condition. The treatment entailed venisection (in the past performed with leeches), having initially two pints and later one pint of blood drawn off each week. It was neither a convenient nor a comfortable backdrop to the events of 1972. On one occasion the television news showed me bounding up the steps of the P&O building. What the viewer did not know was that I had forgotten that it was one of my venisection days. I soon remembered but fortunately, panting and breathless, I had passed out of view.

Denys Brown and I were working well together. Denys, as I have already said, had the highest principles and in this case a sense of outrage that, first, he had been steamrollered and, second, dismissed as irrelevant. Added to this, the more he dug into the origins, the timing and the contacts, the more he became convinced that there had been some less than honourable goings-on; indeed that Lazards had played a questionable role in early developments and now needed to avoid exposure by pushing the bid through as rapidly as possible. Denys' sardonic wit was an attractive feature. It helped on a number of occasions and he was not above a mischievous intervention to discomfit the Establishment when the opportunity offered.

Denys visited me at home one Sunday late in September. 'Gillie, who is that?' asked James, aged five: 'Don't you know, James?' replied Gillian, aged eight, 'That's Denys Brown, Daddy's very, very best friend.'

The publicity I was getting attracted a rather unusual but threatening attack on the domestic front. We had recently bought our house with an option to acquire title to three and a half acres of paddock. We exercised that option in due time, but the vendors refused to transfer the land and we were forced to take legal action. As the dispute wore on we could only assume that the vendors felt that I might well lose my job in case of defeat in the Bovis battle and that they therefore had a tactical advantage in holding out. It was a thoroughly uncomfortable threat and through September and October we had to deal with it in the Inns of Court without putting a foot wrong. Justified anger gave Mona a determination and a winning edge, and our case was resolved satisfactorily.

These domestic events were significant for the family at the time, but as the years passed I realised that they also provided something of a point of reference, of shared values and a measure of mortar between the bricks. The greatest contribution was made by Mona – her steadfastness, her practicality, and on occasion her righteous indignation provided both stimulus and comfort. Her diaries for August to November reveal that life went on: school runs, pantomime rehearsals, dentist, swimming competition, other kids to stay or ours going to friends, my coming home late or being away overnight or longer, and dinners in London with overseas visitors. And Mona made sure that we did not lose touch with friends, so that we still had a steady round of social engagements at home. I could not have coped without her. Knowing how much she had missed her family over the years, hoping that one day we might move to South Africa, she recognised more clearly than I how important it was to preserve normality for the children, yet not to make them feel excluded. Perhaps theirs was a simplistic view of goodies and baddies, but it was a support and frequently provided light relief, as on the occasion when, one Sunday evening, Mona brought the family up to collect me from the office. Before going home we took advantage of the deserted streets to see some of the sights – St Paul's, the Tower, the Bank of England. Then, as we drove down Broad Street, I pointed out Lazards offices. 'Boo, Boo,' chorused the children, giving Lazards an emphatic and enthusiastic thumbs-down.

Our press releases were reaching a fairly wide audience now, not only in the business pages, but increasingly in the general news and we felt strongly that our conviction and our confidence should be put directly to stockholders. As the month closed Denys Brown and Clifford Nancarrow worked on the draft of a circular we hoped to send to all 40,000 P&O stockholders. The logistics were daunting and the cost was immense. Printing and despatch, as estimated by the security printers, Burrup Matheson, would come to £7,500 (equivalent to about half my annual salary).

We asked Lewis Collins, the company secretary, for a copy of the stockholder list. He was guarded in his response, saying it would take time and would cost a lot. He thought that there was only one copy left with the registrars and that reprinting would be a slow business. We felt that there was a hint in this for us. Within the hour we had a representative hand over £350 to the registrars and had the precious volume in our hands together, most conveniently, with a set of addressed labels. Denys took the package home. On the following day an almost apoplectic Geddes accused us of devious behaviour, and of having gone behind the company secretary's back.

Our success obviously rankled. At 5.30 p.m. that day, the chairman's secretary handed Betty Fairclough an invoice for me for £900 'on account of supplying addressed labels of P&O stockholders', coupled with a request for 'a cheque tonight'. As she only had a general idea of where I was and no idea when, or if, I would return, she prudently refused this hot brick by claiming that, as she did not know where I was, she couldn't guarantee delivery that evening. This was not good enough; a cheque was wanted 'tonight'. So a cheque they got – Betty's. It was refused, and this stupid harassment ended with agreement that the invoice be given to me as soon as possible. I returned unexpectedly some forty-five minutes later and my cheque was handed over at 6.35 p.m.

I had asked Geddes to agree that it was appropriate that our views, as a significant minority on the board, should be made available to stockholders and I asked that the cost be borne by the company. But, through a series of delaying tactics, it was not until the board of 1 November that our request was considered formally. We were not surprised when the board decided, backed by predictable explosions from Crichton, that our costs of circularising stockholders would not be made good.

We had already resolved to go ahead on our own account when, as we went to press, Oliver Jessel, who had built up a major holding in P&O and who, for his own reasons, was a powerful opponent of the bid, offered to meet our costs if we were unable to recover them from P&O. I am happy to say that recourse to Oliver was not in the end required.

However much the public posture of the board was to dismiss criticism, the various opposition interests were hitting hard enough to erode confidence in the bid. In our case David Greenslade was invaluable in producing not only ideas, options, arguments and questions, but in ensuring that they were backed by figures assembled with formidable efficiency. He outraged the hierarchy by addressing the chairman directly, accusing him and his colleagues of incompetence, misrepresentation and of being in dereliction of their duty to stockholders. 'Who is this fellow Greenslade – how dare he?'

In an attempt to silence his detractors, Geddes addressed the stockholders. Unfortunately for him, his letter of 29 September could do no better than repeat Ian Fraser's argument on the valuation of the fleet. It saddened me that shipping men I had worked with and respected could put their signatures to such a specious argument. It reinforced my impression that my executive colleagues were content to be ciphers for the 'experts' and that they had thrown in the towel.

In a short press release, we pointed out that the directors of Bovis had stated that 'the current value of building land held for development is very substantially in excess of book value' and expressed our amazement that in the same breath Geddes had repeated that 'it would not be meaningful to put a market value on P&O's fleet'. We reiterated that future profits had been seriously underestimated. At this point Geddes and Lazards let it be known that proxies received for the EGM were heavily in favour of the bid.

Morgan Grenfell put its case to the full Takeover Panel, arguing that the EGM fixed for 12 October should be postponed for the following reasons:

– The further information coming from P&O would be too late for proper consideration;

– P&O's advertisements soliciting proxies in favour of the deal had been published in newspapers before stockholders had received the circular giving the facts on which they could come to a decision;

– P&O's advertisements amounted to a further attempt to pressurise stockholders into a vote in favour.

But Morgans had to concede that the circular they were about to send to stockholders contained nothing new. The Panel turned them down.

In their circular issued on 3 October, Morgans recommended P&O stockholders to vote against, maintaining that P&O, under a more dynamic board with Lord Inchcape in the chair, would achieve the company's full potential. Lord Catto confirmed that he had seen Inchcape, but had not made contact with the other dissidents.

During the evening of 3 October I was with Denys at 40, St Mary Axe when Inchcape appeared, thrusting a piece of paper into our hands and saying: 'You had better see this.' It was a copy of a letter he had just delivered to Ford Geddes:

> My board have recently been considering the current P&O situation and believe that terms for a merger between Inchcape and P&O can be reached which would be more favourable to P&O stockholders than the proposed acquisition of Bovis. For every £2 deferred stock in P&O, one ordinary share of Inchcape plus £2 in cash. . . .

A bombshell.

Denys and I immediately withdrew from St Mary Axe; there must be no suggestion that we were working with or available to Inchcape. The Inchcape & Co. offer removed him from our immediate sphere and thereafter we scrupulously kept our distance.

Operating once more from the P&O building added to the complications of meetings and heightened the need for security. Together with Denys, Betty Fairclough would shred the contents of our wastepaper baskets many times a day. Denys had no secretary and the whole burden now fell on my office. Mike Taylor, P&O's oil man, had offered us any help we needed. We asked to share his secretary, Pat Scrimshaw-Wright. Perhaps it wasn't quite what he intended, but he was generous enough to schedule his work to our requirements.

'Inchcape puts money where his mouth is,' announced the press and in some quarters of P&O there may have been a sense of relief, if not of salvation. But Geddes' message to the staff that he would do his 'utmost to see it [the bid] resolved in your best interests and those of our stockholders' was cold comfort, considering the flak his actions thus far had attracted.

The board's line was to dismiss Inchcape as opportunist and to doubt his ability to follow through. His public opposition had been based on the premise that P&O would do better on its own, but now he was saying that P&O presented 'a major opportunity for the shareholders of Inchcape'. As recently as 24 September, he had maintained in the *Observer*: 'I have no wish to be chairman of P&O. A physical merger has not been considered at all. We don't think it will work. We're merchanting, they're shipping.' It has to be said that his U-turn was hardly convincing.

Whatever the motive, Inchcape's bid had to be taken seriously. With the relative standing of P&O and Inchcape shares that day, the bid could be interpreted as valuing P&O more highly than did the board's bid for Bovis.

The P&O board meeting on 4 October was attended by Inchcape, his colleagues Mackay Tallack and Oliver Brooks, and their advisers Peter Baring and Charles Hambro. The Inchcape team addressed the board in encouraging, co-operative terms and overall presented a logical enough case. Inchcape himself was brusque rather than eloquent. But Mackay Tallack and Oliver Brooks demonstrated a grasp of the issues in sharp contrast to the Geddes/Mitchell team. It seemed to me that Geddes was going through the motions and wanted to be rid of this undesirable situation as rapidly as possible.

The Inchcape bid was a much simpler reverse takeover than the P&O/Bovis proposal, and certainly gave P&O a higher value. It merited serious attention and we three dissidents said so, without in any way retreating from our position that P&O's best course was to continue on its own.

The following morning a hastily-convened board acknowledged

that a standoff from the Inchcape bid would not be in the best interests of stockholders. Lazards, who had been sitting on the fence, suddenly found themselves – more uncomfortably – on the horns of a dilemma. Eloquent in support of the Bovis proposal, they now pleaded that any choice between the two bids was very finely balanced, and that the board should decide.

The board lurched to and fro: an alliance with Inchcape was not a suitable mix; Inchcape, unlike Bovis, generated most of its earnings overseas, so would negate the prospect of utilising tax allowances; Bovis had property expertise; Inchcape had none: Inchcape's proposal involved a dilution of equity greater than Bovis's, and so on.

Enter David Horne, hotfoot from talking to Warburgs, to confer with Ian Fraser. The two retired; and, on return, Fraser spoke for both banks: If the EGM set for 12 October were postponed, Bovis would withdraw – 'and then where would you be?' However, Fraser further reported that Warburgs had requested a meeting with Lazards and Wms Glyn at 2.45 p.m. that day to receive a revised proposal from Bovis embodying variations in the terms of the bid. The board adjourned.

Enter Frank Sanderson – again to the rescue. To ease P&O's problems he now offered to accept terms substantially less favourable to Bovis. Broadly, provided P&O rejected Inchcape and approved Bovis at the EGM on 12 October, he would accept a significant reduction in the share of the enlarged company which would fall to Bovis shareholders.

Such a move was so unexpected as temporarily to throw everyone into confusion. But the financial advisers soon restored order. Having recommended the acceptance of the earlier Bovis figures as being 'in the interests of P&O and its stockholders', they seemed to be not at all embarrassed now to recommend acceptance of this higher valuation for P&O.

We dissidents, excluding Inchcape, were thus enabled to participate in discussions concerning the Inchcape bid and the revised Bovis offer. It was a complicated scene. We pressed for a delayed EGM, as we felt instinctively that even the improved terms would not be sufficiently attractive to overcome the compelling arguments which we were developing. Equally, we were clear that our duty to stockholders was to ensure that the Inchcape offer was carefully considered.

After a marathon session, in total some eleven hours, the board abandoned the attempt to evaluate the rival bids and the meeting closed with support for Geddes's proposal that the EGM arranged for the 12th should be held, but immediately be adjourned to allow time for consideration of the new offer. That decision had been a long time a-coming.

The next episode was fought out in the press. While attempting to find a palatable form of words to justify his move, Frank Sanderson attributed Inchcape's motives to personal ambition and suggested that the dissidents' motives were not concerned with the terms of the bid, 'but were about personalities'. We stuck to facts and did not respond to his smear tactics.

With hindsight I can say that Frank Sanderson accurately pin-pointed Inchcape's motives, but made a mistake with the dissidents, as was later to be proved in my case in a moment of pure farce over tea at the Oriental Club.

When Inchcape dissented, he had given Geddes no quarter and Geddes had failed to recognise the danger of being dismissive. Having gone public, Inchcape promised Geddes that he would not lobby the board for support and that he would not organise a stockholders' pressure group. Admittedly Denys Brown and I had to woo him into the open – but of course that had been only two weeks before he made his own bid. A 'spoiling' bid? It is not fair to judge it so, considering the cost of mounting a bid and the quality and character of his board.

We dissidents succeeded in getting our vote of no confidence in Lazards and Wms Glyn onto the agenda for the directors' meeting on 11 October. In the run-up, we tried to discuss the issue with colleagues, reminding Geddes that on the 5th he had said he would not be pushed around and would take the necessary time; and that Oliver Poole had indicated privately that perhaps P&O would do better to tackle the immediate future with the help of other financial advisers. But, unless our executive colleagues had a change of heart and supported us, we would be defeated even with Poole, Marris and Lloyd abstaining. And so we were.

During this series of meetings in October, Oliver Poole, on more than one occasion, would absent himself at a critical point. He would apologise to the chairman and leave the boardroom, some-times to return later (the impression being that he had been en-gaged on other urgent business). I recall being both surprised and dismayed. Was he trying to avoid being associated with a disputed decision? Was he ensuring some fallback position from which he could claim that, had he been present, he would not have agreed the course taken? These board discussions were certainly the most important to date and of profound significance to the company, yet Poole seemed almost Olympian in his detachment.

The EGM on 12 October was a heady affair. The venue was the panelled hall of The Chartered Insurance Institute, with the directors ranked on a dais in order of seniority and a packed and excited floor. Geddes hoped to get the adjournment through on the nod, and to get some kudos for modernising the voting arrangements. But, before he could start, there was a moment of high drama. Oliver Jessel rose, and in resounding terms proposed a vote of thanks to the dissident directors – Lord Inchcape, Sandy Marshall, Denys Brown and Clifford Nancarrow – for having the courage to stand up for the interests of the stockholders. The chairman huffed and puffed and endeavoured to declare Oliver Jessel out of order. But Jessel rode roughshod over him. His motion was seconded by George Law of Morgan Grenfell and, with a triumphant 'I declare the motion carried with acclamation', Oliver sat down to tremendous applause.

It was not an easy meeting for Geddes. He was faced with a number of technical questions and was criticised for his interpretation of a chairman's moral duty. Stockholders who were frustrated at being short-changed had a field day and put various motions: proposing that the bid be dropped; that Geddes should resign; that Inchcape should take the chair.

The proposal to adjourn was eventually put; but the floor, several hundred strong, was wound up and demanded a vote. By a show of hands the motion was defeated – further applause and cheers. The chairman then exercised his right to take into account the proxy votes cast prior to the meeting. The adjournment was duly carried, but in all the turmoil and to the dismay of the board, the proposal to change the voting structure could not now be put.

Kenneth Fleet, in the next day's *Daily Telegraph*, wrote of the 13 October board meeting that this would be the second time in the history of P&O that a vote would be taken – the first had been on the previous Wednesday when the dissidents proposed that Lazards and Wms Glyn should cease to act as P&O's financial advisers. (He had reported that Poole, Marris and Lloyd had voted against that motion and subsequently had to print a retraction to avoid a libel suit by Poole.) He then went on to say:

> Today's vote is crucial. The dice are loaded in favour of Bovis by virtue of numerical weight: of the committed non-execs, the three bankers are solid, Crichton is behind them, so too is Angus Mackinnon, though less comfortably since he is also a director of Inchcape and owes his seat on the P&O board to Inchcape rather than the Brown Shipley connection. Mitchell is more 'proBo' than Frank Sanderson. It is possible that Adams, Beazley and Parry will have the courage of their convictions and vote against, influenced in their wavering by the knowledge that Sir Donald Anderson and Lord Geddes would like to see the deal dropped. If the vote today goes against him, Geddes would have no option but to resign, a step I understand that has already been put to him but which, understandably, he has so far refused to take.

With scant analysis and an obvious sense of irritation, the board rejected the Inchcape bid. We three dissidents voted against rejection without further in-depth consideration. We did not vote for acceptance as some of our colleagues hinted. On receiving P&O's decision, Hambros and Barings immediately approached the Panel to get a ruling that P&O must provide information on future profitability. Inchcape commented: 'It is hard to understand why the majority of the board has already reached a decision on the rival alternative after adjourning the EGM specifically to allow time for mature consideration of the alternatives facing them.' It was a fair point.

Frank Sanderson then lashed out: 'Inchcape can't be serious, he's clouding the issue, he glibly talks about acquiring UK earnings; if he cared for P&O he would let it rest.' Oliver Brooks took up the cudgels: 'We do not make bids for the fun of it. We only do things at Inchcape which we expect to benefit our shareholders. There is ample room to increase P&O's earnings as well. Using its cash and properties, it is not difficult to generate them. We have also been approached by two of the major property companies offering to help develop the P&O properties if the bid is successful.'

On the 15th, the *Sunday Times* produced a memorable headline: 'Our Ford: any colour as long as it's Bovis.'

On the 16th, Geddes sent another update to staff. In fairness to him I am sure he did not intend to mislead when he wrote: 'I shall not agree to anything that has not been fully explored and considered.' The rival bids did of course give him the opportunity to withdraw and regroup. Instead, with all the stubbornness of a weak man, he was unswerving in pursuit of his downfall.

At the Panel on that Monday, the Inchcape bid ran into a serious snag. Under the Panel's rules of equality, P&O could not be required to give Inchcape a profit projection as they had not given one to Bovis. Oliver Brooks commented that 'the securing of a profits forecast is probably the most important part of the information we have requested from P&O.' And Peter Baring stated: 'Inchcape would not want to go ahead without an indication of P&O's future profitability.' Inchcape was in no mood to take the ruling lying down and wrote to P&O reminding them of the agreement that there would be an exchange of profit forecasts. Deadlock.

A few days later Denys Brown sent me the following chit:

> Leo Seymour telephoned. Betty Fairclough persuaded him to speak to me in your absence. Hoare Govett have decided that they cannot support P&O in the bid for Bovis and therefore feel compelled to resign as the company's brokers. This must be good for us and really is one in the eye for Ford, is it not?!

Greenwell were immediately appointed brokers to P&O. Although Hoare Govett were Inchcape's official brokers, the company had used Rowe & Pitman for their bid and thus Hoare Govett were independent in that respect. As P&O's former brokers, they were forbidden by the Takeover Code from publishing earnings or dividend forecasts for P&O, with or without Bovis, or from publishing circulars expressing opinions on the merits of the merger and the appropriate price for P&O. But they were not inhibited from offering private advice to their clients.

Hoare Govett put forward their investment analyst, Brian Costello, and a very helpful contribution he made. But it was his introduction to our team which sticks in my memory. He had information for me. Betty Fairclough contacted him to arrange a handover. He wanted total discretion, no couriers. Unable to leave the office, she turned to Pat Scrimshaw-Wright for help. Pat was to go to the corner of Leadenhall Street and Bishopsgate where she would find a slim, fair-haired Irishman of medium height wearing a grey flannel suit and dark glasses. He would hand her an envelope. 'No thanks, you go, I'll mind your phone.' 'No, Pat,' said Betty, ' I'll be missed.' 'So will I, if I get the wrong Irishman!'

Hoare Govett's defection – another almost unprecedented move – astonished the City. It was a mighty boost to our morale and invaluable in our approaches to institutional shareholders (on the assumption that they would be able to exercise full voting rights). I had already made my own case to Commercial Union. We had been to the Panel in an endeavour to prevent P&O as trustees voting the pension fund holdings in support of the board (we failed); we had suggested to P&O Australia that stock in their hands should at least be immunised in the light of the dissent on the board. With Leo Seymour, Richard Westmacott, and Laurie Connor of Hoare Govett I now embarked on a marathon round of visits; the Pru and Commercial Union again; to Edinburgh to see the Charlotte Square investment houses (where I played my Scottish card for all it was worth); to Clerical & Medical where Lord G had been chairman and Donald Methven had taken over; M&G, Schroders, and the other merchant banks except, I think, Barings who were advising Inchcape. The list went on and on. My reception was on the whole encouraging and all the time I became better at presenting our case.

The paper war was hotting up. On the 16th, Jessel fired off a broadside to stockholders in his 'Save P&O' campaign. Our own 'Say NO to Bovis' circular was nearing completion.

A happy change of scene came with the naming of Bulk Shipping's *Kildare*, a 150,000 ton OBO, on 17 October at the Eriksberg yard in Gothenburg. Dick Lloyd's wife, Jenny, was to sponsor her. As chief executive of Bulk Shipping I was the host, and, with Mona, accompanied the guests to the yard. A very British occasion: Richard Lloyd, one of the majority on a board determined to beat the dissidents, and myself, a principal dissident, proudly showing off one of the investments which was taking P&O into a new era. I respected Dick for his demeanour and conduct over those stormy weeks and we have remained good friends. The *Kildare* ceremonies provided welcome relief from unremitting pressure.

Before a meeting to be held in Amsterdam, I had arranged a briefing on Associated Bulk Carriers matters. Michael Naess, Neil Freeland and Bo Madsen of Zapata Norness were ushered into my office. Their unusually solemn expressions took me off guard. As I went over to greet Michael he opened his jacket with a flourish to 'flash' one of Jessel's flyers – 'Save P&O: Tell Bovis No!' in large red letters – pinned across his chest. That was a good moment.

There was a series of board meetings on 23 October, but no decision on the new Bovis terms was reached. As Geddes had promised stockholders fourteen days to assess these terms, it seemed possible that the adjourned EGM now called for 9 November would itself have to be postponed.

Negotiations with Bovis were, however, finally concluded late on the 24th. We were given the revised terms at 6.15 p.m.; no full meeting of the board was called; at 7 p.m., after a board committee meeting, the position was presented to the press.

A somewhat complicated valuation of ordinary, deferred and preferred stock – with the introduction of an element of unsecured loan stock and some cash – would result in P&O's stockholders owning 63.48% of the combined equity and Bovis shareholders the balance of 36.52%. Ironically this was not very far from Wms Glyn's original split of 60/40. The EGM would go ahead as planned to consider the proposed change in voting structure; but the EGM scheduled to consider the increase in share capital would be postponed (probably until a week later).

The terms were hardly simpler than the earlier convoluted offers. I rushed out a press release: 'At first sight the new terms are nowhere near good enough. We see no reason why stockholders should accept them. They do not remove the basic lopsidedness of the bargain.' We emphasised that we had only seen the terms forty-five minutes before publication and that a full board had not been called to debate and approve them.

Through Oliver Brooks, Inchcape published his views on 26 October: 'The terms do not seem to have changed very much to us. It only seems to be of marginal benefit and we are still very much in the ring. We had a meeting today and decided on what our course of action will be. We want to see the formal documents first and will then follow up fairly promptly with a statement.'

An offer to get Geddes off the Inchcape hook was not the same as an offer too good for the stockholders to refuse. Sanderson, while astute in his handling of Geddes, failed to see that he needed to demolish a wall of criticism before P&O was his. If he believed our dissent had a personal motive, which may have influenced him to disregard it, he could not make the same assumption about the institutions who also disliked the bid. His inability to see the obvious must later have haunted his dreams.

Towards the end of October, I was approached by Lord Catto of Morgan Grenfell. Catto accepted that I, Denys Brown and Clifford Nancarrow had elected to maintain our independence and that seemed to be working well. There was now a weighty opposition – the institutional scepticism led by Morgans, the minority directors, Inchcape & Co. maintaining that their bid should have consideration, and numerous press and broker critics. Morgans felt they had to have credible proposals for management to follow defeat of the P&O board. Stephen Catto informed me that, now that Inchcape had dealt himself out of the equation, he proposed to advance the name of Sir John Saunders, lately chairman of the Hong Kong Bank, for the chair of P&O. Catto advised me – not seeking my agreement – that he would propose me as managing director. I listened to him. Ancillary to these proposals he would himself expect to join the board and Morgan Grenfell would take over from Lazards as financial advisers.

Jake Saunders was very close to Y. K. Pao, the Hong Kong shipping magnate who was said to be the biggest tanker-owner in the world, and was on the board of 'YK's' World-Wide Shipping Group. I sensed a hidden agenda, but Denys Brown and I agreed to meet him. We liked what we found. Saunders assured us that he had allowed his name to come forward because he felt strongly that P&O should not be 'destroyed' and that he carried no baggage in respect of 'YK'. He would not allow a conflict of interest to arise. Although at this first meeting I felt he knew relatively little of P&O's recent history and that the solution was not as simple as he might think, I was conscious that my initial reaction – 'It's too difficult for an outsider' – was instinctive, predictable and inappropriate. I liked him as a man, he had a good record and his approach was straightforward.

So, when Morgan Grenfell produced their plan a week or so later, I was able to say that I would find no difficulty in working with Jake Saunders if that was the wish of a reconstructed board. I emphasised that I believed implicitly in the separation of the roles of chairman and CEO and that, therefore, I supported the appointment of a non-executive chairman of P&O. As for the other proposals which Catto had advanced, I emphasised that these would be matters for the board to decide in due course.

Next came an approach from a *Daily Express* journalist who asked if we could meet in the West End. I proposed tea at the Oriental Club, where I was well known and there could be no suggestion of a clandestine meeting. The gentleman concerned stressed that this was an individual, off-the-record approach. He 'happened to be a close friend' of Frank Sanderson, for whom he had an 'exceptionally high regard'. He also had a high regard for me, and nothing would give him more pleasure, and of course be more advantageous for P&O and Bovis, than to bring us together. He of course had no brief, but he knew that Sanderson anticipated great benefits from his association with P&O. I, on the other hand, was facing catastrophic loss of reputation, loss of employment and a life in the wilderness. How unnecessary and what a waste. As I was feeling pretty unsure of the outcome of the whole affair already, I did not appreciate his point. Nor did I like what I suspected I was hearing. I terminated the tea-party abruptly. I sometimes wonder whether a Swiss bank account might have figured had I stayed longer.

I was indeed unsure. While the opposition had loud and widespread support, we still had to reckon with the sheer mountain of the bid. Warburgs, Lazards and Greenwell were no lightweights. Geddes constantly drew attention to the fragmented opposition, 'each operating to his own agenda'. He impugned our motives and even disparaged one of us personally. The new Bovis terms were certainly more digestible and probably, to some, acceptable. One-for-one voting would favour the institutional vote – more likely to vote on the figures than on niceties. Yet each vote for the proposal would still mean a vote for a bunch of directors and their advisers who had made fools of themselves, had given up on their duty and who could not possibly carry forward a major new venture with confidence.

As the final EGM approached, logistics again became an issue. The bid had run for almost 100 days and, under Panel rules, could not now go past 17 November. Oliver Jessel, who campaigned ferociously and won some admiration for having the gall to flypost the City, asked all those who followed his advice to send their proxies to Morgan Grenfell. So did Inchcape; it seemed sensible for us to do the same. Morgans had the facilities to cope, to count and to deliver.

On 31 October came the culmination of weeks of hard work and secrecy. Our circular proclaimed:

NO TO BOVIS
A Recommendation to Reject the Merger Resolutions and to
Re-affirm Confidence in an Independent Future for P&O.

This circular was signed by me and on behalf of Denys Brown
and Clifford Nancarrow, and was despatched to stockholders – the
opening salvo in a bombardment that for the next two weeks had
the Post Office delivering exhortations almost daily to P&O stockholders:

Say No to Bovis;
Say Yes to Bovis;
Ignore this;
Support that . . . .

The enclosures were multicoloured 'for simplicity', but when P&O
and Morgans, even P&O and Bovis, used red and blue for conflicting purposes, it only added to the ordinary stockholders' feelings of
frustration as they opened (or binned) in rapid succession:

– P&O's official offer document for Bovis with new proxy cards
and urgent recommendations to vote for the resolution and to lodge
proxies by 15 November.

– Inchcape & Co: 'Reject the Bovis bid and allow Inchcapes the
opportunity to carry forward its merger proposals with the then
P&O Board.'

– P&O: 'Disregard any circulars from the opposition – Jessel,
Morgans, Inchcape and the dissident directors – and do not fill in or
despatch any of their proxies.'

– Barings' and Hambros' recommendation of the Inchcape bid.

– Morgan Grenfell: 'Stay independent of Bovis, strengthen the
Board and Management of P&O.'

– Oliver Jessel: 'Save P&O; the future of P&O as a great independent company is at stake.'

– P&O: 'You may be bored by all these circulars, but you cannot
afford to be bored; record your vote for the resolution.'

Full-page advertisements placed by P&O and Bovis in the press
were countered by others on behalf of Inchcape, Jessel and Morgans.
Advertising costs greatly exceeded those incurred in any previous
takeover.

Morgan's new-look board was initially considered a more
credible alternative than either Bovis's or Inchcape & Co.'s – Catto
felt that the board should also include Inchcape 'if he feels able to

continue'. Geddes said this move showed Morgans and their aides 'in their true colours. Having stated on the 3rd that they were taking a completely independent and objective position Lord Catto shows his independence and objectivity by seeking appointment to the P&O board.' On the chairmanship, he produced his best quote of the whole affair: 'I do not know Sir John Saunders. But I was not aware I had resigned. The office is not available at the moment.'

Our statement of 31 October emphasised that my position and that of my fellow dissidents was an independent one. While praising the work Morgans had done for stockholders, I said of the suggested board changes: 'These will be matters for the board as it may then exist. If they choose to elect me as managing director I shall be glad to turn my hand to it.' There was a telling new point in that the board's statement on tax allowances implied an average annual profit level for P&O alone in excess of £20m for the next two financial years. This estimate, which had been cleared by the Takeover Panel, was based on figures from P&O accounts and information published in connection with a prospectus for ship-financing for Panocean. It was John Maltby of Panocean, stalwart in support throughout, who guided us to this nugget.

The press picked up the story that the majority of the board had refused to finance our circular out of company funds and that the £7,500 cost had been borne by the dissident directors.

It had not gone unnoticed that other opponents of the deal had avoided supporting the Inchcape bid. Morgans said that this bid could hardly be considered 'until there is a public P&O profit forecast and Inchcape are a bit more forthcoming about their intentions'.

Within our camp, we may perhaps be forgiven for feeling elated by the elegance and weight of the opposition campaign. But, in the world outside, the Bovis bid still attracted a wide range of supporters, from those who traditionally gave their backing to the board in any event to those who were now thoroughly impatient with the endless wrangling and who felt that the sooner Bovis took over the better. Also, the new terms were certainly more attractive. So we were bound to recognise that the market was drifting inexorably towards acceptance of the bid.

I had called on Donald Anderson, Freddie Harmer and Lord G. All were dismayed at the P&O spectacle. They were initially reluctant to take a public position, but assured me that they supported the dissenters and each assured me that he considered the bid should be withdrawn before more damage was done.

This was encouraging, but we desperately needed public endorsement. With faultless timing, Donald Anderson turned up trumps. On 9 November, the day of the EGM, the *Daily Telegraph* gave prominence to an interview with him by Kenneth Fleet in which DFA declared that he disliked the bid and would vote against it. This was the right stuff for individual P&O stockholders, of whom we expected a good turnout at the meeting that afternoon. So we ran off hundreds of copies of the inverview for Betty Fairclough and Pat Scrimshaw-Wright to distribute. They stood alongside a bevy of girls handing out Oliver Jessel's broadsheet, and put up with some barracking; but the 'outing for nice young ladies representing Mr Sandy Marshall' made good copy.

There was only one item on the agenda – the alteration in the voting structure to a one-for-one basis. Having put the motion to the meeting, and endured some decidedly unpleasant jeers, Geddes took a few questions from the floor and passed swiftly to the vote. Undoubtedly with vivid memories of the last vitriolic meeting, he warned that he would demand a poll regardless of the result of the vote by a show of hands. The motion was carried on the floor, but he still called for a poll, urged stockholders to read the winning results in the newspapers, and closed proceedings. In about nine minutes P&O had modernised its voting structure.

The Donald Anderson interview and the attribution of the tax allowances were powerful arguments in support of our stand. Not having the resources to circulate all the stockholders again, we compromised on a circular to the major fund-holders together with a press release to ram these points home. With a week to go to the final EGM, we needed all the help we could get. My sister Edith, in indignation and with great enthusiasm, had come south to give moral support. She and Mona came to my office to help by stuffing envelopes. There was very little room and they happily sat on the floor.

The closer we came to the finale, the more I realised that I had placed my career and family in jeopardy. What are my memories of those torrid days of up and down emotion? Mona remembers me sitting on the edge of an unmade bed, in pyjamas, unshaven, glued to the telephone on a Sunday morning. My own recollection is of tiredness and yet exhilaration. In P&O's official circles there was tension and some apprehension. But I was buoyed up, above all by the stalwart support of Mona, who added a burning anger to her love and loyalty; by support from the wider family and from outside the company; from people I respected and by the commitment of our team which was working so smoothly that we were always able to react promptly and with authority as developments occurred. Denys Brown remained calm, rational and focused. He had proved his point of, to say the least, 'ill-handling' by Lazards and had the pleasure of seeing this acknowledged in public. He never lost sight of the main objective – to save P&O from destroying itself; and he insisted throughout that we maintain the highest standards in our statements and behaviour.

On 14 November, the last posting day for proxies, the press took the opportunity to advise stockholders how to vote. However, Donald Anderson, supported by Freddie Harmer and Lord G, had intervened once more to allay stockholders' fears as to who would steer P&O if the bid failed. His intervention made headlines: 'Lord Inchcape agrees to chair P&O if Bovis merger is rejected.' Ignoring the small matter of his own bid which was still on the table, Inchcape had told Sir Donald that he 'would be prepared to accept the chairmanship for a limited period of, say, up to three years'. He saw his prime task during this period as 'to re-establish harmony and confidence, to reassess P&O's future profitability on its own or in conjunction with another, to establish its course in the light of this assessment and organise a succession'. Morgans interpreted this to mean that Inchcape would be a caretaker, with Sir John on the board and likely to take over as chairman later.

For us the day was brightened briefly by *The Times*, which published a letter from Denys Brown detailing the chronology of the bid and demonstrating the inadequacies of the board's handling of its responsibilities.

Morgan Grenfell filed a number of opposition proxies on Wednesday 15th and P&O/Lazards seemed to assume that these represented the bulk of the opposition. Photographs of Geddes and Sanderson watching the proxy count appeared in the evening press, which reported their confidence in an overwhelming victory for P&O and Bovis, and a reaffirmation of their support for the deal on the part of our seven executive colleagues.

It was a miserable day. But late in the evening, when I was rounding up the tally with George Law on the telephone, he told me, in confidence, that Morgans had a few more proxies up their sleeve and to 'stay with it'. Just before the deadline of 3 p.m. on Thursday the 16th, Morgans delivered a huge vote, some ten million, to the registrar. As the count went ahead it became clear that the stockholders had voted firmly against the bid – small individual holders overwhelmingly so.

The EGM, at the now familiar venue of The Chartered Insurance Institute, on Friday, 17 November was again packed. The board filed onto the dais. Geddes announced that the proxy count showed that, if a poll was demanded, the board's proposal to bid for Bovis would be defeated by three to one. He added that he and Dawes would resign. There were extraordinary scenes in the hall. Oliver Poole, seen by many as the villain of the piece, was booed. Geddes, who behaved with considerable dignity on a day which must have shattered him, had asked me to speak at the end of the meeting.

The *Sunday Times* described the scene:

> The 99-day battle over the future of P&O reached its climax beneath the stained glass windows of the Chartered Insurance Institute hall in the heart of the City shortly after 3 o'clock last Friday afternoon. But the most telling moment for the company, its staff and its 40,000 shareholders came not when chairman Ford Geddes conceded defeat over his plan to merge with construction group Bovis, nor even when Geddes revealed his intention to resign tomorrow.
>
> That moment came when the tall, stern-faced figure of Alexander Badenoch Marshall immediately stood up and echoed Geddes' plea for the meeting to dispense with a discussion of the events which made up the bitterest, yet most fascinating, takeover struggle of the 70s. 'The time has come', said Marshall, 'for us to get on with our work again.' It was a moment which said eloquently, the king is dead, long live the king.

The drama seemed to be over – but it was not. As the directors filed out, the press tackled Kenneth Inchcape who confirmed that 'Bovis having been seen off, Inchcape & Company will renew its bid for P&O.'

7

The Dream Team

We wanted to find a company with good assets and rotten management. We found it in P&O. *Frank Sanderson, at an impromptu press conference immediately after losing the battle.*

From today's perspective it is difficult to appreciate the impact the affair was to have on established City practice. For years the takeover had been 'the anvil for the new efficient Britain'. The faster and higher a company's share price rose the better. Progress was represented by the takeover and often by asset-stripping. Management which felt threatened put itself in thrall to financial advisers.

If nothing else, the P&O/Bovis story made clear that not even the merchant banker has a monopoly of financial wisdom. The assumption that the City knows best was fractured beyond repair. The conduct of takeovers would be reformed; corporate governance and boardroom democracy would be afforded more importance.

Did we celebrate our victory? Neither Mona nor I can remember. I believe Clifford Nancarrow held something of a party, but we didn't attend. I could not help but be sad for Geddes. However ineptly Ford had handled the Bovis affair, he and I shared deep roots in P&O – I understood his present desolation and felt compassion for him. There was work to be done on our return to the office. A board meeting was called for Monday morning. The press release which Denys and I had drafted was finalised and despatched. I made and received a number of calls and left for home – not early, but certainly not late. I wanted to spend every minute of that weekend with the family.

At the board on Monday, 20 November, Geddes immediately announced his resignation from both board and company. He handed over the chair to his deputy, Bill Dawes, and left the room. Dawes followed suit. Inchcape then proposed that I should take the chair for this meeting. John Mitchell, smugly wrapped in his three-year contract, resigned and departed. In short order, Denny Marris, Dick Lloyd and Oliver Poole withdrew – Poole having confirmed that

Lazards would resign their position as financial advisers and would make no charges in respect of the failed bid.

Inchcape informed the board that, with the rejection of the Bovis bid and in line with the offer made in October, his company would be seeking an agreed bid with P&O. No doubt that would be considered as a matter of urgency and, pending a conclusion, he felt it appropriate to seek leave of absence from the board. He then also withdrew.

Only Andrew Crichton and Angus Mackinnon remained at the table as sitting non-executive directors. It was the latter who broke the stunned silence which followed the exodus by proposing that Andrew Crichton, due to his seniority and experience, should be elected chairman.

I asked Crichton to withdraw while we discussed this outrageous suggestion. I made it absolutely clear that if the board were to consider such an appointment appropriate I would resign immediately and make my reasons public. No director supported Mackinnon. Crichton returned and was informed.

Mac Sidey then proposed that I be appointed managing director. The minute specifically reflected my earlier public statement that I regarded the separation of the roles of chairman and chief executive as vitally important. We had enough immediate experience of how the concentration of authority in one person can exercise undue influence. But I undertook to act, for an interim period, as chairman of the board 'in order to facilitate the conduct of business'.

With collar turned around, Andrew Crichton would have made a convincing Vicar of Bray, hence it was in character for him to deny the objective he had fought so vociferously to attain, in order to avoid loss of salary, loss of status and the anonymity of enforced retirement. As the years confirmed, Crichton never forgave me for keeping him out of the chair. He would duck and weave in egregious fashion, attaching himself ever closer to Inchcape upon whom he realised his seat on the board depended.

Even in retrospect it is difficult to understand Mackinnon's motives in this extraordinary episode. It is highly improbable that he would not first have discussed his intention with Inchcape. On the other hand Inchcape, who undoubtedly wanted the chair for himself, would surely not have given his blessing except on the basis that Crichton's proposed appointment be strictly temporary. But Mackinnon had given no indication that such a limitation was envisaged. As a member of the Inchcape board Mackinnon backed their approach to P&O, but as a member of the P&O board he was staunchly pro-Bovis. The most charitable conclusion is that he truly believed P&O's best interests lay in being taken over, no matter by whom. Mackinnon's progress down the Yellow Book road must have been bumpy. After the meeting he resigned. It was not a distinguished note on which to bring to an end over 100 years of family association.

Thus I found myself responsible for the company's survival. True, I had, over the years, aspired to being chief executive, but I would have wished this to come about in a more orthodox fashion. I needed time to learn more about the ways of the City – I had not been won over by all I had seen so far, and I regretted that, with his company's bid still on the table, Inchcape could not take the chair at once.

The press predicted a blood bath. But I believed that the Group would best be served by the strength that derived from continuity, and that time would heal our wounds. I knew, however, that this decision would require of me some painful adjustments.

Andrew Crichton? He would still be the Vicar of Bray, sir, but he was chairman of Overseas Containers Limited (OCL), whose successful performance was essential to P&O. He seemed to accept the new regime, and I had no wish to rock the OCL boat where he was doing a good job. I needed time to assess the consequences before contemplating change there, so Crichton stayed put.

Mac Sidey, a military man who ran European & Air Transport like the brigadier he had been, had supported the Bovis bid. He now wrote to congratulate me, and acknowledged that he had been wrong. He pledged his loyalty – from which he never deviated.

Adams felt that he had done his duty in supporting Geddes and, indeed, had once broken his customary silence by issuing a limp manifesto which purported to question the motives of the dissidents and to raise doubts about their experience. He was no entrepreneur, but he was competent, ran a tight ship and could be trusted to oversee the rundown – already underway – of the traditional cargo fleet.

Beazley, who had sat on the fence none too comfortably, was probably relieved at the outcome; a Bovis/P&O future would have held no future for him. He was well liked within the Group, and could provide much-needed reassurance for our residual New Zealand Company people who might be perturbed by the departure of Bill Dawes, the last in the line of the Dawes family who had contributed much over the years to the line known throughout New Zealand simply as 'The Shipping Company'.

Parry had maintained an almost invisible profile, essentially a pawn on the board, for the board, and – had the Bovis bid found favour – for the bid. But he was loyal to the company, and was playing his part in the important shift of emphasis from trans-ocean passenger services to holiday cruises.

All these men knew their jobs, and I believed they would run their divisions well.

At board level we now had to get back to work – fast. We had been sixteen; now we were nine, with one – Inchcape – counted out for the time being. My first priority was to ensure business as usual, but questions remained:

– A large block of stockholders, mainly institutions, had backed the old board. Would they now sell and in so doing devalue our stock?

– During the course of the bid, P&O had acquired some 10% of the Bovis equity, valued at £15m – would that stock hold its value?

– How would our customers and associates around the world react to us, after watching P&O tear itself apart?

As to the Inchcape bid, we could not dismiss it out of hand; a proportion of our stockholders would probably be willing to accept it; we had to assess it on its merits. So:

– David Greenslade took on the role of acting finance director. Unwilling to commit myself to Morgan Grenfell as financial advisers, vital though they had been in opposition, I turned to Michael Verey and David Airlie of Schroders, who were wholly independent of P&O, of Inchcape and of Bovis. Geoffrey Williams, with Anthony Loehnis (a son-in-law of Donald Anderson, but still independent), immediately started work solely on the Inchcape bid. It would take them some three weeks to report.

– Greenwells having resigned as brokers, I invited Leo Seymour and Hoare Govett to resume their role.

Quickly we began to settle down. I had to tackle the management structure. I needed to find a new head of Bulk Shipping, although Jim Bayley would hold the fort well; I was concerned about Deloittes, our auditors; there were loyalties to recover and confidence to inspire across the Group; I told Frank Sanderson that I could not give him an immediate undertaking about P&O's holding in Bovis's equity, but that we would not jeopardise its current value by dumping. Above all, I had to ensure that P&O would deliver the profits that we dissidents had forecast – profits on a scale not contemplated hitherto.

While at times I felt somewhat lonely and exposed, I soon realised what a tremendous spirit we had unleashed. Throughout the Group – ashore, afloat and around the world – staff were receiving a new message. Instead of the doom, gloom and near despair of Geddes, they were now hearing 'Of course we can do it'. The response was tremendous and it became clear that, despite the boardroom games, the ongoing business had, thank goodness, been managed effectively during the 100 days and no momentum had been lost. But I was not so sure about our associates overseas.

Ford Geddes's wife, Barbara, had been invited to name Bulk Shipping's new OBO, the 250,000-ton *Lauderdale*, at the Mitsubishi yard in Nagasaki, in December. I now proposed that Mona should assume that role and that I should accompany her. In Japan I would emphasise to Mitsui, Hitachi, Nippon Steel, Sumitomo, C. Itoh and other important clients, that, in P&O, it was 'business as usual'. On our arrival it was brought home to me that I had been right to sense a problem. Corporate rebellion was unthinkable in Japan at that time and these major clients had been dismayed. Fortunately, I was fairly well known to the top management of the shipyards, steel mills and trading houses and was able to reassure them. I got Bo Madsen to go out for Associated Bulk Carriers shortly afterwards to reinforce the message.

En route to Japan, I visited as many other offices and associates as possible: New York for Zapata Norness, Mundo Gas and, for old time's sake, Funch Edie, general cargo agents. Then off to Houston to see Zapata. (It was at Houston that Mona watched our baggage being loaded. Her hat box was seen being kicked up the ramp, but perhaps it missed the cargo door as that was the last she saw of it until it arrived home months later. She had to borrow a hat for the *Lauderdale* naming festivities from Margaret MacCallum of Swires.) In Los Angeles I met Stan Macdonald of Princess Cruises, who was very excited about prospects in his business and this confirmed my own enthusiasm. After Japan, I spent twenty-four hours in Hong Kong and then dropped in at Bombay to see the Mackinnons people, from whom I received a very warm welcome.

We were abroad for ten days, saw eight offices, numerous staff and some of the Group's most important clients and associated companies. Some years later Crichton, then feeling more secure, wrote in a note to Inchcape: 'Of course you will remember that Marshall went off on a jolly to the Far East as soon as he took over.' With his long experience of the East it was surprising that Crichton refused to recognise the value of my trip. I suspect he had a different agenda. Those ten days, of minimum fuss but much exertion, convinced me that I had conveyed a very necessary and very well-received message: 'Forget the aberration of the past four months – P&O is in good hands and we look forward.'

I arranged a board meeting on 19 December to consider Schroders' report and our response to Inchcape & Co. There was perhaps a residual and nostalgic inclination among some members, such as Adams and Parry, to attach more value to the Inchcape offer than was strictly justified by the figures and, in some ways too, they may simply have felt bid-weary. A merger with Inchcape would close the circle; could be seen as logical historically; and would, to some extent, justify their earlier decision to abandon ship.

But the new leadership was imbued with conviction and confidence and I do not believe Inchcape & Co. expected any reply other than a negative one. I conveyed our reply to Kenneth Inchcape on 19 December and asked if I could propose him as chairman. He agreed immediately. He also agreed that it would not do to seem to be in indecent haste and that it would be suitable to deal with his appointment at the next board meeting which was scheduled, appropriately, for 4 January at the beginning of a brave new year.

In announcing our rejection of the Inchcape offer we made it clear that we hoped the long-standing co-operation between our two companies would continue. On the same day I wrote to Inchcape:

Dear Kenneth,
I feel the somewhat formal statement being made to the press today, and our exchange this afternoon, perhaps do not convey adequately the real concern that the present Board had in considering the approach by Inchcape & Company Ltd.

One of the results of the last few months, however, is quite clearly a feeling of considerably more self-confidence in the Board and in the Company's capability to make good the sort of profits which we have 'on paper'.

When your first approach was made in October there was, as I think you know, a great deal of goodwill attached to it in P&O. As things developed you and your colleagues can, and I believe will, feel that your initiative has contributed in no small way to establishing our appreciation of our own strength. The context in which your approach has been considered over the past weeks is quite different from that in which it was originally made.

I am sure we are both convinced that P&O has a great future and, at the same time, I hope that our two Groups will extend our long-standing connections across the world.

Finally it is, I know, of great importance to your colleagues on the Board and to myself to know that you are going to remain with us. The early lead you personally gave at the end of August has enhanced your position throughout P&O.

Yours sincerely,

SANDY

This letter was to be important for the record when Andrew Crichton later accused me of wanting to be chairman myself and of having attempted to block Inchcape.

Over the weeks following my appointment it was heart-warming to receive a huge volume of congratulatory letters from colleagues in the shipping industry (David Gresham of BP headed the list); from UK and overseas, from our own people around the world, from old India friends, from relatives in Scotland, including my uncles Bertie and Alfred, from friends of my parents, P&O pensioners; the list seemed endless.

I was looking forward to establishing and working within the new structure which Denys Brown and I had planned, with the encouragement of Inchcape and with thoughtful contributions from my McKinsey friends. A key task was to define the separate but interlocking and complementary responsibilities of non-executive chairman and chief executive to promote a relationship of co-operation and confidence. It would be most satisfactory if this were sufficient, for it can be argued that definition is essentially restrictive and inhibits development of effective interplay. Experience has taught me, however, that one should define responsibilities in fairly general terms, emphasise common objectives and require the incumbents to set down their respective approaches and to work them through and forward together.

Inchcape, firmly standing in his grandfather's shoes, felt comfortable surrounded by Mackinnons and BI people; it was his milieu. He gave every appearance of being wholly in support of me. But I now see that the role of chairman was, for him, a symbol of ownership rather than a job to be done. Much attention was paid to his office and its furnishings – out went the contemporary design so carefully put together by Sir Colin Anderson, who was both a director of P&O and a distinguished connoisseur of the arts. In came net curtains and mock Regency. He was not at ease outside his own social circle and his willingness to 'meet the troops' was spasmodic. Hierarchy was important to him and he always wanted to know who was to become a member of the senior lunch mess. He jumped to opinions about people very quickly – sometimes to my dismay. He was not a sharer of thoughts: one has to note, as Denys Brown did sharply on more than one occasion, that perhaps he did not have many to share; rather he seemed to expect one to provide him with what he should be thinking. Over the years this became a real thorn in the flesh because, frankly, his focus was too often narrow and short term. One's patience was sorely tried – it was frequently difficult to get him to concentrate on the major issues. But this is for the future: at the beginning of 1973 we were the 'dream team'.

Helmut Sohmen of World-Wide Shipping, speaking at Lancaster University on 7 September 1980 said:

> When you reflect that if in 1970 somebody had suggested that in ten years' time half the tanker fleet would be looking for spot cargoes, that Shell and BP would be chartering surplus tonnage to other operators, that Japanese shipyards would have reduced their capacity to 40% and go begging for orders, that owners would spend in excess of US$10m to re-engine individual vessels from turbines to diesels, that very large and ultra large crude carriers (VLCCs and ULCCs) would be scrapped before reaching the tender age of twelve or even ten years, that European shipowners would part with something like 25 million deadweight tons of relatively modern ships over a period of only three years, that Korea and Poland would be two of the world's leading shipbuilding countries, that we would generally worry about energy supply and consumption, or that interest rate levels for the US dollar would be at 20%,

we would certainly have declared him a depressive maniac and not let him join the shipowning fraternity.

This aptly summarises some of the difficulties which lay ahead of us. While P&O was making history in the City, momentous events were in train on the world scene. 1972 saw the opening round of the oil crisis. The Organisation of Oil Exporting Countries (OPEC) was becoming a household word; the Seven Sisters, the major international oil companies which virtually controlled oil production and distribution and through which national governments exercised policy, were under strain. OPEC had secured an increase in price of 8.5% giving their producers an extra $700m per annum – an enormous figure and sufficient to influence patterns of trade, but peanuts compared with what was to come.

Britain joined the European Economic Community (EEC) early in 1972, and the country's external trade changed in direction and volume quite dramatically over the next few years as ties with the Commonwealth loosened. The short-sea routes to Europe saw a huge increase in passenger and freight traffic carried by RoRo ferries. P&O's traditional passenger services to Australia were effectively undermined by the relaxation of air charter rules, and the writing was on the wall for the other line voyages. At the beginning of the year the book value of the passenger fleet had been written down by 50%.

The oil price increase forced the industry to adopt a new approach to propulsion systems, accelerated the improvement of cargo-handling methods, hugely influenced the design of ship and shore facilities and affected energy trading patterns. Trade in LPG and LNG increased as their use became economically viable; oil exploration in the non-OPEC areas became a priority. Oil transportation was particularly vulnerable. The standard practice of the independent tanker owners had been to gear their shipbuilding programmes to the oil companies' projections, which assumed 7% compound annual increase in oil consumption. But now the majors' inability to exercise their customary absolute control disrupted the smooth running of the oil industry and presaged the tanker surplus which depressed the market in the 1970s and early 1980s.

As we approached the year's end, with Heath's think-tank predicting nil growth and 20% inflation for the UK, the shipping industry was being forced both to address major challenges and to examine a range of opportunities. Thanks to Donald Anderson's foresight, I was confident that we at least had an appropriate management structure in place.

The first item of business at P&O's first board meeting of 1973 was to appoint Inchcape chairman. Next the board approved my contract of service as chief executive officer. This flowed from Mac Sidey's proposal that I be put on a three-year contract, given my exposure during the Bovis battle. I had also by now forecast, although of course with the full backing of the executive, a doubling of profits in the current year. My contract had been drawn up by Peter Peddie of Freshfields – now that David Stebbings, who had been so closely involved with the bid, had withdrawn discreetly into the background. The board approved it 'subject to such minor adjustments as necessary being approved by the chairman' and Inchcape duly signed on behalf of the company.

I had been considering a circular to stockholders to sum up the P&O/Bovis saga, but it was not issued as we decided that no triumphalism should be sounded. However, its content provided a valuable platform for stockholder information for the year ahead. Inchcape had made his contribution, in particular on our decision to separate the functions of non-executive chairman and CEO. He wrote: 'Clearly at the moment this separation is the best thing for P&O as we believe it will make the Chairman of the Board and the Chief Executive of the Group better able to serve the Company.'

Inchcape as chairman felt right to the City and also right to us, the executive. I was personally pleased. Although never close to Kenneth, I had known him for over twenty years. In Calcutta, on his extended visits, relations were cordial, even jolly on the tennis court. Mona and I had been to Glenapp, Inchcape's turreted Victorian castle in Galloway, for his daughter Lucinda's twenty-first birthday party, and social contacts in London revolved around Calcutta Dinners, Oriental Club events and his annual cocktail party at Hanover Gate. I was a junior member of a long-established and quite hierarchical club. He was always 'the boss' and always an accepted figure of authority. His wide range of board memberships should enable him to have a feel for the progress of OPEC and of the oil factor in world economic affairs. We had stood together in 1972 and he had been enthusiastic in his support of my appointment, saying that his role was 'to counsel and support the chief executive'. I believed I could trust him. I was wrong.

It felt good to be able to conclude my first New Year message to staff, afloat and ashore, by telling them that, on my visit to Los Angeles in December, I had heard how well our newly acquired cruise ship, *Spirit of London*, had been received on the West Coast. As I left the office one of our American staff had handed me a marketing pamphlet: 'There is a new Spirit in P&O.'

With the help of John Maccoy and the advice of Bo Madsen, I was swiftly in discussion with Derek Hall of Seabridge for the position of head of Bulk Shipping. He was more a marketing man than a ship manager and I welcomed that – we already had plenty of technical knowledge and experience, but I wanted to develop our commercial clout alongside our Zapata colleagues. For him, it was a great opportunity to head the leading British independent tanker fleet and a growing state-of-the-art bulk carrier fleet with extensive development in gas and chemicals carriage and storage. He became a director of P&O and always pulled his weight.

The vacant finance director slot was more difficult. The obvious candidate was David Greenslade and I deeply regretted that I could not decide in his favour. Perhaps he was too black-and-white – no shades of grey. He demanded of others the same high standards he set for himself, and could not tolerate any compromise. A man of great qualities but not, sadly, one who would work well within a team. Gradually I developed my template: someone of courage and integrity, independent-minded, with commercial sense and an ability to think in risk/reward terms; he would, of course, need experience of the book-keeping side and an appreciation of the contribution that management accounting and information can make to understanding the dynamics of a business. He would be the fiscal and financial conscience of the team and so must have strength of character together with breadth of vision. When, to my surprise, my paradigm became available and we were able to bring Oliver Brooks on board from Inchcape, David Greenslade resigned. He had been a stalwart ally, and for a long time I felt his loss.

I already knew a bit about Oliver. My father, through his association with Gray Dawes and the Mackay family, had known the Inchcape people well and had secured Oliver's help as investment adviser to the Carnegie Trust. They held each other in mutual regard and after Father's death in 1961, Oliver continued his work with the Trust. I had, of course, noted the weight Inchcape gave to his advice on the financial aspects of the Bovis affair and, more crucially, in the preparation of the Inchcape bid. I was glad to have his support.

Sir John Saunders, with whom I had kept in touch since Bovis, agreed to join the board on 15 January; Derek Hall was appointed on 1 May and Oliver Brooks on 1 July.

We established a Planning Secretariat – a classic central function of its day – under Jim Lindars. Together with Finance Division, the Planning Secretariat was to be a powerful resource. It looked forward, asked questions of the operating divisions, did 'What if?' studies and altogether gave us a much more professional edge, so that the board and senior management could feel confident that our database was sound and decision-making would follow good analysis. We looked into the new world of computer-modelling for the bulk and tanker trades. It took a long time, perhaps too much management time, to ensure the input of all relevant data. It inevitably involved more and more experts, some rather unorthodox, so that the tail began to wag the dog. However, that we were prepared to grasp these new techniques says something for the confidence with which we set off.

Returning from my lightning round-the-world trip in December 1972 I made a rather smug remark to Powell in the car: 'You know, I've visited eight overseas offices in ten days'. 'Yes,' said my driver, 'but not many of the UK staff have seen you.' It was a sobering comment, so I set out to repair this omission. During the early months of 1973, I undertook a series of 'meet the staff' engagements: fifty or more in various canteens from 5.00 to 6.30 p.m. – a brief statement – questions and, I trust, constructive responses. Known by name to many from my Trident days and because of my appointment as the first executive director of P&O, I was nevertheless conscious that my 'rebellion' in 1972 might have upset some; also, perhaps, I was still seen as a member of the 'Mackinnons/BI mafia'. Now I wanted to put across my enthusiastic commitment to the Group staff around the world.

My theme was a compelling desire to achieve the quality performance of which we knew P&O to be capable: to achieve the development of people, the modernisation and professionalism of management, the jettisoning of much in the way of traditional practice without throwing tradition overboard and continuing the trend to become customer- rather than product-oriented. The company must be balanced, protected as far as possible from a collapse in any one market adversely affecting the whole. To sum up – delivery of our full potential by a well-motivated and responsive staff, maintaining quality of service and, by example and performance, retaining pole position in our various businesses. These canteen meetings were by turns stimulating and humbling. We had a wide range of capability and commitment; but it became clear that the management reorganisation and the Bovis bid had left deep scars in some quarters.

A significant problem flowed from the formation of the Group Personnel Services Division (PSD) as recommended by McKinsey. Management consultants may, with sweet reason, put new company structures in place, but the companies themselves have to cope with the ensuing culture shock. The letting go of staff as a result of rationalisation disturbed those who had assumed a job for life, and Group Personnel, which had delivered many unpalatable messages, was bombarded with as many critical responses. Frank Thomassen, the self important head of PSD, who drove us to distraction with professional jargon, soon moved on. His successor, Colin Lawrence, faced a bumpy few years. The maritime unions conducted national negotiations with employers in a relatively antagonistic spirit. The Employment Protection Act and the disturbed climate within P&O ashore gave ASTMS fertile ground for recruitment. Their interminable meetings occupied much valuable management and staff time, which could have been more productively spent for mutual benefit. The Bullock Report on industrial democracy, a politically correct, time-consuming parade of platitude and exhortation, contributed nothing to productivity or efficiency and much to the arguments of the traditional trades unionists. I had a personal regard for Jack Jones and Clive Jenkins, two of the most prominent union leaders, but little time for their politics. Over the ensuing years this negative, dead hand, unchallenged by the socialist government, tightened its grip on industry and unwittingly paved the way to the Thatcher era.

I needed a level-headed director to oversee Personnel and, in November 1972, had wanted Harry Beazley to take this responsibility. He was very reluctant to do so and I concluded that it would be stupid to put someone who lacked commitment into so sensitive a role. It was a relief when Denys Brown gallantly volunteered to take it on.

We also had to grasp the nettle of Public Relations. Peter Thomas, who had played a somewhat creepy role during the bid, had gone, to be succeeded by Bill Parkinson, about whom I recall little except that there was no way, after being volubly 'pro-Bovis' in November, he could present the new look in December. There was also the matter of 'chemistry,' about which both Denys Brown and I felt strongly. So Robin Sanders was recruited to take on PR. He was to be a committed and loyal supporter. He did a very good, professional job in communication with staff – particularly with *Wavelength*, the Group newspaper – and also managed to cope with the chairman's often strange and inconsistent requirements.

It was Robin who later worked with Wally Olins, of the consultants Woolf Olins, to produce what must be one of the definitive corporate symbols of the last twenty-five years. We needed a device to link the many companies and often disparate activities of the Group. We tried the P&O logo, but it had no 'aura'. So developed the symbol – yes, it is the P&O flag, but we insisted it should not be so described. We wanted the tradition embraced in the colours, but did not want to be circumscribed by a flagstaff and house flags lowered at sunset. Hence the blue sky and the flaring, confident 'flag' which could be applied in every situation. It seemed to say it all – tradition, but upward and onward with spirit. It has been a most attractive and worthwhile symbol and a legacy of which I am proud.

As well as his role in Personnel, Denys Brown had responsibility for co-ordinating the annual report. All annual reports are important but this, our first, assumed enormous significance. I was confident, from experience of Denys's skills during the bid, that we would have an informative, succinct and elegant document. But in March, Denys collapsed from exhaustion and on medical advice was despatched to a health farm. Betty Fairclough, who took over, used to report to him every evening 'after his carrot juice,' as she put it. It was a difficult time but I was sympathetic – Denys had taken on more than he had bargained for and, as it turned out, more than he was capable of doing. I should have recognised this.

Meanwhile, under Derek Hall, Bulk Shipping continued its rapid development – much of it driven by our clear policy of moving into more sophisticated types of shipping, which took advantage of the technological advances which were transforming the carriage of oil and gas.

Half-way through 1973, we were faced with a challenge and an opportunity. Corporate pressures forced Zapata to sell Zapata Norness, our 50% partners in Associated Bulk Carriers. We were surprised and alarmed to hear that Zapata's chief executive, Bill Flynn, was close to a deal with the Norwegian shipowner, Hilmar Reksten of Bergen. Hilmar had had his ups and downs. They say that in 1967 he was on his way to 'give himself up to his bankers' when news came of the Israeli attack on Suez. He turned back to his office and, with soaring tanker rates, made a fortune. He was not, at first sight, thought to be the most attractive partner in ABC, and we intervened. After some lateral thinking, we ended up with an agreement whereby P&O and Reksten would each buy 50% of Zapata Norness – so that we, P&O, would thus 'speak' for 75% of Associated Bulk Carriers.

P&O paid $104m for its 50% shareholding in Anglo Nordic, as we now named the company – the highest cost of an acquisition to date and, as the *Financial Times* pointed out, a demonstration that the new management of P&O not only recognised a good bargain, but was commendably quick on its feet. The bulk interest thus enlarged was for years afterwards an important enterprise in the P&O portfolio and in due course P&O bought out Reksten's holding in Anglo Nordic. I was proud of the development and of its legacy and, twenty-five years later, it is again a matter of pride to see the name of Associated Bulk Carriers being revived by P&O for their joint venture with a group of Chinese steel mills.

During July, I decided that the Passenger Division, headed by Peter Parry, needed new leadership. Peter had made little impact at the time of the Bovis bid, but in its immediate aftermath I acknowledged that he had been responsible for initiating an in-depth study of the future for the passenger fleet. His report had already been accepted by the board and I saw no reason, despite some grey areas, not to allow him to see it through.

It was going to be a difficult task to transform the classic A to B passenger trades into a leisure-oriented cruising business – the ships designed for the former were less than ideal for the latter. Results from the division were poor and the prospects of securing funds for rebuilding or refurbishing were not bright. Unfortunately, Peter Parry did not display the leadership required and had probably lost credibility during the Bovis bid to such an extent that he was not likely to recover his confidence. So I had to suggest that Peter 'retire'. Inchcape fully supported me at the time, but years later suggested that 'he had always felt that I had been unfairly critical of Parry'. In fact, Peter's successor, my old friend Harry Spanton, grasped the opportunity and led the change so effectively that he was able to justify P&O's huge further investment in the development of Princess Cruises.

Dick Adams – formally titled Group Executive Director – was effectively my second-in-command, overseeing a number of operating and staff divisions. A long-time Mackinnons and BI friend, he was intellectually capable, but somehow lacked fire in the belly. Perhaps he recognised that his Bovis performance had been less than distinguished. He became a conservator – even a demolition expert – rather than a developer and a leader. He and I were very closely involved in the executive and in the development of policy, yet I was to realise later that he managed somehow to distance himself when I was targeted. Dick was a Wykehamist and his manners were impeccable, but it seemed he was a No. 2 to the manner born.

In September an interesting proposal came from Y. K. Pao that P&O and World-Wide should each put up to six VLCCs into a joint company in Bermuda, to be managed commercially by World-Wide. We chose not to pursue this, but it confirmed our significance in the tanker field ('YK' then had the world's biggest tanker fleet). It also emphasised that we had to perform; our supporters would not appreciate our reluctance to associate with someone of YK's flair if we failed to deliver.

We grappled with our substantial property interests, doing such dull but necessary work as establishing sensible market rentals for operating divisions, introducing better accounting methods and improving management information. We recruited a group property manager and sought advice from those in the business. I was amazed at how amateurish in this field P&O had been over the years.

I instigated a pattern of Friday morning meetings of all available executive directors. I deliberately kept the meetings in my office informal to encourage an open and free-flowing exchange of ideas. Over the years these meetings encouraged co-ordination and co-operation in an easy atmosphere and thus ensured that we kept in touch with all that was going on throughout the Group. Although no formal minutes were kept, decisions made and actions required were confirmed in writing.

We withdrew from an ill-starred venture into deep-sea fishing by selling Ranger Fishing to British United Trawlers. We acquired a substantial holding in HYCO, a Canadian company constructing and operating mini-submarines used for work in offshore oil fields, for survey, pipeline maintenance, etc. We inaugurated a new RoRo passenger and freight service to Spain and Portugal. Following the initiative of Anglo Nordic, who before we acquired our shareholding had been negotiating for a 400,000-ton ULCC, a similar vessel was ordered at Mitsui. By the end of 1973, Technical Services Division, under Douglas Kerr, was working on eighteen Group ships for delivery over the next four years. The value of these orders was some £100m.

Profits for the year to end-September 1973 would be reported at £34m, up £21.7m from £12.3m in 1972. In rejecting the Inchcape bid in December 1972 the board had been prepared, on the basis of the work the opposition had done during the Bovis bid and the very studied reappraisal by Finance Division and Schroders during the five weeks since 17 November, to forecast profits 'in excess of £20m'. This £34m was almost three times as much as P&O had ever before achieved. We did have the benefit of a booming bulk market but that, of course, was what we were building for and what we had emphasised to stockholders during the 100 days. The results were well received, and the 'new management' was regarded as having taken a useful first step. Within the company it was a significant morale booster for everyone: 'We can do it.'

OPEC was pushing the price of oil up and up. In October 1973, Egypt and Syria attacked Israel in the Negev and on the Golan. Another OPEC conference broke up, and so events were set in motion which were to transform the economy of the West. President Nixon snubbed the Arab Foreign Ministers when they visited Washington, an oil embargo on USA and the Netherlands was implemented, OPEC cut back production, and the price per barrel rose in irregular jumps to $11.65 in December – quadrupled within two months. The industry, the country, indeed the world was entering uncharted waters.

In the autumn I made what was then the traditional tour of Australia – the state capital cities and Canberra. It was a demanding schedule and on later visits I simply had to curtail the itinerary. Canberra, however, was an essential stop with formal calls on the politicians in power, on top civil servants and on opposition MPs waiting in the wings – of whom I remember Andrew Peacock as one of the more colourful – and on the UK High Commissioner of the day. John House, our representative, had marvellous access and a highly developed sense of fun, which was desirable in Canberra's somewhat artificial atmosphere.

A highlight of that 1973 tour was a week in Western Australia. At Mount Tom Price, the Hammersley ore mine, I saw a town with permanent residents in artificially green suburbs, an amazing development in the bush. A few miles away the mountain was being quarried and dug – enormous earth movers crept like huge beetles, 150-ton grabs inched forward and there were dump trucks which could carry a house, while on the railway the wagons freewheeled down hill to Dampier. I saw one of our OBOs loading ore for Japan. While it was an impressive performance by shore and ship, perhaps we did not then pay enough attention to the stresses involved. There have been more structural failures, indeed total losses of bulk carriers out of Australia than anywhere else. Speed of loading and distribution of ore is now recognised as highly relevant.

I flew by oil-company helicopter from Port Hedland to one of the drilling ships working offshore. I was counted on board and was glad to get a seat (a canvas jump-seat) forward near the door. I realised later that the more experienced had scuttled deep into the chopper's cabin. The door (if indeed there was one) remained open and the impression of speed and exposure was extreme as we hurtled over the ocean 50 ft above the surface.

On to Broome, the pearl fishing centre of Western Australia and, during the war, a target for Japanese bombers. The atmosphere was very laid back. We had three Australian offshore supply boats stationed there working with the North West Shelf drilling rigs in extreme conditions. Our representative had arranged that I should host a drinks party at the Broome Motel for our customers, local dignitaries and our own people. After a dusty day I freshened up, put on a clean shirt and tie and thus smartly attired made my way to the private rooms. The route was through the beer garden where by 5 p.m. the tables were crowded – all men, mostly wearing shorts, T-shirts and thongs on their feet. The three in my party were very kenspeckle and a hush fell. Then I heard a low whisper: 'Must be the Government'. This was taken up accompanied by banging of beer cans and bottles on the tables: 'The Government, the Government'. Such is the distinction granted by pressed shorts and a tie. Having been greeted thus noisily, we may have been apprehensive about our departure, but there was no cause for worry – two hours of beer in temperatures in the high 80s had reduced the clientele to bleary somnolence.

From Perth I flew back to the UK via Singapore and India, where 'I should be able to see our people over the weekend.' My greatest pleasure was, whenever possible, to fly home via Johannesburg. In the early days the South African flight required a refuelling stop at the Cocos Islands followed by a very long ocean flight to Mauritius where there was an overnight stay. The Super-G Constellation was, in first class, wonderfully spacious, but it was a most noisy aircraft. Today the non-stop flight is easy, but it's a little sad that one loses the stop-over. More than once, after making landfall on the Mozambique coast, I have been able to look down on the South African border, the Crocodile river, Havelock asbestos mine to the left in Swaziland and, almost underneath on the right, the distinctive outline of the Kruger Park hills and Logogote and, by now with a lump in my throat, the trim slopes of The Fountains.

On 15 December 1973, I gave the board an initial assessment of the effects of the oil crisis on P&O. This included:

– The need to absorb a significant increase in operating costs;

– A report on P&O's, and Anglo Nordic's, limited exposure if the tanker market were to collapse (which it soon did);

– Enhanced purchasing power for the oil-producing countries coupled with a negative impact on oil consumers would require adjustment in trading patterns;

– The opportunity for the UK to benefit if North Sea oil could be brought on stream soon.

I also reported that, pending review, all delegated authority for capital expenditure had been withdrawn.

Given that every aspect of the Group's business would to some degree be affected by the crisis, and given his business and political background, Inchcape's lack of contribution to the discussion that followed my critical analysis disappointed me greatly. In the tanker sector P&O was battening down; yet Burmah Oil, where he was vice-chairman, was going for growth. It seemed inconceivable that Inchcape, a member of the boards of two companies adopting diametrically opposite policies in the same market sector, found virtually nothing to say – after all we couldn't both be right. He might have helped both companies in the decision-making process. But no; lack of involvement was his style. I saw an interesting contrast with my old chairman, Lord G. He had an opinion on most things and was always prepared to discuss and debate, but he would then say 'You've heard me, now it's your decision'. I cannot recall a major issue which we could not resolve in this way. But Inchcape was unable to accept his role – he seemed often not to want to offer a view, and was frequently unwilling to be associated with a decision.

As 1973 drew to a close, P&O suffered some bad publicity. On a cruise from New York *Canberra* fell victim to technical faults and to catering problems of a bizarre nature. The ensuing ridicule made Dick Adams inclined to call it a day and sell her for scrap, for she was in any case a greedy consumer of increasingly expensive fuel. But the division, and Harry Spanton in particular, resolutely maintained that her problems were short-term. They sorted her out and twenty-five years later Canberra remained a popular favourite with UK holidaymakers.

The UK house-building bubble finally burst and, more particularly, property values tumbled, putting pressure on the secondary (and tertiary) banks engaged in the mortgage and second mortgage business. In the autumn Bovis had sacked their chairman, Frank Sanderson. The company was under strain and Sanderson's plans to float 20th Century Bank seemed to hover even closer to cloud-cuckooland than they had a year earlier. In December Bovis directors Neville Vincent and Malcolm Paris came to see me. P&O still held 10% of Bovis shares (written down to recognise the collapse in value since P&O had warehoused them in August/November, 1972). They came straight to the point. Would P&O consider making another bid? For me the logic of strategic diversification still stood, but now the price must be realistic. On the other hand, with the instability in the oil market and UK inflation averaging 10.61% over 1973 and rising, should we take on another problem?

The proposal demanded much due diligence and consideration of image. The public tended to regard us – my chairman and me – as anti-Bovis. Even some of our biggest stockholders expressed reservations. Hambros, Reksten and Jessel owned between them about 30% of our stock: Jessel's held since 1972, Hambros' partly the same and partly of more recent acquisition. Reksten's vast holding had been built up through and following the Bovis battle and was in itself a matter of concern. Dilution had its attractions.

There were black holes in Bovis. 20th Century was a potential problem and provisions had to be earmarked against potential losses on property. We persuaded National Westminster Bank (George Burnett) to underwrite some of that exposure. I went to see the regulatory people at the Bank of England. They were not very helpful; their rather slim file on 20th Century contained no more than the Report & Accounts for the previous year. But they obviously thought it would be a good thing if we took over.

On 8 February 1974 our formal offer for Bovis, valuing the company at £27m compared with £170m at its peak during the 1972 bid, was issued and recommended by the Bovis board. We were alarmed when Jessel, Hambros and Reksten advised that they would vote against. Jessel simply did not believe that Bovis was a good enough business and felt that its acquisition would depress P&O. The motives of the other two were unclear: they said that they wanted us to stick to our last, but we suspected that they did not want their holdings to be diluted and that they might well be building a platform from which to launch a bid for P&O.

The weeks before the EGM at which the proposal would be put to stockholders were tense. I toured the institutions in London and Edinburgh. The chairman wrote to stockholders arguing that the strategy was sound and that this time the price was right; that we could give P&O an important new 'leg', and that the balance of the Group could be improved. It was a hectic and difficult time and in the end a close-run thing – the voting in favour was too narrow to be comfortable. We had to make the acquisition work quickly, and we did. It provided a significant contribution to balancing our portfolio. Bovis flourished within P&O and delivered impressive profits in the businesses it knew well, repaying the Group many times over for the 1974 rescue. Later in the year the Jessel shares were placed with a wide spread of institutions. That in itself was a major operation smoothly undertaken by Hoare Govett. It was the end of an interesting speculation, and I wrote to Oliver Jessel to record how important his role had been in saving P&O in 1972.

At the same time, the Reksten Group, highly geared and severely exposed in the tanker market, was under increasing financial pressure. Andrew Robb in Bulk Shipping estimated from our knowledge of their tanker fleet that, on that side of the business, losses must be running at $60m p.a. I entered extensive discussions with Hambros, sometimes in tandem with Inchcape, sometimes with Oliver Brooks, about the future of the Reksten holding, and twice I went to Bergen to see Hilmar. There was an ominous rumour that the Reksten shares, together with Hambros' holding, might be sold as a package to Arab interests. We had to know – as far as possible in a rather complex situation – what was happening, so I maintained close contact with Hilmar's advisers, Charlie Hambro and John Clay. My aim was to ensure that the Reksten and Hambros holdings were kept apart and, indeed, dispersed as widely as possible. I also kept Sir Peter Thornton of the DTI informed, as at one stage it seemed that, if Reksten collapsed, P&O might suddenly have to pick up his 50% of Anglo Nordic. To do so would have put an intolerable strain on our balance sheet and bring with it a gross imbalance in our tanker exposure. We were much relieved when this threat was lifted with no fuss and no disturbance to our market. The Hambros holding was trickled out and in 1975 the Reksten stock was placed. Thus, from having a somewhat daunting 30% in three hands (holdings which could be regarded as potential concert-goers), we were once again widely-held in a more normal pattern. They had been interesting months requiring coolness and patience.

I remember one discussion with Hilmar in his penthouse in Park Lane when he urged me to 'get that man Crichton off the board'. I had to explain that Crichton was chairman of OCL, a very important joint venture for P&O and said that I could not risk damage there, but it was interesting that his antipathy to Crichton was so strong. I should have listened to him and found a way. Hilmar was a buccaneer, and I liked him. Mona and I well remember our first visit to his home in Fjøsanger. We gazed in awe at his collection of old English silver, of oriental carpets, his Picasso drawings and his paintings by Munch. Eventually, Hilmar's empire foundered – a messy and sad affair. The Norwegian Government hounded him for alleged tax evasion, giving scant recognition to his service to his country during the Second World War and to his notable contribution to Norway's shipping industry. Following his death, the legal wrangles over his Estate continue to this day.

As oil prices soared and the obligation to supply the boycotted USA and Netherlands reduced the quota for Europe, the National Union of Mineworkers in the UK seized its opportunity. Arthur Scargill placed a ban on overtime and weekend work 'in order to defend the coal industry'. The government's response was to introduce a three-day working week in an attempt to conserve energy supplies. Fortunately for me, we had an emergency diesel generator at P&O and my office continued to work a full week. Heath's Conservative government staggered through January, at the end of which the NUM embarked on an extended and increasingly ugly full-scale strike. A general election was called for the end of February on a 'Who rules Britain?' manifesto, and Harold Wilson became Prime Minister of a Labour government.

In January, 1974, P&O formed Energy Division to focus attention on oil and gas production in the USA and on our increasing range of offshore services in the North Sea. Our anonymous advertisement for a senior executive to lead this new division elicited a response from Dr Rodney Leach who had been a member of the 1970–1 P&O McKinsey team. I got hold of him quickly, making Mac Sidey head of Energy and bringing Rodney on board as head of European and Air Transport Division (E&AT), where his background in logistics would be invaluable. We needed to develop E&AT into a large-scale business able to carry the infrastructure and the quality and financial controls essential to an integrated transportation system. Over the next few years, Rodney was to develop a highly professional, techni-cally-advanced business with a reputation for innovation and for quality service.

We were also actively seeking one or two additional non-executive directors. We felt able to offer a stable, progressive company with clear objectives and at least a short-term performance record. Denys Brown had suggested Keith Joseph if the Heath government lost the election. Keith had family connections and board experience at Bovis and would have been an interesting colleague. However, he was deeply committed to the Conservative party's think-tank and the suggestion was not followed up, although I later got to know him quite well when he was Minister of Technology.

Kenneth Inchcape secured the interest of the Earl of Cromer, lately UK ambassador in Washington and former Governor of the Bank of England. He was a distinguished and valuable addition to the board. He added breadth to our discussions and took a continu-ing interest between meetings. He gave notes to me on the Trilateral Commission, and to Derek Hall on US energy policy, and he would send me copies of speeches of relevance to our business. In turn, he would tap us for input when preparing himself for a conference.

Inchcape also approached Eric Drake, chairman of BP, regarded – particularly by Energy Division – as a very attractive prospect. He could not accept because of his BP commitments, but was to join us later in rather different circumstances.

Another useful recruit was Ian Denholm of the eponymous Glasgow shipowners and managers. He had earlier been on the board of Anglo Norness and was well known to us through his presidency of the Chamber of Shipping. He was forty-six. I suggested to Inchcape that it might be wise, when appointing young non-executive directors with some twenty-five years to normal retiring age, to establish at the outset that such directors might after, say, ten years 'discuss with the then chairman if it is of mutual interest that he or she continues'. This would be a mild proposal today, but Inchcape was outraged: 'Not bloody likely.' Even Lord Cromer (and – predictably – Crichton), when advised of my suggestion, said that such a condition 'would mean that P&O would never attract suitable non-executive directors.' This is just one example of the anguished protectionism that would greet any proposal that might seem to rock the Establishment boat.

Despite the threat of further oil price hikes and the depressed economies around the world, new ships were still in strong demand. For many years, advances in ship technology had been relatively marginal but now, as I have said, under the pressure of increased fuel costs, huge strides were being made. Steam was replaced by diesel in even the largest vessel, specialised and more efficient ships were being designed, drilling rigs and support vessels for developing environments in the North Sea, Australia and China were required. The proliferation of RoRos continued and the concept of catamarans for short-sea passenger traffic was taking shape.

It was vital to develop alternatives to oil. Historically, gas had been stripped from oil at the point of production and had been flared. Although the technology for the transport of liquefied petroleum and natural gas (LPG and LNG) under pressure or refrigeration had been well known, only now did the economics look like making it viable on a large scale. Times were good for those shipyards equipped to build these sophisticated vessels and berths were at a premium. Norwegian owners were building LPG carriers, Ocean and Nedlloyd LNG carriers, our associate company, Panocean, was completing a programme of chemical carriers and Stolt Nielsen was racing ahead with state-of-the-art stainless steel tankers.

In June 1974 we increased our shareholding in Mundo Gas to 43%

by acquiring part of Mobil's interest and in July placed orders worth £75m at the Rheinstahl yard in Germany for four 53,000 cbm LPG vessels. The rationale for the order was well presented by Bulk Shipping Division. Production of LPG was planned to increase substantially, not only in the Persian Gulf – Kuwait in particular – but also in the North Sea. Relatively long-haul transportation would be required to meet rising demand in the USA and Japan. We had the market knowledge and a competent international trading vehicle in Mundo Gas. Bulk Shipping's analysis was fully supported by independent international agencies and by oil company predictions. At the same time, the commitment of £75m was massive, and the P&O board deliberated long and hard before approving this investment. I recall considerable enthusiasm for the project and no dissenting voice.

To hedge our position Bulk Shipping proposed, and the board agreed, that the first and second of these ships be for trading on our own account and that the fourth certainly, and the third provisionally, be earmarked for sale or bareboat prior to delivery. This reflected the scarcity of building berths – the conclusion was that by holding those two slots we could later make a profit by getting a premium for the berths or, ultimately, selling the ships themselves. P&O had embraced the philosophy of being the operator rather than necessarily the owner of ships and was poised to trade the units of production where appropriate. Regrettably, the confident assumption of our ability to get one or two of these ships off our balance sheet at a profit turned out to have been a major misjudgement. They were to become known as 'the notorious Rheinstahls.' It may be said that it was only a matter of timing, but that is quite sufficient in itself to turn such a project sour. Economic conditions delayed the worldwide development of LPG systems. The Rheinstahls, scheduled for delivery from late 1976 to late 1978, were the subject of much negotiation including postponement of the second, third and fourth by twelve months, and represented a heavy burden of debt when the Deutschmark began its dramatic rise against sterling and while government exchange controls prevented us from covering adequately the forward exposure.

Unfortunately for the maritime industry as a whole the shipping finance departments of international and domestic banks were hyper-active. Countries such as Brazil, South Korea and Poland were expanding their shipbuilding capacity. Credit for shipbuilding was to be had for the asking, and the industry was booming. Not a single key player in the fragmented shipowning community could contemplate falling behind the pack, and all were disinclined to recognise that surplus tonnage in the tanker, bulk carrier and – eventually – container classes lay just around the corner.

8

A Changing World

P&O's acquisition of Bovis in 1974 brought with it a range of activities and problems around the world which vividly illustrated the somewhat ill-controlled, almost insatiable, appetite for growth which had characterised Bovis in the late 1960s. Among these were two in south-east Asia which entailed enormous cost and much delicate negotiation. Accompanied by Mona, I went to Singapore where P&O interests were now largely Bovis-related.

The first issue was an outstanding claim by Bovis against the Singapore defence authorities. Bovis had constructed extensions to the jetties at Pulau Brani naval base. The piling had been tricky and laborious, costs had overrun, and the authorities had declined to pay. These were complex matters. UK counsel were there in force and at high cost, but early on it became clear that Bovis's case could not be brought to trial with any confidence. A swift out-of-court settlement was the answer.

The second could have been seen as an opportunity. There is little indigenous rock and stone in Malaysia, whose infrastructure and industry were developing rapidly. Bovis had initiated an imaginative venture whereby much-needed stone would be quarried on Karimun, an island across the Malacca straits several hours by sea from Singapore. However Karimun belongs to Indonesia and so the project required a joint venture between Bovis and local 'interests'. These interests tended, in the end, to be self-selecting and it was no surprise to Bovis to find itself in bed with a number of politically-inclined businessmen not too distantly related to the wife of President Suharto. If all had gone well this might have worked, but it was not a comfortable structure when difficulties arose. The problem was that the reward to the Indonesian element was to be related to production, while Bovis's reward was to be related to sales. However, no sales had been made, yet quarrying went on apace and stockpiles of granite continued to grow.

We abandoned Karimun the following year – a lesson, for those who wanted to learn, in not stepping too far away from known ground. Bovis, a housebuilder and civil engineer with expertise in UK road construction, was simply not capable of taking on a major overseas project – not capable in management terms, in political awareness, or in logistical support. Today, under Frank Lampl, Bovis International has acquired such capabilities with commendable skill and success.

In London, on the management front and in my relationship with Inchcape, there had also been some problems. In April 1974, Denys Brown suffered another breakdown. He had been a staff officer of the highest quality, but the pressures in an operational role – of living up to the confident predictions made in 1972 and to the changes in management style which we had, together, introduced – had become too much for him. Denys had volunteered for the Personnel assignment in November 1972 and tackled it to the best of his ability, but had, I fear, overestimated his own capacity. His depression intensified during absences on sick leave and he came to believe that a reason for his decline was that I had ceased to value his contribution. Denys put the case to Inchcape that he had been unreasonably pressured into taking on Personnel, a responsibility for which he was not suited, and, now that he had 'failed', that I wanted to get rid of him.

He wished to revert to the job for which he had been recruited originally – Government Relations and International Affairs. By now the General Council of British Shipping (GCBS, formerly the Chamber of Shipping) under the leadership of Johnnie Wood was increasingly able to provide effective representation for the industry and, as Denys must have known in his heart, P&O could not justify running its own man. However strongly I might emphasise the importance of having reserve fire-power, the situations in which Denys's particular and undoubted skills would provide the answer were few and far between. Gradually it emerged that he had in mind early retirement on terms above-and-beyond standard practice, which would boost his already index-linked Foreign Office pension.

Inchcape did not discuss Denys's accusations with me; instead he decided I was victimising him: 'I won't have it. You should be able to use him.' But surely Inchcape would agree that we could not carry a passenger at board level when we were cutting staff numbers throughout the group. 'Oh, I know you are cutting, but that's among the clerks,' he said, apparently quite unaware of the crassness of such comment.

I should have bitten the bullet, for the outcome was a fudge. Ostensibly we found enough for Denys to do, but we had a dissatisfied colleague and my close relationship with him was fractured beyond repair. The loss of his friendship has always disturbed me – we had worked so well together, whether angry or laughing.

Harry Beazley, quietly-spoken and innately courteous, was the man for Personnel. He was reluctant to leave General Cargo for what he felt to be a demotion, but Dick Adams and I formally advised Inchcape that in our view Personnel needed the top quality oversight which Beazley could provide. He would retain responsibility for our OCL investment, in itself an important role.

Inchcape would have none of it. Apparently Crichton had told him that Adams and I were plotting to get rid not only of Brown but also of Beazley, by 'forcing' him to refuse Personnel. Inchcape shot from the hip and called a meeting of the non-executive directors ' to decide'. It was all nonsense – when faced with the logic, the obvious support both Dick Adams and I gave to Beazley and our sympathy for Brown, the chairman caved in. Harry Beazley went on to carry the personnel function with great success. Ian Denholm told me afterwards that Crichton had tried to 'nobble' him. He also wrote to me: 'It is of the utmost importance that there should be no misunderstanding – the chairman's position in P&O is of importance because of his general standing, but the chief executive must manage, as, ultimately, it is he who carries the responsibility.'

In August I was on holiday with the family. Inchcape was also on holiday. At P&O Betty Fairclough was opening Inchcape's mail and saw a letter from Lord G indicating that Inchcape had accepted the vice-presidency of the GCBS. On my return, Betty was as embarrassed as I. Had she misinterpreted Lord G's letter? I checked with Ian Denholm, who was flabbergasted that I did not know. He had assumed that Inchcape 'would have cleared it with you and that you are fully in support.'

I told Inchcape of my dismay that he had not informed me of something of such importance to the company. He blustered that he had been sworn to secrecy and 'specifically not to inform anyone in P&O'. The then president, Lindsay Alexander, told me: 'I am simply astonished.' Inchcape had never played a part in GCBS affairs, and had frequently shown impatience or disdain at 'the time you are over there.' But when the call came his attitude changed overnight. Indeed, eighteen months later he reminded the industry of his inherent fitness for the position by opening his presidential address with the words: 'It is seventy-three years ago since my grandfather first became president, and fifty-seven years since he last did so.'

The tension between us must have been becoming obvious. I gritted my teeth and arranged for a personal assistant from P&O to help Inchcape organise his papers and to provide liaison so that he could be armed with a shipowner's point of view on the range of matters he would be required to discuss at GCBS. The first incumbent was Sandy Stirling, a competent executive who had just completed a two-year secondment to government. As ever in such cases, reintegration was proving tricky. The job did not appeal to him and Sandy soon resigned. I was then able to propose Leo Hudson, a quiet, determined man, very experienced in industry affairs. I was apprehensive that, without such competent backing, both my chairman and the company could well be embarrassed.

I also suggested that, as Inchcape would have extensive commitments at GCBS, it might now be appropriate for me, as CEO, to take over the chair of the Executive Committee. I had always felt it inappropriate that he, a non-executive chairman, should chair that committee, but had accepted it as a way to keep him in touch. I emphasised in my memo that 'this will enable the executive to function effectively *within the limits laid down by the board,* without imposing on you, but at the same time it will enable me to keep you fully-informed on the main issues before the Group.'

Between this memo and Inchcape's response, I made a trip to Australia. En route I stopped over in Fiji to see one of our more exotic new interests. A few years earlier we had taken a 10% holding in Southern Pacific Properties (SPP), a company headed by a Canadian entrepreneur, Peter Munk, which was developing a leisure complex on the south and, as it turned out, the wrong, i.e. the rainy, side of the island. SPP was also engaged in purchasing the Australian Travelodge chain of motels in order to get some cash flow into their business. We, meanwhile, increased our shareholding in SPP to 40% with the intention of later backing it into P&O Australia (POAL), so that when we came to flotation, POAL would have a wider asset base.

I found a concept beginning to stumble. Increased oil prices meant fewer holidaymakers and a dearth of jumbo jet-loads of Japanese golfers. Even in those expansionist days, Pacific Harbour was a development too far. A happy result of the visit, however, was meeting again a Canmore school classmate of forty years earlier, Sir

Robert Sanders, KBE, long-time Colonial servant and now Chief Minister of Fiji. Even he, with the interests of his domain at heart, could not raise much enthusiasm for the scheme.

On a happier note, POAL's bold move into leisure showed promise as they acquired some of the 'mom and pop' resort businesses in the Whitsunday Islands and, in the case of Heron Island, on the Barrier Reef. These island resorts needed capital investment and professional management and, from small beginnings, POAL built a major tourist business. The development of Heron was not easy: marrying a marine reserve and research station with volume if not mass tourism had problems, but it had a unique attraction and later became a useful part of their portfolio of resorts. I retain a particular regard for that island because of the strange noddy terns and mutton birds, and the great flapping manta rays in the shallows. On Lindeman, in the Whitsundays, the emphasis was on beach and water sports. But Mona and I remember it even more vividly for the casual way in which the pilot of our mini-flying boat lost his life – a week after he had shown us how easy it was, he flipped over on touching down.

In January 1975 – two months after I had suggested arrangements to cover Inchcape's GCBS role and, in a helpful spirit, that I relieve him of his commitment as chairman of P&O's Executive Committee – I received his reply. By this time he saw my proposals as 'an attempt by you to seize control'. I can only assume that the trigger for such a paranoid reaction was Burmah Oil where Inchcape was vice-chairman.

In the previous October, the *Investors Review* published an article: 'Burmah's Tanker Fleet heading for the Rocks'. I thought Inchcape might want to discuss this with me, but was taken aback when he handed me a copy of an in-house analysis of Burmah's tanker operations prepared by Elias Kulukundis, Burmah's rather unconventional head of shipping. I supposed, with some amusement, that the chairman of P&O must have advised the vice-chairman of Burmah Oil that it would be sensible to share this explosively price-sensitive document with the chief executive of P&O, and I recalled that ten months earlier the attention of P&O's chairman – or perhaps of Burmah's vice-chairman – had been drawn to the dramatic difference between the tanker policies being adopted by the two companies.

Together with John Maccoy and Derek Hall, I gave Inchcape an assessment of Burmah's position. In P&O, we were taking a conservative line, but Kulukundis was taking Burmah on a roller-coaster ride – something a privately-owned enterprise, an Onassis, Reksten or Niarchos might risk, but most imprudent for a public company, particularly Burmah, 'the Scottish widows' and orphans' company'. We advised Inchcape that the exposure was excessive and potentially hazardous; and that, if he could not secure a change in the proposals, he should quickly distance himself. If he did anything as a result of our advice, he did it so discreetly as to leave no mark. He certainly recoiled from overt action: 'Sandy, I don't want to be known as a maverick.' At this second opportunity, he had a much better-researched case for standing against the crowd than he did in August 1972.

Two months later, on 31 December, Burmah collapsed. Dramatic action was taken to effect a rescue – the most important being that the Bank of England bought Burmah's substantial shareholding in BP at what turned out to be the bottom of the market. This led to widespread recriminations and to a court case which was not concluded until 1981. Everyone involved took cover. Kulukundis was blamed. Nicky Williams, the chief executive, was criticised for exceeding his authority. Senior executives and directors protested that until early December they did not have 'any inkling' of how desperate the situation was. Robin Bradley of Barings later commented that the Burmah board 'was not treating it as a crisis'. Inchcape said that the 'forced' sale of BP shares was a scandal and that the BP price was artificially low – 'clearly a temporary situation and it was bound to recover in a matter of time.'

Press and City criticism of the Burmah board was unrelenting, and the effect on Inchcape was devastating. He was a major City figure, assumed to have a deep understanding not only of Burmah's business, but that of Inchcape & Co., of BP and of P&O, and to be a symbol of secure guardianship for the Scottish investors. He had been warned specifically of the danger of Burmah's shipping policy by three of the most experienced and respected figures in the British industry. I knew that he knew. Indeed he knew that I knew that he knew! 1975 was a bad year in our relationship and I am sure now that this was largely because of the Burmah hangover. Yet despite his evident, and public, failure at Burmah, Inchcape was appointed vice-president of GCBS in February 1975.

I was pleased to have been able to advise the board that P&O's involvement with Burmah was slight and also that I considered our system of checks and balances, levels of authority, etc. would ensure that a Burmah situation could not develop. Even so, in consultation with the executive directors over the next month, I proposed a reduction in the extent of authority delegated to senior management.

The 1974 economic scene, despite the mid-year lifting of the Arab oil embargo on USA, had been sluggish. In the UK the annual inflation rate had risen to 19.16% and the pound was losing strength. Western demand for oil had fallen and the outlook was uncertain. We took action to maintain our cash flow with some draconian programmes to defer capital expenditure and to reduce costs. Within the new Energy Division we tidied up a number of ventures which were too long-term or too small to be cost-effective and, in a major step, we sold the IOS fleet of twenty-five offshore supply vessels, full control of which had only been purchased in 1972. They were not suitable for the new oil-fields in the North Sea and we received a sizeable offer, $29m, from Tidewater of New Orleans – an offer described by OIL, the Inchcape-Ocean joint venture, as 'ridiculously high'.

We were able to report profits for 1974 at £48.5m, a figure which would have been regarded by Ford Geddes and his colleagues two years earlier as impossible to achieve. The profits from operations before taking into account various financial adjustments were:

	£		£
Bulk Shipping	13.4 m	Bovis (six months)	4.5 m
General Cargo	16.8 m	Property	3.4 m
Passenger Services	0.9 m	20th Century Bank	0.2 m
European & Air Transport	1.5 m	Energy	(1.9 m)
General Holdings	2.5 m	(Loss due to set-up costs)	

An overview of the following year would indicate that 1975 was a year of retrenchment. The high oil prices had driven the world into recession; increased spending by the producers did not balance the loss of spending capacity among consumers. The developing nations were burdened with soaring interest charges; Third World debt threatened the international banking system; the Australian dollar was devalued. In the UK, inflation was at a frightening 24.9%; Bovis housebuilding suffered severely and construction contracts were delayed. It was estimated that world demand for oil required only 60% of current tanker capacity.

In March, I accompanied Lindsay Alexander, president of GCBS, to Tokyo for discussions with Japanese shipowners. I was now chairman of the GCBS Foreign Shipping Policy Committee. We wanted to explore Japanese thinking on a number of matters: UN-CTAD, where there was now a threat to the bulk trades; national shipbuilding subsidies which were contributing so markedly to over-supply; clarification of Sanko's position (Sanko was a Japanese company speculating in the tanker market on an extraordinary scale and we were worried that a collapse could destabilise others). There were also issues over flags of convenience about which the Japanese were somewhat ambivalent. They were not then operating under such flags to any great extent and apparently took little interest in promoting international standards of safety and pollution control. This last was to change for the better in short order, so perhaps we did achieve some success, but our impression at the time was that we did not influence much nor did we leave very much better-informed. In reality it was heavy going, although we were most hospitably received and the visit was splendidly organised by the P&O and OCL agents, Swires, ably led by Graham MacCallum, my contemporary at Glenalmond and Oxford.

During the next few months, sometimes with the president, sometimes on my own, I was involved in similar discussions with the Germans, the Danes, the French and the Dutch – trying to develop common ground in our response to growing governmental intervention and growing threats from the developing nations with their state-owned shipping.

In April, I was faced with what could have been a difficult management problem, had it not been for the quality of those involved and their understanding of our overall objectives. I had always encouraged the operating divisions to take a broad and innovative approach. Two projects within that category were the fruit of an imaginative team in General Holdings, principally Euan Geddes and Ann Thornton, and it was unfortunate that both schemes turned out to be rather ahead of their time. A proposal for deep-water dredging of aggregates off the south coast to support infrastructure for the 1974 Channel tunnel project had to be terminated when national confidence faltered in 1975 and enthusiasm for the tunnel collapsed.

Next, transport of pulp and paper direct from the northern Baltic to mills in the UK, using ice-breaking articulated tug and barge units, offered great benefits when compared with the costly seasonal pattern of shipping. Again, the economic climate of 1975 raised uncertainties and merchants were reluctant to make forward commitments. In both these cases we knew when to call a halt and contain our costs, but I was glad that we still retained the ability to 'think big'.

Throughout 1975, indeed throughout my tenure of office, there runs a continuing theme: that of improving the management process, something in which all the executive directors were involved and to which Denys Brown was able to make a valuable contribution. A review committee to assess the result of each investment compared with the original proposal was working well and lessons were being learned. These procedures did contribute to a well-informed board which could consider strategy, investment and disinvestment proposals, developed in a professional manner and processed efficiently. Nothing came forward which had not been appraised and signed off by those responsible – the divisional management, Corporate Planning and the Finance Division including Treasury. After Bovis in 1972 and reflecting my outside experience, I was particularly careful that in no circumstance should the P&O board feel bulldozed. Of course, as chief executive, I played a full part and led on major issues. In the case of operational matters, the responsibility of the divisions, I would support or temper the presentation as appropriate. It would simply have been impossible for me – quite apart from my innate distaste for such action – to push anything through the executive and the board of which the directors did not approve and which was outwith my delegated authority.

The Suez Canal was reopened in June and general cargo ships returned early to that route. It was, however, to be several months before the big container vessels and the bulk fleet could pass through safely.

The New Zealand Shipping Company general cargo vessels continued to follow the traditional route through Panama and across the Pacific, and I was glad to help secure passage in *Taupo* for my niece Kirsty Robertson and her friend Cath, both young farmers. Years later, at a pensioners' lunch held in Southampton in 1994, a retired captain introduced himself as having been in command of *Taupo* when Kirsty 'was the life and soul of the voyage'. She herself recalls the journey with great pleasure, not because of special treatment but, rather, that they could feel part of the team. Recently I came across a note I sent to General Cargo towards the end of that year asking for prompt submission of an account for the girls' fares. We were meticulous.

In the autumn, Inchcape produced a 'draft comment' on the financial situation in which he drew a picture of possible crisis 'if nothing is done'. He concluded by urging management to find 'a major diversification outside shipping, non-dilutive and with immediate profit'. We might have been forgiven for a sardonic chorus of 'and so say all of us'; or even 'the difficult takes time and the impossible a little longer'.

Oliver Brooks, Dick Adams and I wrote a detailed response to the chairman covering action already taken and in hand and reminded him that there might be just such scope for diversification within the existing portfolio, in Bovis and in Energy, both relatively new developments being nurtured steadily and carefully into growth.

We noted papers already agreed or in the course of consideration by the board concerning improvement of earnings, deferral of capital expenditure, limiting new capital expenditure to immediate profit earners, reduction of costs, etc. We detailed for example

– the successful renegotiation by Anglo Nordic of their contract for four ULCCs into five, or, at their option, six bulk carriers of 70,000 dwt which would operate in a more stable market;

– renegotiation of the P&O order for one ULCC to follow;

– delivery of four refrigerated vessels being built in Norway postponed;

– three of the four Rheinstahl LPG ships delayed for twelve months;

– the attempt to swap one Rheinstahl for another type of vessel;

– bank stand-by facilities being discussed and a share issue considered but, with the share price at just over par, not pursued;

– restructuring of the cross-channel services and withdrawal of the service to Spain and Portugal (a pity, as trade with the Iberian Peninsula was P&O's earliest venture);

– peripheral interests for disposal including Hall Thermotank, engineering and air-conditioning; the ship-repair companies; Australind, a dormant shipping company which had big accrued tax losses; parts of Bovis, e.g. civil engineering.

We made special mention of Cathay Pacific, in which P&O had held 15% since the airline's early days. It had been one of the Group's most rewarding investments – somewhat ironic in the light of the 1st Earl's pre-war decision not to accept the Imperial Airways agency, but with Swire in control and a large holding in the hands of the Hong Kong and Shanghai Bank, there was no synergy and no strategic objective for P&O to grasp. When, in 1975, Cathay put forward bold new plans for expansion requiring an injection of capital it was time to call it a day. The handsome funds released by the sale would be available for P&O's more focused businesses.

It was a good management document – a clear statement reminding the chairman that we had recognised the potential problems and had instigated a recovery programme, every item of which had, over recent months, been discussed and approved by the directors. Inchcape so approved this programme that he incorporated it in a regurgitated document which was presented to the board as 'The Chairman's Proposals'. I recall Oliver Brooks saying that if it made him feel better to represent it as his own initiative, we should not worry. It was not Inchcape's claiming all the credit that irritated me, but the fact that the whole exercise was an unnecessary diversion. I feel now that, with Burmah still casting its long shadow, he was endeavouring to safeguard his reputation against possible future criticism.

I had been working on another paper which I was able to submit soon afterwards. I wanted the directors to recognise strengths as much as they acknowledged weaknesses, on which I feared we might spend too much time. I traced the development of the Group, highlighting the dynamics of the various businesses and explaining the rationale which lay behind the development of our activities: increasingly sophisticated, technologically-advanced, requiring quality manpower, modern systems and modern management. This comprehensive review relied on considerable input from colleagues and from senior management in the operating and staff divisions. It represented an appraisal, based on the facts, of how we had arrived where we were, the lessons we had learned from the experience, and a view of where the future might lie. The latter part of my paper was intended to generate discussion which would be useful input for our five-year planning process.

Inchcape dismissed my review as 'bumph of use perhaps for PR but not for the board'. He produced his own 'Not-a-five-year-plan', which Dick Adams criticised, saying that it was 'extremely restrictive simply to label P&O a shipping company'. I proposed that, in the light of the proliferation of documents and his evident concern, we should have a special board meeting to discuss strategy. The chairman dismissed this as unnecessary: 'The non-execs don't like extra boards, especially Eric Drake, who has already agreed the dates for 1976. In any case, any well-organised board can deal with strategy at an ordinary meeting.' He was becoming hard to deal with.

In January 1976, a rather exotic guest came to lunch. Peter Munk, our associate in Southern Pacific Properties (SPP), had persuaded Adnan Khashoggi, the Saudi/Egyptian/Lebanese 'fixer', allegedly the prototype for the central character in Harold Robbins's racy novel *The Pirate*, to make a modest investment in SPP. Munk now sought his help in a more imaginative venture, led by SPP with the support of Bovis, to develop a leisure complex in Egypt. The layout of this ambitious scheme was to be in the shape of the ankh, a symbol of profound mystical and religious significance from the time of the Pharoahs. The site itself was stony desert bordering the cultivated area alongside the Nile, with the pyramids as backdrop.

The lunch table was adorned with P&O's Egyptian silver – a clock, two columns and a sphinx. During the 1850s, before the Suez Canal was built, P&O had urged the Khedive of Egypt to improve the overland route from Alexandria to Suez. To assist the somewhat impecunious Said Pasha, P&O made him a loan of a quarter of a million pounds. The railway from Alexandria to Suez via Cairo was completed in 1859 and over the next few years the loan was repaid. In recognition of the P&O contribution, Ismail Pasha, who succeeded Said in 1863, presented the company with these rather monstrous mementoes. Admiral Zaki, Egypt's Minister of Tourism, admired them over lunch, saying that he could read the Arabic inscriptions, but that he could not decipher the hieroglyphs. I was so intrigued that I got the British Museum to have a look. It was a let-down to be told that these treasured objects might well have been manufactured in Birmingham, that such art was in vogue in Victorian times and that the hieroglyphs were merely decorative – the Rosetta stone had not at that time been deciphered.

The lunch was interesting but inconclusive. Although Khashoggi remained non-committal, the Cairo project continued to bubble and in February I went out to get a feel for it. During the visit I was glad to re-meet Michael Weir, another of Miss Veitch's pupils at Canmore School, now ambassador to Egypt. Increasingly over those years, the foreign service was becoming more business-aware and Michael was most helpful in our lengthy negotiations. I was very glad, on my only free afternoon, to enjoy an exhilarating desert ride on a great white stallion, where space and sand stretched so far as to exhaust my Arab steed.

My trip to Cairo came in the wake of a whirlwind tour of the Persian Gulf (as it was still known). I have mentioned earlier the impetus given to our general cargo shipping after the oil price hikes. The traditional break-bulk ships and their trades were being marketed as StrathServices and, instead of presiding over their demise, General Cargo was looking aggressively for new opportunities, particularly in areas as yet unable to sustain the investment in infrastructure required by containerisation. The Persian Gulf was the focus of much of this enterprise. Oil wealth had increased purchasing power to an enormous extent. While the major ports at Jebel Ali, Kuwait and Dammam could handle containers, many others around the Gulf could not. It was in this field that traditional ships found their niche so successfully that General Cargo was soon able to justify Combo ships (vessels with break-bulk, container capacity and sometimes RoRo facilities).

I felt it was now time to refresh my knowledge of this rapidly changing area. Alan Hatchett, head of General Cargo, accompanied me. We found Basra and Umm Said much as before, slow turn-round and modest cargoes. Strains between Iraq and Iran made the transit between the two a delicate business, but Ian Malcolm of Grey Mackenzie in Teheran had influence. As major users, we talked long with the authorities about port congestion and I saw Bovis at work on a hospital and a school. The Shah was still in power, Teheran was elegant and the social activity intense.

On to Kuwait, where our ambassador, Archie Lamb, was a powerful supporter of British commercial interests. LPG exports were high on my agenda and Fred Jackson of Mundo Gas joined me in seeking Kuwait's recognition of our growing capacity.

Then to Qatar, Bahrain, Abu Dhabi and Dubai, where formal calls on the rulers took rather too long in our high-speed programme, but were essential in terms of keeping P&O's name to the fore. In Dubai I met Sheikh Rashid in company with George Chapman, long-time resident manager of Grey Mackenzie, our agents. 'Tell me Mr Marshall, do you see much change in Dubai since you first came twenty-five years ago?' 'Your Highness, there seem to me to be only two institutions which have not changed – Your Highness himself and George Chapman.'

We moved on to Riyadh where, in addition to looking at our cargo interests at Jeddah and Dammam, I wanted to discuss long-range road haulage from UK to Saudi Arabia; openings for Bovis in a number of major construction projects for Riyadh's Defence Agency; and a possible joint venture VLCC operation which one of the royal princes had put forward. We kicked our heels in ante-rooms, while appointments with officials were delayed an hour, two hours, twenty-four hours. Once in the great man's office, one had the coffee routine, and the discussion was constantly interrupted by telephone calls which the official seemed to think it would be discourteous to divert. We were treated not as potential partners, but as suppliants. To cap it all, when Alan and I retired to Riyadh's finest hotel we found ourselves sharing a bedroom, and at dinner the 'wine' waiter proffered a bottle of vintage apple juice. I was glad to leave for Cairo and, on my return home, to share with Gillian my Arab steed adventure.

In March, prime minister Harold Wilson stood down and bequeathed to Jim Callaghan a raft of political and economic problems which were to lead to a sterling crisis later in the year, with Denis Healey, then Chancellor of the Exchequer, being forced to call in the IMF. Prudently we went to see the NatWest, our lead bankers, in the persons of its chairman John Prideaux, chief executive Alex Dibbs and George Burnett. Almost a year earlier, we had given them a forecast of a £34m profit for 1976, well down from 1974's £48m. Now we expected to report a mere £28m. In fact Inchcape gave our estimate as £23m, and £33m for 1977. We were asking NatWest for a £30m overdraft facility, despite forecasting that in 1978-9 our overall borrowing would peak at £600m. Inchcape emphasised that this total was largely accounted for by 20th Century Bank and by the Bovis property side, and did not allow for possible disposals. The bankers declared themselves satisfied with our policies, and we got our facility. Our estimates were comfortably exceeded: 1976 saw a profit of £31m, and in 1977 we achieved £42m.

There was some light relief in March when Mona and I took the children to France for the weekend. We travelled on *Lion*, P&O's RoRo ferry which was inaugurating a new Dover/Boulogne service and in my rusty Oxford French I formally declared the route open. After a very enjoyable couple of days in Normandy we returned on the leisurely overnight ferry from Le Havre to Southampton.

I was to undergo renewed difficulty with Inchcape, this time over the audit of the 1975 accounts which were nearing completion. Our auditors, Deloittes, always remembered my sharp criticism of them when, in 1972, they had been prepared to endorse the Bovis offer documents even though these put a nil value on P&O's fleet. Trevor Spittle, the partner responsible for P&O, now complained to the chairman that Oliver Brooks and I were antagonistic, that Oliver would exclude him from meetings, and so forth. On investigation it was clear that Oliver did not get on particularly well with Spittle, and there had been a disagreement between them, now resolved, about property values. A storm in a tea-cup, except that Inchcape used the opportunity to accuse me of being obstructive and aggressive: 'You can't treat the auditor that way.' He wanted evidence to his Chairman's Committee and, 'As you obviously cannot be trusted to deal properly with the auditors, I will set up an audit committee.' I criticise myself for having, later in the year, dissuaded Inchcape from going ahead with an audit committee. I thought it inappropriate at the time, yet not long afterwards I came to believe that a well-found and well-serviced audit committee is of great value to shareholders and, in a very practical way, to all directors.

Inchcape was now preparing for his year as president of GCBS. He had not 'found Leo Hudson of much help' and wanted a panel to advise him. More likely, the position was that Leo Hudson, a cerebral character, found it impossible to get through to Inchcape on matters of which he had no previous understanding. Leo was not particularly patient. He probably let it show.

After Sir Eric Drake had been six months on the board, and recently appointed – with my enthusiastic support – deputy chairman, I had a talk with him. In addition to routine business we had been advising the board each month on profit-improvement plans and capital claw-back measures, and I wanted to know whether he felt, from his background in BP, that he was getting the appropriate information. His response was crisp and clear. There was too much waffle at board meetings. The executive directors should discuss board matters in advance and resolve lines of policy which I could then present to the board, thus saving time on unnecessary detail – precisely the purpose I had intended for the Executive Committee. Drake also said that he had no need of certain technical reports and no wish to deal with operating divisions below board level.

He enquired after my relationship with Inchcape, saying: 'He's a funny little man – never said a word at the BP board.' I gave him, I hope, a fair picture and when he said that the difficulties were for me to sort out, I agreed, but suggested that on occasion I might have to seek his advice and help. I found Drake rather good news.

In April 1976, I delivered the Grout Memorial lecture at the GCBS. It was ten years since Lord G had spoken of the origins of the VLCC and I proposed to look back at how these ships, now the workhorses of the oil trade, had performed. I was concerned about structural strength, pollution control, ship-to-shore interface and, in particular, the importance of internationally agreed rules and standards. The lecture was a demanding chore, but something more or less required of all leading shipowners in turn, and to be forced to take stock in this way before an informed audience exercises a useful discipline.

In June, Shell sought a provisional tender for two large LPG vessels and I asked Derek Hall to pursue the possibility of their taking one or two of our Rheinstahls on bareboat or timecharter, joint venture or purchase. But it transpired that, for Shell at least, long-term commitments were not the flavour of the month. The project petered out.

In September, our North Sea 'ship' came home. The first wild-cat exploratory well in Block 11/30 had revealed a significant field, Beatrice, estimated to yield 150m barrels. We were astonished at this swift strike and so were the operators, Mesa Petroleum. Cheering news in most difficult times.

Beatrice was to play a significant role in P&O affairs over the next few years, but there were some unexpected obstacles to overcome. In order to get early production, the consortium planned to use floating storage and a shuttle tanker to bring the oil ashore, but as Beatrice is only eleven miles out to sea this was vetoed by the DTI because of the risk of pollution. Permission for a permanent off-shore loading system was also refused. Delivery ashore was now beginning to look very costly. With the early-1977 oil price having fallen to about $14 per barrel, we could still look to a comfortable margin, but not on the scale – formerly based on $35 per barrel – that had raised our hopes. A pipeline to Nigg on the Black Isle had to be laid and, because of the viscosity of the waxy crude, this had to be heat-traced. Costs soared, and production – and thus cash flow – was delayed.

Today Beatrice remains the closest inshore field – its gear can be seen from the mainland coast. Now controlled by BP, it is almost exhausted, having yielded some 170,000 barrels. Beatrice has been a consistent earner throughout, a successful gamble, but one which many in the old P&O hierarchy seemed unable to trust.

Through 1976, *Nordic Clansman*, a VLCC, was building at Lithgow's yard on the Clyde for Anglo Nordic. She was timechartered to Elf, but was running months late. There was by now no profit for the yard and the owners were anxious not to lose rewarding employment. Relations were not easy. Nonetheless the niceties had to be observed and Caroline Inchcape was duly invited to name the vessel. She let it be known that she did not want the usual gift of 'another bit of jewellery'. After discreet enquiries, Bo Madsen of Anglo Nordic and Ross Belch for the builders were stunned to be informed that her wish was a motorised horse box. The cost would far exceed the yard's budget. Careful negotiation led to Lithgow's contributing a proportion of the cost and Kenneth Inchcape the balance. There was much amused comment on the protocol of which end the builders would present – the front of the 'orse or the arse.

A proactive employers' group, IRIS, on which I represented the shipping industry, endeavoured, by disseminating sound information, to stiffen the resolve of those courageous labour leaders prepared to resist the onslaught of the doctrinaire and destructive power of the unions. IRIS, of course, had its detractors. Some labelled it sinister. But to have any success it had to act discreetly and in confidence. Political affiliations were across party, and for much of my time Lord Robens of Woldingham was chairman. Alf Robens was a down-to-earth, realistic man, who had been through the mill during the depressed thirties and had seen an alternative to confrontation.

During the bitter months of 1974, and in the years up to the 1978–9 'winter of discontent', IRIS tried hard to support the moderates and counter the extremists. At the end of this time, the socialist government under Callaghan had lost its way and whatever common sense there was in facing individual issues was swept up in what became an 'outbreak of barbarity'. One might claim, however, that behind the scenes IRIS made some modest contribution to the massive political and social shift which began in the summer of 1979.

P&O staff, like so many British people, were conscious of the malignant atmosphere over these years. They had suffered from the three-day week and they endured almost daily disruption of transport, power and public services. Yet I believe that at all levels within the office and in our dealings with customers and associates there was no despair, we had developed a real sense of self-worth and were prepared to confront the demons. I made a particular point of seeing and being seen – on ships, in ports, at road haulage depots and on building sites – morale was of the utmost importance.

In October I undertook a major visit to our burgeoning oil and gas interests in USA. Mona was with me and we moved fast to take in as much as possible. First to Washington and New York, largely on GCBS shipping policy matters. It was heartening, after leaving the troubled UK, to hear, as we touched down at Dulles airport in one of the first Concordes, a round of enthusiastic applause from the mostly American passengers.

Mona stayed in Washington while I went up to New York for a day's business. She was to meet me in New Orleans at 6 p.m., but there was no sign of her at the appointed time. As J. E. Fowler of Falco, our Louisiana oil and gas distribution company, pressed the airlines for information, our dinner guests, mostly clients of Falco, were assembling at the Marie Antoinette. Through some network or other, 'JE' discovered that Mona would be arriving three hours later than intended on an Eastern flight via Atlanta. She changed in the back of the car which brought us from the airport and joined the guests, who had courteously declined to start eating before we arrived, but who had not neglected the booze. The party in one of the South's best restaurants became a bit of a shambles. It was Howard du Temple of Mundo Gas who had arranged for Mona to be taken to the airport in Washington. Her limo driver talked non-stop about his clientele – Bobby Kennedy, Telly Savalas, etc. Mona expressed surprise at getting to the airport so quickly, for which the driver took full credit. Howard's secretary shook hands on the kerbside and was whisked away, leaving Mona to discover that she was at National when she should have been at Dulles. It was a nightmare for her, compounded, when we eventually fetched up at the very elegant Royal Hotel at 2.30 a.m. by the realisation that we had only four and a half hours in which to enjoy it.

Falco, a recent P&O acquisition, was going well and there were prospects of increasingly useful links with our producing interests, with the trading business we were setting up in the UK and perhaps with Bulk Shipping. It was interesting to meet the people on the ground, particularly Clair Smith whom we had recruited to take over when J. E. Fowler retired. It would be some fifty years since 'JE' and his wife had started with one truck and a hand pump; Falco was now turning over in excess of $100m per year. Sadly, a couple of years later, he was killed in a light aircraft crash on his way to hunting camp.

From Shreveport we flew to Oklahoma City in a private jet borrowed by Larry Nicholls, from whom we had purchased his majority interest in Devon Oil Corporation. The Nichollses lived in Nicholls Street, Nicholsville – high, wide and handsome. Dick Povey of Energy Division made sure that I got a good overview of the producing properties, which were scattered over a wide patch. I had lunched at the Oil Clubs in Houston and Dallas and now we were taken to the Oil Club in Oklahoma City by our Kerr McGhee partners in Beatrice. Devotees of the TV series 'Dallas' will know the style of these see-and-be-seen establishments.

It was on this trip that I made a side visit to Bartlesville, the home of Philipps Oil – we were trying to negotiate an LPG deal involving Bulk Shipping and Mundo Gas. At that time, not many visitors seemed to go to 'Bartles where?'.

At Denver, we were taken up into the mountains to see a prospective investment in exploration for gas. It was a particularly dull area overshadowed by dramatic, stark scenery – Wyatt Earp country, I believe. Anyhow, I was not sufficiently technical to understand why the vibes were so good. In later years I often thought that our elder son Alastair and his wife Sue, geologist and geophysicist respectively, would have thoroughly enjoyed being involved in a developing business like P&O Energy. An unpleasant memory of Denver, and particularly Browns Hotel, is that Mona experienced the first of the debilitating migraines which were to plague her for years afterwards. It might have been the altitude at which we dined which triggered it, but it was very severe.

From Denver to Houston, back to commercial air service now, and then on to Mexico City where Harry Spanton of P&O Cruises joined us. At last we had a day off – and what a day. Acapulco's Los Brisas hotel was then one of those out-of-this-world places – individual villas with private pools – 300 of them. Bougainvillaea abounded, a man with a bucket of blossoms floated hibiscus in the pool and room service arrived, borne high in the air, by moped. Mona was in her element – photographs, flowers, seed-pods, people.

I recall, however, that she was perhaps too tense to take a photograph of me being macho and probably rather irresponsible. Parascending was then in its infancy and I decided to have a go. I took off from a barge, soared round Acapulco Bay enjoying a spectacular view and a very exhilarating ride before landing back on my feet. It all seemed quite easy and I was surprised at how many who followed me ended up in the sea. Afterwards we heard of some who were swept by a gust of wind into the cliffs or, because of a change of wind, found it very difficult to get down at all.

Sun Princess took us up the coast to Mazatlan. It was fascinating to experience US cruising in one of TV's 'Love Boats' and, as we were to be again twenty-five years later, we were very impressed with the professionalism and the customer-friendliness of the crew. Captain Mike Bradford, lately of *Oriana*, was in command and he indulged me. Since my naval days, and stimulated by experience with the ships in Calcutta, I have always been interested in the hardware. In *Sun Princess* I climbed from top to bottom and end to end, appreciating the calm control of the engineers and the exuberance of the Pakistani crew when they realised that I was one of the old sahibs.

Because of Mexican cabotage, Mona and I could only be landed at Mazatlan on a medical certificate – I needed 'urgent attention', so Harry Spanton came too as my bag carrier. Mazatlan was battened down ahead of an imminent cyclone and we were glad to get away in a hurry. In LA we had a huge show biz 'Love Boat' reception with Cary Grant and other lesser stars. Thanks to television, Princess Cruises was becoming a household name, but as the executives put it, perhaps less than 1% of Americans had taken a cruise. What about the other 99% from coast to coast, before even contemplating the repeat market?

At P&O, we had to manage many difficulties thrown up by the general economic turmoil. We continued to make progress in reducing peripheral activities and, when the opportunity to dispose of our insurance broking interests came up, we sold – to Inchcape & Co. This was timely as I had established a compelling case for us to manage our own marine insurance by in-house underwriting and had found a first-class experienced man in Neil Matthews to set this up. We were satisfied, in all the circumstances of what had been a difficult year, to be able to report profits before tax for 1976 at £31.1m.

In February 1977, Derek Hall, supported by Howard du Temple and Charlie Scott from Mundo Gas, made a comprehensive presentation to the board on 'P&O and Gas' and, in March, I discussed Beatrice with Monty Pennell and Jack Birks of BP. We were prepared to consider a sale of part of our interest to help fund the development or indeed to sell the whole if the price was right. Perhaps because it was our first exploration venture and we regarded ourselves as having scored a triumph, sights were set high, but, whatever the reason, we were not talking in the same range. I recall also that the British National Oil Corporation had prior rights to acquire participations which were for sale. The talks came to nothing, but illustrate that even at that early stage I had no hang-up about trading our participation. It was useful, too, that Peter Walters, chairman of BP, told me that BP would gladly purchase our full share of production, while Shell and Home Oil among others also showed interest.

Early in the year I was suggesting to Alan Hatchett and his team in General Cargo that they keep well abreast of opportunities in China, the sleeping giant. Soon afterwards, Brian Baillie of P&O Australia began to develop his cargo handling and port management interests in China and he rapidly became the Group authority on dealings there. There were, however, as many threats as there were opportunities in the Far East. The Soviet state enterprise, Far East Shipping Co. (FESCO), which had already intervened in the Europe/Australia trade, began operating from Japan to New Zealand. FESCO's potential link with the Trans-Siberian Railway posed a danger to our traditional trading pattern and, among other issues with the Soviets, this was to take up much time during the ensuing months.

Throughout the Group the imperative of making assets work was now understood. We tried to establish priorities and to conserve resources, but new developments were given a fair wind if justified by the profit potential. The process of analysis was being steadily improved. New ships joined the LPG and reefer fleets and in February I advised the board of a revolutionary passenger service we proposed to introduce in June from the heart of London, at the Tower, to Zeebrugge, for Brussels. Boeing had developed a jetfoil craft using their aerospace engineering and design skills. The jetfoils operated a successful Hong Kong/Macao service and Boeing wanted a showcase in Europe. It looked as though there would be ample traffic potential – the attraction of going from the City to the centre of Europe in speed and comfort. From P&O's point of view, an important aspect was that Boeing would underwrite a substantial part of the operation. European & Air Transport launched on programme in June – the Lord Mayor attended with the chairman and, while it was impressive to see this revolutionary craft sweep off the landing stage at St Katherine's Dock on her way down-river, that was not half as impressive as the return voyage. She came up-river on her foils as far as Greenwich, leaning into the bends and, although at high speed, leaving little wake. It was a dramatic arrival as the City unfolded ahead, Tower Bridge, St Paul's and, beyond, Westminster. We saw this one red, sunset evening when I took the boys on a round trip.

The service was to be short-lived. It proved yet again that sea conditions cannot be taken for granted. Too often the sea state in open waters compelled the jetfoil to drop onto her hull, when the ride became not only slow but very uncomfortable. There were too many technical faults in this rather difficult environment. Customer acceptance was never fully established and the core traffic, business- and EEC-oriented, was not of high enough volume, while tourist traffic was seasonal. The service eventually folded in 1978, but at no loss to P&O.

In June 1977 the Queen reviewed the Fleet at Spithead to mark her Silver Jubilee. It was a gallant attempt to recreate reviews of the past when the navy could muster an imposing array of warships. But still, it was staged with meticulous pomp and ceremony, and I enjoyed a nostalgic day on board P&O's *Manapouri* as she lay at a buoy in the trot of merchant vessels. The weather was grey and blustery, but *Britannia*, steaming through the lines, made an impressive sight as ships manned the side and gave three cheers for Her Majesty. Eric Drake, as an Elder Brother of Trinity House, was on board *Patricia*, leading the Queen; Kenneth Inchcape chose to be in a BP tanker. *Manapouri* did the P&O Group proud. Sadly there may be no more reviews – we haven't enough ships now to make a proper show.

9

The Inchcape Rock

For some months I had felt that Clifford Nancarrow was developing his own agenda. He had always been a bit of a loner. He viewed a number of his colleagues with evident contempt and was not, frankly, a team player. He was intellectually capable but not a good leader and the senior members of his General Holdings Division found him inconsistent. He had made a number of decisions which exceeded his authority and I was losing confidence.

We were negotiating sale of the ship-repair interests to the newly nationalised British Shipbuilders; we were preparing to go public in Australia with 25% of the shares which would change the relationship with P&O Australia; because of competition for the available resources it seemed the growth of General Holdings would have to be held back. I suggested to Nancarrow that his future might be more attractive elsewhere. We agreed he should have six months to look around from the advantage of his P&O base.

The Chairman's Committee, on this occasion under Eric Drake's chairmanship, was in full support but, while confirming this, at the same time criticised me for not bringing good executives onto the board. We then had a board of thirteen – six non-executives and seven executives, of whom one, Mac Sidey, was about to retire and now Nancarrow's days were numbered – so the seven executives would be reduced to five. I had been consistent in not wanting appointment to the board to go automatically to specific executive positions and in resisting any revival of P&O's traditional practice, a board of divisional barons. I thought that a board of twelve was a workable size and was not concerned at having more non-executives than executives. But I was conscious of the need to plan succession. I had wanted for some time to bring Jim Lindars in, thus adding intellectual capacity. Inchcape would not agree as he was 'not a shipping man'. In any case he refused to discuss board membership until after the end of his GCBS presidency. Drake's remark that 'the board don't know anything about the next level' came as quite a surprise. Since his explicit comment a year earlier that he did not feel it necessary to deal with management below board level, he had given no indication of a change in approach. Between Drake and Inchcape it was becoming Catch 22 for me.

With our retrenchment and development plans, a great deal was brought to the board both for information and decision – the board was being asked to work hard. I had another word with Drake. He asked me bluntly why I didn't get on with Inchcape. He still found him 'a funny little man' but he was chairman and it was my job to keep him happy. I agreed up to a point, but explained that it was difficult to be constructive when black could become white and yes could mean no. Could he, Eric Drake, with all his experience and authority, perhaps help to resolve the problem especially as Inchcape's concern seemed to take up a disproportionate amount of his time and energy? Drake's response was unequivocal. He hadn't joined the P & O board for hassle – he had welcomed the prospect of a congenial board after his retirement from BP, and he enjoyed cruising. So that was that.

Drake's business career had been entirely within BP and he judged everything by BP standards. For him, theirs was not simply the best but the *only* way. He tended to be critical rather than constructive, to question rather than to suggest, to be cynical rather than supportive. In view of the crisis that the oil companies had brought upon the world, his was perhaps not the most convincing stance. Many in P&O management found his contribution minimal and regarded him as a spent rocket.

Inchcape's year as president of the GCBS came to an end in May 1977. In office he had spoken up strongly for the need to contribute in time and experience to the work of the Council and had expressed the view that successful negotiations with government at industry level could well contribute more to a company's performance than much in-house activity. This was politically correct for the leader of the shipping industry, but strangely at odds with his personal attitude. A pronounced reluctance to engage with socialist ministers was a particular problem for the officials. The antipathy was reciprocated and I recall being faintly shocked when I heard Dennis Healey, with whom I was dining, refer to him as 'that fat cat'. Inchcape's year as President was not, as I recall, a distinguished one. Council meetings were all too often meandering and, indeed, embarrassing in showing up his lack of grasp of the issues. He was propped up by Johnnie Wood, Bruce Farthing and others in GCBS and sustained by his image. We all rallied round to ensure that he did not fail.

From 1974–9 I was chairman of the GCBS Foreign Shipping Policy Committee and much involved with the various European national associations. We endeavoured to get our act together to present a common and powerful front in defending our interests vis-à-vis the USA, the developing Third World fleets, represented by Group B in UNCTAD, and the state-owned fleets of the Eastern bloc.

The US scene was complicated by the many departments and agencies involved in maritime affairs. The Federal Maritime Commission (FMC), the Department of Justice, with its proclivity to apply anti-trust legislation extraterritorially, the White House advisers, Transport and Commerce all had a position. Uncertainty tended to make for confrontation in OECD, in the GATT and generally in any issue touching liner trades to the USA.

In UNCTAD the Liner Code, designed to protect 40% of trade for ships of the exporting nation, 40% for ships of the importing nation and 20% for outsiders or cross-traders, was lumbering its way to adoption. In the end, perhaps, it was the least unattractive of some pretty poor options. Efforts to prevent the inclusion of bulk trades were, fortunately, successful.

For some years the ageing, inefficient Soviet fleet had been undergoing substantial renewal – tankers, bulk and log carriers, ferries, general cargo ships and even what were represented as cruise ships, all began to appear, up-to-date in design and with much improved facilities. The corollary of improved efficiency was not immediately apparent and was evidently not a priority. Their priority was hard currency and, with no requirement to service the capital investment, the ships were operated on a cash basis.

A very significant threat was presented by LASH (Lighter Aboard Ship) vessels – the Soviets' equivalent of container ships designed to fit readily into the fleet train during naval operations. In peacetime they had to find a living in trades to Central and South America, Africa and the Pacific Basin, where they ran hard against many British interests.

On the North Atlantic the FMC encouraged an accommodation of Soviet aspirations without requiring conformity with the obligations of conference membership. As I took every opportunity to point out, it was ironic that US regulators could by direct action, or in some cases by inaction, so encourage the nationalised Soviet fleet that Western free enterprise shipping could be squeezed to the point of having themselves to seek governmental aid.

There was such disquiet over the Soviets that the Department of Trade & Industry sent a small delegation to Moscow in August 1977 – Gerry Lanchin, a deputy secretary in the DTI led, with Bruce Farthing, deputy director-general of GCBS, David Tomlinson, a staff member, and myself. I mugged up on the existing fleet and on what I could glean about future construction. Everything I learned confirmed the threat. The formal agenda was built around the Anglo-Soviet Trade Agreement, but our main objective was to work towards agreed parameters for Soviet aspirations within the areas of Western shipping interest. Our European colleagues were consulted and gave us general endorsement so that we could speak with a broad-based authority

Moscow is hot in high summer, and just before leaving London we heard that the Soviets proposed to hold the substantive discussions on board one of their cruise ships in the Black Sea. Relief at being out of Moscow was tempered with some concern that we might be isolated. Our working host was Igor Averin of the Ministry of Shipping, a very personable and respected figure in international circles. On our first evening he entertained us royally in a noisy, crowded restaurant. He always gave the impression of understanding one's problems, indeed of sympathising and intending to do something about them, although of course 'this could be difficult' sometimes, because of the structure of the industry, the Soviet bureaucracy and so on. It was a not unsuccessful negotiating technique.

We were briefed at the UK embassy – a fine building in the shadow of the Kremlin. I don't know if we looked in need of it, but there was a repetition of London's warning about the dangers of being compromised by friendly females. Next, we saw the acting Minister of Shipping, Guzhenko. He was a great bear of a man, bluff and doubtless rough, an ex-stoker in *Revenge* – a British battleship transferred to the Soviet Navy during the war, which was based in Archangel. He spoke little English, but we hit it off during what was essentially a rather formal exchange of greetings.

When we flew down to Sochi, a holiday resort on the eastern shore of the Black Sea, we found beaches of large pebbles with wooden walkways leading down to the water from the hotels (more like hostels). We noticed the absence of advertising and of amenities;

deck chairs were regimented, the crowded holidaymakers took their role seriously and the sea was an eponymous black – turgid and seriously unrefreshing.

As our cruise ship, *Captain Kareliya*, was being employed to reward the modern equivalent of Stakhanovites, the passengers were a mixed bunch from all over the USSR and there were few, if any, normal fare-paying travellers. *Kareliya* was modern and well kept with accommodation more akin to a North Sea ferry than a cruise ship. The organisation was simple – two sittings for meals, late-night buffet, home-grown entertainment, daily tote and so on. But we were not there for a holiday.

The pattern to be adopted for the discussions took time to agree. Averin suggested that we should all have a quiet morning, lunch, and then meet from 2–6 p.m. before adjourning for drinks and whatever entertainment was available. Recalling my earlier experience of Russian eating and drinking I, for one, knew that an arrangement on these lines would be disastrous for my metabolism. Gerry Lanchin was firm – morning discussions, afternoons free, more discussions if necessary and then time for fun. The Russians protested as this could impinge on their planned excursions ashore. But we did not budge.

The negotiations were standard – there was the hard man/soft man approach. Gerry Lanchin was, throughout, sensitive to the possibility of criticism from his West European counterparts, particularly Christopher Hinz, the acerbic West German official, that we might be persuaded to concede on the broader issues in order to win a point or two on Anglo-Soviet bilateral interests – for example, improved cargo-sharing in the Baltic trades. It was pretty pedestrian, but the ship's programme put down some markers and we concluded a note of understanding before arrival in Odessa.

We did after all find time for sightseeing. At Novorossisk the Soviet Black Sea Fleet was an impressive but rather sinister spectacle. The war memorial was a vivid reminder of the enormous slaughter in the Crimea in 1942–4. There were crowds of ordinary Soviet civilians, families, standing, staring, shuffling – all profoundly engaged with memories. At Yalta we saw the dachas and villas of the Czars and the dictators, and the rooms where the world was divided into spheres of influence by Churchill, Roosevelt and Stalin in 1945.

Our last night aboard *Kareliya* was a gala evening with a fairly alcoholic dinner and a cabaret by the ship's company, followed by a talent contest for the passengers. The various items illustrated well the cultures of various Soviet republics. As the night gathered pace there was more audience participation and the Brits were popular targets. It was most unfortunate that, at the end of a week in which he had put in a great effort, Bruce Farthing was spun off his feet in a mazurka. At first we thought that he had simply twisted his knee, but sadly that wasn't the case; he suffered permanent damage.

Landing in Odessa we climbed the sweeping Borodin steps, made a quick tour of the city – drab, ill-kempt and sad. We saw another war memorial and the changing of the guard, with high-stepping marines supported by very solemn teenage boy scouts. The Ukrainians seemed, understandably, determined not to forget. The minister had come from Moscow to sign the agreement and to offer appropriate toasts before, late in the day, we swept into the VIP suite for our return flight to Moscow. As we walked out to the plane I noticed that it was a TU33 – a copy of the Comet. There was a rather rudimentary set of access steps, the carpet was worn through, the seats seemed like cast-iron garden furniture and the stewardess looked like a caricature of the Russian heavy. I felt distinctly nervous and, seeking comfort, made some comment about this being rather an old design of aircraft. 'Oh, yes, Mr Marshall,' was the minister's reply, 'you are quite right – Aeroflot only use these TU33s when there is exceptionally heavy traffic.' And with that we were away, rattling and bumping to take-off.

Did our negotiations achieve anything lasting? We were able to assess the immediacy of the threat posed by the Soviets' rapid expansion and convey our concern, with some authority, to the Americans. We learned too, that the apparatchiks in the Shipping Ministry could understand our worries at the development of the Trans-Siberian Railway with its theoretically unlimited capacity, although they claimed to have no influence or even opinion on that threat. Despite the limitations to their willingness, even ability to co-operate, I believe our very clear exposition caused them to begin to accept that some form of co-operation and stability could benefit them in the long run. Our European colleagues to whom we reported fully, were enthusiastically complimentary. In the following years the Soviets' and their satellites' liner shipping increasingly associated with and joined Western liner conferences. At the personal level, I was warmed by the friendship of Igor Averin and continued to see him for some years. It is good to know that he is well-established in the burgeoning private sector of Russian shipping.

A few months later, in October 1977, we were planning the corporate changes needed to bring local capital into P&O Australia and I visited Canberra with Bob Rose, POAL's managing director. We called on Malcolm Fraser the premier, on Donald Tebbit the UK High Commissioner and others on the Canberra circuit. In the corridors, Bob introduced me to Gough Whitlam, the premier who had been 'dissolved' by the governor-general, using the Queen's prerogative. There was, as usual, a fair amount of anti-monarchy rhetoric, both in the country and in parliament, but Whitlam was wonderfully relaxed: 'Yeah, P&O, you've been around for a few years and I suppose you will be for some time yet – just like the Queen.'

Fraser, on the other hand, was uptight and spiky. I thought our plans for POAL would be welcome but he seemed predisposed to criticism of the shipping industry as a whole. Australian politicians have always tended to assume exploitation by overseas interests. Yet not infrequent investigations concluded that the conference system, which had long managed the liner trades, had been the least bad system. Australian endeavours to maintain a home-grown shipping line have never been successful.

I arrived with the view that the climate was not favourable for our flotation; that we might, for the time being, have missed the boat. But, after a wide canvassing of opinion, I was persuaded to 'go'. The part-flotation was a success, with the 25% of shares on offer well over-subscribed. I was very happy. Management of a wholly-owned subsidiary in Australia had always seemed a problem and to have an Australian dimension would, I hoped, give the management a different perspective, so that there would be more co-operation and less confrontation. My attitude implied no particular criticism of POAL, but was reinforced not only by the benefits which now began to flow to the parent company, the Australian shareholder and the management, but also by my subsequent similar experience in Bestobell, Commercial Union and Royal Bank of Canada.

On that trip I managed to fit in a visit to New Zealand. Our subsidiary was struggling to find a role to compensate for the progressive loss of its traditional liner agency business. They were anxious to show me the recently-acquired passenger launches on the Bay of Islands, the 'cream boats', so-called because their first role had been to collect churns of milk from the dairy farmers on the shores of the bay. They were still the post boats and delivery service for a scattered community, but carried more and more tourists in this spectacularly beautiful area.

The local manager was very keen that I should go deep-sea fishing outside The Heads, and to meet a tight schedule we did so at 5 a.m. There was much tension until, at the last moment, I hooked a 55 lb kingfish. We were hustled ashore, photographed, and raced by car to catch a flight to Auckland in time for a 9.30 a.m. meeting. It was with wry amusement that, three months later, I saw a photograph in *Wavelength*, the P&O house newspaper, captioned: 'Managing Director relaxes on fishing trip in New Zealand.'

I did relax on a visit to Invercargill at the tip of South Island, where Marshall relations abound. There a cousin of my father's, whose parents emigrated from Scotland at the turn of the century, presided over a family the mirror image of my own. The colouring, the names, the style were that of their counterparts at home. I enjoyed, too, Uncle Jim's conducted tour of Southland – the green of the grazing country, the backdrop of mountains and wall-to-wall sheep. The warmth of a Scottish welcome left me with a great feeling of kinship.

The end of 1977 saw some major changes on the shipping side of P&O. We sold fourteen general cargo ships, a reflection of the continued development of the container trades, with the New Zealand trade going to Overseas Containers, and a dramatic improvement in port conditions in the Persian Gulf on the back of increased oil revenues. Anglo Nordic had managed to finesse their Japanese new-building orders yet again and they were now likely to emerge with two 83,000 ton tankers suitable for East Coast North America. They had sold two older tankers to Burmah Oil. A particularly noteworthy event was that we were able to bring our white elephant, *LNG Challenger*, out of lay-up for modest employment as a storage vessel. She had been one of the last ships to benefit from the investment grant available to UK shipowners, but even that had not been able to overcome stagnant market conditions when she was delivered in 1974 to joint owners P&O, A. P. Møller and Fearnley & Eger of Oslo, and she spent almost three years in expensive lay-up.

Among the non-shipping interests, we had sold P&O property developments to the value of £40m. The ship repair businesses went to British Shipbuilders. With Clifford Nancarrow's resignation, on programme in December, General Holdings Division was disbanded and its remaining activities were absorbed by other divisions, although a special secretariat was set up under Michael Kenny to look after relations with Australia and New Zealand together with the remaining Mackinnons companies in the east.

Not all cash flow was in our favour: devaluation of the pound sterling to the equivalent of $1.75 put up the cost of borrowings that year by £14m, but it was a busy and productive period and at the end of the year we would deliver profits at £42.5m, not far off the record set in 1974.

It was unfortunate, in personal terms, that there was an unnecessary incident with the chairman in December. For over a year, I had been discussing with the Bovis directors the make-up of their board in anticipation of the next move forward. Neville Vincent, Bovis's non-executive chairman, had agreed that he had made his major contribution and should retire in 1978 and the question of his successor was on the table. Dear Sir Brian Horrocks was eighty-three and Sir Richard Powell was approaching seventy. We had agreed that they would not be 'shoved out', and we all felt that, given his war record as the distinguished commander of 21st Army's XXX Corps in North West Europe, Brian was rather special. He would be retained as a consultant in the West Country to provide, as it were, a pension. Our discussion had been open and constructive and Neville Vincent had been closely involved.

Then Neville met Andrew Crichton in the street and remarked, quite understandably, that, after a lifetime in the business, he was sad to be standing down (although he also was to be retained as a consultant for some time because of his relationship with Marks & Spencer). Crichton immediately reported to Inchcape that Marshall was sacking Vincent. Inchcape immediately launched into print to all the non-executive directors, to the effect that the chief executive was 'again exceeding his authority, pushing Vincent out'.

When the whole position, the extensive discussions and the need to plan forward were explained and when Neville had written to express his regret at the misunderstandings and his satisfaction with the arrangements, Inchcape acknowledged that I had acted entirely properly and sensibly. However the damage had been done; Crichton resented the fact that he had picked up the wrong end of the stick (or, and at this stage I wouldn't have put it past him, simply to have misrepresented Vincent's comments); Inchcape logged the 'case', bringing it up triumphantly some months later: 'And we didn't let you get away with sacking Vincent and old Horrocks.'

We had a good start to 1978, with inflation continuing its downward trend (the average for the year would be 8.39%) and the pound strengthening. Alan Hatchett, Rodney Leach and Harry Spanton joined the board – but Inchcape's hang-up about Jim Lindars persisted. I hoped to see the new recruits developing as Group directors. Derek Hall had been a powerful spokesman for Bulk Shipping and had also succeeded in taking a broader view. Rodney Leach was a very useful addition in this way, but in my time I felt that neither Hatchett nor, strangely – because he was a confident individual – Spanton, quite developed into the role.

In February, again for GCBS, I led a shipowners' delegation to Washington to see the Departments of Commerce and Transportation, the Federal Maritime Commission and the White House maritime adviser. This was the first formal visit for some fifteen years and was born of exasperation at the fragmented approach to maritime policy in the USA. There were numerous agencies, departments and advisers, all with an individual agenda, sometimes a highly political agenda and an approach which too often seemed legislation-driven. George King of BP, Bill Slater of Cunard and Bruce Farthing were in my team and Peter Walters, then president of GCBS, joined us at a dinner for all our contacts. Peter Jay, who was the UK ambassador at the time, was first-class in his support. He had informed himself very fully on the issues of extraterritoriality, the conference system, the Soviet threat and the FMC, and he ensured access and assured follow-up.

In March the Australians were feeling their new semi-independence and I was writing to Bob Rose urging consolidation and organic development 'in these times of high inflation'. In April, I heard Mrs Thatcher speak on industrial relations. She was beginning to impress as leader of the opposition.

In May, I produced a management briefing paper on the poor performance of the world shipping industry in what were, and looked like continuing to be, adverse world trading conditions. A plank of P&O strategy was, and I used the term frequently, to secure a balance in our business so that there was at least the chance that not all sections would go down together; that within shipping we might see the bulk business strong while cruising was struggling; ferries might flourish while deep-sea containers were depressed; even that domestic house-building might carry the burden, although world trade was slow. However, it was obvious to us all that this time all sectors and all commercial activities would be adversely affected. We were in for a tough time, but management, and particularly the top executive team, firmly believed that we had the measure of it and would weather the storm. We abjured brushing problems under the carpet; we wanted no hostages to fortune. The board was well-informed and expressed full support for our plans.

My regular Friday morning meetings of executive directors continued to be an invaluable management resource for the team. With hindsight I can say that they were even more important in bad times than in good. I see that on 1 June that year we opened (as always during the difficult years) with the progress of profit improvement plans; we considered renegotiation of bunker contracts with BP – be it reduced prices or increased cargoes for our ships; we reviewed a draft of the chairman's AGM speech and a list of possible questions and answers; we considered CBI policy on exchange rates and its recommendations to government; there were items for information, such as a letter from Peter Laister, CEO of Ellermans, about the Mediterranean trade; and there were questions: were House of Commons dinners with MPs proving useful?

Ladies' Day at Ascot gave us a day off. P&O had inherited a box with the acquisition of Bovis and we managed to persuade ourselves that our hospitality made good commercial sense. Our guests were Ronnie and Charmian Swayne of OCL, Peter and Trish Walters of BP, Fran and Lynn Howard of Charter Consolidated, Hugh and Anne Barnes of Community Re and Gordon and Jo Bisset of Thyssen Bournemiza. We had a wonderful day – colourful and enjoyable with the ladies looking exquisite

The next day, the 19th, I wrote to Derek Hall on the need to bite the bullet. Should we not simply renege on the fourth Rheinstahl (LPG) contract even if it cost us damages in court? Should we not somehow get out of LNG Carriers? (Fearnley & Eger did just that later in the year). What about disposing of the remaining three *Ards* (VLCCs)? And, most cruel perhaps, we must at least consider selling our flourishing Mundo Gas interest.

Two days later I noted the changes which recent board appointments and the restructuring of the operating divisions imposed in terms of those statutorily responsible for safety at sea. I asked Leach,

Hatchett and Spanton to confirm that appropriate arrangements had been made to pick up these responsibilities in Ferries, StrathServices and Cruises. I continued:

> While this may cover statutory requirements can you also confirm that you and your management are satisfied that adequate arrangements are in force for safety, organisation and training on board vessels within your division. I have in mind particularly the rapidly developing use of RoRos, with a certain lack, to date, of statutory regulation, leaving more responsibility on the operator; the pressures on operators through the necessity to economise at all levels and the additional spotlight which is being directed on operators through increasing awareness of health and safety requirements, environmental accidents and the like.

In the light of the high-profile disasters of the late 1980s and mid-1990s, it is interesting to note the emphasis on RoRo regulation and practice.

I was preparing an important paper for delivery in June to the British North American Committee. It followed up Admiral Sir John Treacher's presentation the year before on 'The Soviet Threat: a Naval Analysis'. My paper was on 'The Threat to Western Shipping Presented by the Soviet Merchant Marine'. Sometimes I did feel 'Here I go again', but I took comfort from Adlai Stevenson's advice that 'mankind needs the repetition of the obvious more than the elucidation of the obscure'. And this time I would not be preaching to the converted, but to a broad-based audience which should have a close interest in the survival of a strong and viable Western shipping industry, but which was unlikely, yet, to appreciate the threat. I was much helped in my preparation by Krys von Sidow of the Swedish Brostrom Group. He and his team had developed an important database on Soviet shipping. The whole exercise was useful too as a curtain raiser to the major policy speech I was due to give for British shipping in New York in September.

In July, I prepared the ground with colleagues for the divisional budgeting process. There was, as in planning, a top-down, bottom-up approach. The emphasis was on cost-cutting while, at the same time, looking for investment opportunities which would make an immediate return. We discussed relocation and recognised that this would involve decentralisation. I had no objection in principle, provided we secured management and economic benefits and I had no problem about the likelihood of the process being reversed after some years, provided there were again recognisable benefits. Our City-based activities could be moved to Worcester Park, where the Maori Club, the social and athletic club of the old New Zealand Shipping Company owned some 35 acres of greenfield site. Frank Heaton, formerly a logistics expert in the navy, headed a team to assess the practicalities.

I tried out on the chairman a 'Statement of Business Principles'. There was widespread talk of the benefits to all stakeholders of such a commitment. It was what later came to be known as a Mission Statement, part broad objectives and part a declaration of business ethics. Inchcape was dismissive of 'those papers'. I could see that the speed of change through the 1970s was exercising pressure on his old-fashioned, arrogant style of management. He could neither comprehend nor accept. He would need careful nursing through the rest of his chairmanship. Yet I was encouraged by the positive climate of the spring and summer months. Aside from the inevitable hiccough, Inchcape and I were working reasonably well together with, I felt, a common purpose and, within the executive, we had a really strong commitment to teamwork.

Oliver Brooks, the finance director, was a key member of the team, indeed the colleague with whom I worked most closely. From his arrival in 1973 in time to advise on the acquisition of Zapata Norness, he had been at the heart of the executive management, involved in financial planning, in acquisitions and disposals and in strategic developments like Bovis, energy, and gas carriers. I was comfortable with him and valued his input enormously. Indeed he was one of the very few with whom I shared my concerns over Inchcape. He was always supportive and would always stiffen my resolve.

The half-year results to be announced at the board meeting on Tuesday 29 August would be bad, and under Oliver's guidance the board had already agreed to take the maximum pain immediately, thus ensuring that the recovery reported at the year-end would be all the better. And we all knew that as a result of action taken, the basis for recovery had been well laid. In the five years since 1973, the number of ships in the fleet had been halved. We had sold many ships and had brought into service vessels which made the fleet hugely more cost-effective. We had achieved major improvements on the non-shipping side. We were getting the core of the Group into fighting shape. While, therefore, not looking forward to announcing a half-year result of only £1.8m profit compared with £42m for the full year 1977, we agreed that the accompanying statement should not be down-beat. It was with no major concern that I went off with the family to Norway.

Peter Berg, the owner of the Drammen yard, had asked Mona to launch *Ragni Berg*, a sleek, swift reefer. It was a happy family occasion – the school band played, the choir sang and the town turned out in force. We then had a marvellous week with the Bergs at their summer cottage – swimming, water-skiing, sailing, a visit to Geiranger Fjord and a hair-raising motor trip on corkscrew mountain roads. We sailed back from Gothenburg in North Sea Ferries' *Elk*, later to distinguish herself in the Falklands campaign. Rodney Leach and Alan Hatchett and their families were also on board. We arrived at Immingham on Sunday evening, 27 August.

When I went into the office on Monday, Betty Fairclough said that the chairman wished to see me later that morning. Inchcape, without introduction, handed me a piece of paper: 'You should see the resolution I propose, with all your colleagues' support, to put to the board tomorrow.' It stated that in view of the 'serious situation' facing the company, Inchcape would, with immediate effect, assume the role of chief executive as well as that of chairman. I would continue as managing director with particular responsibility for 'problem' areas including Bulk Shipping and Energy.

It was shattering. I was appalled as much by the handling of the resolution as by its content. I did manage to pull my scattered wits together and question whether and how 'all colleagues' had agreed this proposal, particularly as I was confident neither Leach nor Hatchett could have been consulted. Inchcape would not meet my eyes; he just swept up his papers and departed, 'for a meeting'.

His was a classic manoeuvre. In my absence, he and Andrew Crichton had seen the available directors individually. Derek Hall told me that Inchcape had informed him that 'everyone has agreed', inferring that he was the last to be consulted and as Derek said to Mona: 'I had my own position and my family to consider.' Both Rodney Leach and Alan Hatchett saw the chairman after I did. They were told that all the other directors had agreed the proposal and that I had accepted it. The irony is that in having agreed to take all the negative factors into the first half of the year I had, with the guarantee of recovery in the second half, made the bullets and loaded the gun. All that remained was for Inchcape to aim and fire.

I was now the titular managing director, assured by Inchcape of continuing authority within my defined areas of responsibility. He made a particular point also of assuring me of his continued support for my involvement in industry affairs, especially in going forward to become vice-president of GCBS in 1979, and president the following year. When the Interim Statement was issued on 6 September, my role had been fattened for public consumption 'to supervise and coordinate the company's operations'.

Immediately, however, I had work to do and commitments to discharge. Another mission to Washington for GCBS was to be followed by a challenge to the American administration in a speech in New York on 15 September, using *Canberra* to provide an appropriate platform. Victor Matthews, Chief Executive of Trafalgar House (Cunard) had offered the delegation, with Mona as official hostess, passage in *QE II*. The voyage itself was not without drama: we had to heave to in mid-Atlantic on the edge of a hurricane when a succession of 90 ft waves bore down upon us. We were wakened on the first night of the storm by the crashing of potted plants and glasses as they were swept off the dressing table. Even more alarming was a swish and spray which drenched the stateroom. To our relief, but dismay, a bottle of champagne had popped. It was as fierce a sea as I had ever seen, even from a ship as large as *QE II*. After initial instability, we both found our sea-legs and some perverse enjoyment in being among the few 'survivors' in the Princess Grill. I was invited to the bridge and heard from the master, Captain Ridley, just how close a call it had been. Had he failed to hold her head into the sea at the height of the storm (and there was little up his sleeve after steaming full ahead on the starboard screw), we might have broached and been overwhelmed.

Perhaps taking advantage of *QE II* rather than staying at my desk and flying over a few days later was a gesture of bravado. But these engagements could not be jeopardised – they were too important for British and European shipping – and I needed a break from the fetid atmosphere of the tenth floor. The *Oriana* storm in 1972 had heralded my chief executive years. Now this *QE II* storm, appropriately ferocious, would mark the beginning of the end. But I found a certain symbolism in our facing and surviving such an onslaught.

I found time, too, for reflection. I did not understand how Oliver Brooks had been influenced, coerced or persuaded to deny me: what had happened during those ten days in August? Cromer and Saunders would not have fallen in with Inchcape's scheme had not definitely Brooks, and probably Adams, supported him. Brooks's conversion remains an enigma, but all his working life he had been an Inchcape man: perhaps he simply decided to 'cling to nurse'. Adams was easier to fathom: he would, of course, see it as his duty to follow his chairman.

QE II was thirty-six hours late in reaching New York – but it was a sparkling day as we came under the Verrazano Bridge sharing a farewell glass of champagne with friends made on the passage. As soon as we secured I had to be rushed off in order to get the shuttle to Washington for an early meeting with Bill Johnson, the shipping policy man at the White House. This entailed standing by in the bowels of the ship, dealing with immigration as the official boarded and then being whisked to a waiting car. While I dashed through, Mona found herself faced with a barrage of press photographers and journalists clamouring for a story. 'It was a great experience – no I was not frightened – I had every confidence in Captain Ridley. Yes, I would certainly sail on *QE II* again – a fine ship and the ship's company did a very good job.' Later that evening Mona saw the television reports. Lord Boothby: 'I was on my knees.' Others reported a frightening experience, with 'the Brits singing Nearer my God to Thee.' With its overtones of the *Titanic*, all this was much better grist to the newshounds' mill than Mona's studiedly cool response.

Following my delegation's visit to Washington earlier in the year we had now determined to take the argument on US maritime policy, or the lack of it, to a wider audience. I had a full programme on the Hill and went the rounds of 'the usual suspects' and then shuttled back to New York, where, with the help and advice of colleagues I had invited an impressive range of opinion-formers to a dinner on board *Canberra*, berthed at Pier 80 for the occasion. It was a glittering event – the backdrop of the Empire State Building and other skyscrapers was spectacular. Michael Medlicott was a very efficient staff officer, while Captain Scott Masson and the ship's staff were superb. It was a great opportunity to show off *Canberra*; she was, that night, the flagship of British shipping.

My speech was a good one (see page 300). The message was

designed to be a marker for a range of initiatives planned for the months ahead to secure an improved understanding with the Americans. I felt stirred up so that I spoke with some passion. Congressman Murphy, a leading figure in the maritime field, was sufficiently impressed to enter the speech in the records of Congress.

Almost as memorable as the formal banquet was the party afterwards – Bo and Janeke Madsen took us off to a Greek restaurant. We danced and drank and smashed as many plates as any Greek. It certainly helped me to unwind and to appreciate that I did have many friends and was regarded with some affection and respect.

I had left the UK with my *Canberra* speech unpolished. I arranged with Betty Fairclough that I would work on it on *QE II*, and develop the final version by telex. Something of which I was not aware was that she had been subjected to unexpected hassle in communicating with me. She avoided making it an issue by using Bulk Shipping and Anglo Nordic channels, but it was unhappy that within the chairman's sphere this pressure was applied to her. The incident left a bad taste in the mouth, as it came perilously close to an attempt to scupper my duty to the industry.

The *Canberra* speech marked perhaps the most important démarche by a European shipowner for some years and its intent and content had been widely canvassed beforehand with our international colleagues. As the (new) chief executive of P&O, it should have been of great importance to Inchcape, for our container lines, and cruising interests especially, were at severe risk. He simply ignored it, together with my report on the Washington visit, as being one of 'the extraneous issues on which ABM spends too much time'. For the rest of this critical year for P&O too much of its management was played out in personal terms. I had become something of a lame duck, while my colleagues, acutely conscious of their supine acquiescence, tended to protect themselves by cross-checking ideas and decisions with the emerging kitchen cabinet.

For seven years I had had responsibility for and a total commitment to P&O which I could not disregard. At the end of September, continuing the practice pursued through those years, I presented the monthly management report to the board. We had sold two OBOs and five general cargo ships; Associated Bulk Carriers had settled a long standing claim against Broken Hill in Australia for $4.75m; we had reached agreement with Boeing that they would pick up all losses on the experimental London to Zeebrugge jetfoil service, and we had concluded the purchase of *Kungsholm* (to be named *Sea Princess*) – significant confirmation of our intention to develop the cruising business.

These were not the results of dramatic decisions taken in September 1978, when the supposedly 'dire' situation came to light. They were the result of carefully considered assessment over the preceding months, a balancing of risk and potential return and decisions taken after wide consultation: in other words, part of a continuing conservative and professional management process.

Increasingly I realised how very difficult it was going to be to work within the new system. I endeavoured to operate as an executive managing director and inevitably, in the light of history, I had a view or, as I would put it, a constructive suggestion to make on matters not within the bounds of my new role. Inchcape would hear my view, tuck it away for future use and then frequently and rudely shout that it was none of my business any more and I should stick to what the board had asked me to do.

Energy *was* within my bailiwick. Because of the unexpectedly high front-end costs of developing Beatrice, the scale of our early contributions might be too large for comfort. As already demonstrated, I had no objection, in principle, and subject to certain conditions, to selling, if the price was right, and in October I so advised Leo Pliatski, Permanent Secretary at the Department of Trade.

But when, in November, the board was persuaded to sell, provided we received simply reimbursement of expenditure to date, I balked. The case was put, in a surprising volte-face, by Oliver Brooks, surrendering within a few weeks much of what he, himself, had played such a large part in building up. I argued that this should be no fire-sale and that we should pace our negotiations to ensure as much as possible of an auction. I felt that in the light of Beatrice's close inshore position we should be aiming for a substantial premium. There were enough players looking for concessions in a politically stable environment; the oil price had started to move and our losses on the roundabouts made it imperative that we win on the swings. There was a general election looming and a growing disinclination in the country to endure more years of trade union rule. The economy, freer trade and 'less government' might well signal a change in the business environment. I had rarely argued a more propitious case. Derek Hall joined me, declaring that to decide on such a price would be bound to colour negotiations.

Astonishingly, there was little if any contribution from other directors, who seemed overborne by worries about matters external to P&O. It was a time for steady nerves, but they were in short supply. Derek and I lost the debate.

Inchcape seemed to regard Beatrice as a millstone rather than as a truly remarkable story, one in which success had rewarded the bold. The fact that the negotiations were protracted, that in the meantime the second Iranian oil price hike struck and that BP finally offered several times the board's original target price does not exonerate the judgement of the directors. Luck saved the day.

In December 1978, Inchcape expressed the hope that I was not overdoing it. When I expressed some surprise, he referred to 'your health problem'. This turned out to be the haemochromatosis of which he must have been aware for years. It had not inhibited me in 1972 or since. His concern was touching, but in the circumstances I was wary of Greeks bearing gifts, and not surprised when it emerged that he was hinting at retirement on the grounds of ill-health. I trust I was able to express appropriate pleasure at this evidence of his thought for my well-being and the subject was taken no further.

Also in December Inchcape indicated that he considered management, particularly myself and Derek Hall, had been less than committed to the sale or joint-venturing of one or two of the Rheinstahl gas ships. Rubbish of course, but it appeared he had suddenly remembered a peg on which to hang an attack. Apparently John Maccoy, prior to his leaving P&O in September – three months earlier – had informed him that he had brought a proposal for sale to me and that I had turned it down. I explained, by reference to the board diary and management reports, that there was no foundation for such allegations. I expressed astonishment that John could have made any such suggestion. I contacted him and recorded in a memo to Inchcape that 'JGM regrets any misunderstanding [. . .] he acknowledged that the negotiations were probably as effective and productive as they could have been. JGM did not recall having said to you that he had brought forward a proposition for sale of one or two of these vessels which was in any way firm and that certainly there was no question of my having "turned down" any idea he put before me.' I concluded: 'I thought it would be helpful for us both to set out this record.' Despite a subsequent and very comprehensive review by Derek Hall detailing the complete history of the Rheinstahl project, Inchcape did not acknowledge my memo and clung to his misguided version.

Although interest rates were high, inflation rising again and the 'winter of discontent' was approaching, our circumstances in the last two months of 1978 were not deteriorating. Markets were difficult, but the values of both ships and properties were above book and, while the energy scene was uncertain, the risks for P&O were all on the upside. For those prepared to see, the signs of improvement were there. Yet, in January 1979, running true to form, the majority of the board bowed to what had now become an all-powerful Brooks/Inchcape axis and agreed to sell P&O Oil Corporation of North America. Again the price was to be recovery of expenditure to date – a mere $11m. I was very angry indeed.

The arrival of Ayatollah Khomeini on the scene had just thrown the world energy outlook into disarray. I argued that while we might decide in principle to sell, we should not start discussions for at least six months. It was quite evident that in all the turmoil of the market there was every likelihood that the oil price would be markedly higher in June than it was in January. The price per barrel was in the $14 range through 1978: in January, 1979, it was $15.50: in June, $23.20 and by the end of the year $30. The price soared to $40 in 1980 and remained in the upper $30s throughout 1981.

Fortunately the complexity of title in the Louisiana, Oklahoma and Texas parishes and the need to prove clear title overcame the Brooks/Inchcape plan and the sale of the Devon oil interests was only concluded a year later. Thus the timing was, as it turned out, nigh perfect. The price was some $130m and of course the board took credit for its skill in selling assets at such an immense book profit.

Dick Adams became joint managing director in January 1979 – his prize for loyalty.

By now the reasons why my colleagues had followed Inchcape were becoming clearer. He had presented a case to them so seductive and rewarding as to persuade them either to excuse or to ignore its lack of integrity or wisdom. Having accepted it, they had to live with it. They were going down the dangerous and slippery slope where it is not the actions of bullies which keeps them in power; rather it is the collusion of ordinarily decent people who should have known better and acted differently, but did not.

During the early months of 1979 there was, at least outwardly, an appearance of work as normal. I was very involved in our Overseas Containers investment. OCL, too, had felt the impact of the strong

Deutschmark and its collapse in profit during 1978 directly affected P&O. I was discussing with Alan Hatchett possible developments in the South American trade and with Roland Escombe the opportunities in China. The Foreign Shipping Policy Committee was, as ever, embroiled in UNCTAD and the Trans-Siberian Railway and I was engaged in handing over the chair to Henry Karsten of Ocean in anticipation of my appointment as vice-president of GCBS. I was, even in early February, preparing for P&O's annual general meeting in June and considering papers for another International Tanker Safety Conference in the autumn.

But the ground was slipping from under my feet.

Out of the blue, Henry Keswick of Jardine Matheson approached me to see whether I might be interested in leaving P&O right away and taking on a senior post in Rennies Holdings, Jardine's South African arm. This was both comforting and reassuring. Mona was excited. I took a week's leave and we went to Johannesburg and Durban to meet Charles Fiddian-Green of Rennies and, as it happened, David Newbigging and John Hayman from Hong Kong, Jardines' headquarters. The job would be that of shipping director in Durban with a seat on the main board in succession to Guy Radmore, a friend from years earlier. Jardines wanted a new face at the top table, someone with a track record outside the rather inward-looking, defensive atmosphere so prevalent in South Africa at the time. Although a relatively low-key start, it seemed there could be considerable potential. We got a warm welcome in Durban from Ivor Edwardes (ex Mackinnons, Calcutta, and now Lord Kensington) and Francis Baker whom Mona had known in White River as a child.

In addition to hearing about the job, an important factor was the domestic one – housing and schools. We saw some lovely houses in Kloof; we raced up to see schools in the hills, first Hilton College, then Michaelhouse, whose headmster knew all about Mona from our old friend Wendy Rosselli in Zimbabwe. James would be happy at either and if Gillian went to St Anne's she could take her horse with her. Alastair would have to stay in the UK as he would soon be starting his university career.

South Africa was not then as isolated as it became in the 1980s but Mandela was still in gaol, the school boycotts had created much tension and there was widespread talk of hedging of bets, getting funds out of the country, etc. Nevertheless, there were many of our friends, who were liberals and working for improvement in the political sphere (although at the same time living the privileged life that the system allowed.) There were many attractions – a clean break from P&O, a new life in an exciting environment; for Mona there was a particular family pull, the life-style would be very much better, we could have five years of a new sense of freedom for the children. It is strange, today, to recall our use, then, of the term 'freedom'.

We flew back full of enthusiasm, perhaps a reflection of the warmth of our reception. Then there was the most unexpected twist. It wasn't only because it began to seem unreasonable to ship Gillian's horse Firefly all that way! We thought long and hard and finally concluded that while it might not be a bad decision to go, it might not be the better course. The first consideration was, I believe, that we were both disinclined to do anything which might be interpreted as running away and secondly, I was worried about re-entry to the UK business scene after five years abroad. Mona, bless her, despite all the attractions for her and for the children, came down against the move and it was, thank goodness, very much a joint decision.

Henry Keswick was understanding. Jardines had invested a lot of time and some expense and it was disappointing to let them down. I have always been most grateful to Henry and his colleagues for alerting me to the opportunities which were available.

The final trigger for my leaving P&O was a very personal one. Betty Fairclough had seen a scribbled 'speaking note' which was evidently for the GCBS hierarchy. It disclosed that Inchcape had withdrawn his support for my nomination as vice-president. Perhaps it had never been there. He had, after all, dissembled for months. He offered no explanation for going back on his undertaking. Given my knowledge of his initiative at the GCBS, it was his attempt to put the onus on others for his withdrawing my candidacy which was immediately sickening. I had a quick talk with my lawyer Stuart Menzies of Allen & Overy, who advised me to sit tight and let 'them' make the running. Meanwhile he did his homework.

Inchcape's varied efforts to steer me to resignation would have been laughable were they not so pathetic. He might as well have said that I should have known that his September 1978 undertakings were simply window-dressing designed to give him time to erode my position so that I would fade away before I could claim any credit as the results began to improve. It was indicative of his level of preparations that when I said I would put my lawyers in touch with Freshfields, he immediately replied 'we won't be using Freshfields for this, they are too close. You should speak to Herbert Smith'.

I recall that over the next ten days I was somewhat detached. Allen & Overy negotiated the terms of severance and they seemed not unreasonable in financial terms at more or less three times salary to be applied as far as possible to pension. I accepted more in sorrow than in anger. Somehow it didn't seem to matter very much and I wasn't going to give them any scope for attack. Looking back, the withdrawal of stock options was slippery and I suspect it was not valid; certainly it was mean-spirited. The amazing thing about the whole approach taken by Inchcape and Crichton at this time was their readiness to disregard my thirty-two years' service and particularly my last seven years. Crichton was overheard remarking to Inchcape: 'Well that went very smoothly, I thought he might be difficult.'

The executive directors were protecting their own position to a man. They kept their heads down and I did my best to emphasise to Inchcape the quality of a number of the other people I was leaving behind; people such as Jim Lindars, Andrew Robb, Steve Carter, Euan Geddes, Robin Sanders and others who had been in Planning, Finance and Energy. Of particular concern was P&O Australia, where Bob Rose and his chairman, Alvin Burton Taylor, having done so well, were dismayed at the turn of events as it affected them. They did not relish having Spanton imposed upon them and it was little comfort for them to hear Inchcape's dismissive comment: 'They put up with Nancarrow for years, they can put up with HFS.'

I informed Inchcape that I would have a drinks party on my last evening. There was a bit of bluster and protest, but I paid no attention (nor did the catering staff) and on 20 March we had open house on the tenth floor. Mona, thank goodness, held my hand because it was a very emotional occasion with a great turnout of colleagues from all levels. (It was nice to hear fifteen years later at the new *Oriana* ceremonies that the head telephonist had been there: 'You were always so courteous on the phone.') Regrettably my departure did affect adversely a number of careers in P&O and in fairly short order many good executives, male and female, moved on.

I was afforded the Whitehall Court flat as a base from which to clear my desk. My sadness in leaving was mixed with anger as the meanness of Inchcape and his minions began to exert pressure. My facilities, the flat, car, and secretarial were soon threatened. I maintained a dignified and reasonable attitude and in the end achieved a fairly tidy parting; but however tidy, nothing could compensate, then, for the feeling that I had lost my company.

Demise of the Dream Team

*The Earl of Inchcape's memory is quite clearly not to be trusted. Mr Justice
Walton giving judgment in the High Court in the case of Burmah Oil v The
Bank of England on 3 July 1981.*

*Kenneth doesn't like anyone getting too close to him. Mackay Tallack,
Chief Executive of Inchcape & Company and a cousin of Lord Inchcape.*

Life has been so good to me since my departure from P&O that it has
become second nature to gloss over the most unpleasant incidents.
But I realise that I have raised a number of questions which, if the
reader is to make sense of the whole, I must attempt to answer.

I have found myself dismayed – dismayed that certain incidents
took place at all. When they occurred I dismissed them as isolated
outbursts, but I now realise that they had a deeper significance; that
they were the symptoms of a chronic malaise in the relationship
between Inchcape and myself and that their effect was cumulative. It
certainly never occurred to me that I was being progressively undermined.

Inchcape's attitude to P&O was feudal; he saw, as his birthright,
the preservation of the Group in the form created by his
grandfather. I believe that in his mind I grew to figure as a threat, to
his prestige and to his power. It was an ill-fated misconception for us
both. I saw him as a respected pillar of the City, a chairman I was
glad to serve, and my aim as chief executive was to make P&O work
successfully. I poured all my energies into that task and paid too
little attention to the underlying inconsonance between us.

When Sir Donald Anderson was chairman of P&O in the 1960s,
Inchcape proposed a merger and was rebuffed – it is said abruptly.
Could this be the explanation for his attitude at the time of the
Bovis bid? Was he tongue-in-cheek when he supported me and led
the call for a go-it-alone stand? To launch his full-scale bid for P&O
only a week after publicly declaring, on 24 September 1972, that a
merger between Inchcape and P&O 'would never work', clearly
indicated that his preparations must have been well advanced. It is

reasonable to conclude that my opposition, offering a credible new management and thus a third option – P&O's independence, robbed Inchcape of a straight fight between himself and Bovis.

Without my support, Inchcape's renewed bid in November could not succeed. My fellow dissenters and I had already received the backing of the majority of stockholders and the plaudits of the media: 'Let the new management get on with the job.' Even though P&O had rejected his offer, Inchcape emerged with his reputation enhanced: *he* had initially stood against Bovis. In settling for the chairmanship, one can only surmise that he took the pragmatic course.

I see now that, on being appointed, he assumed a continuation of his accustomed management style which, for the P&O board, would entail a damaging return to the old ways. P&O was *his* and the Inchcape dynasty restored, hence in his dealings with me he saw no need to discuss or to explain his actions. The preservation of the distinctions of rank became the order of the day. He paid only lip-service to the changes being made to ensure a more professional management.

As we cleared the decks and started P&O on its new course, I had no reason to look beyond his public reputation, which I, in common with the City and the company, saw as a bonus for us. Only gradually did I come to realise that he lacked substance.

The first sign of trouble was when, in March 1974, eighteen months after Inchcape became chairman, Denys Brown suffered a second breakdown. My handling of this crisis (see chapter eight) resulted in overt tension between Inchcape and me, which disturbed all the non-executive directors apart from Crichton, who rejoiced in stoking the fire. Both Denholm and Saunders were open and frank with me. Denholm was appalled at Crichton's 'aggressive attitude', and Jake Saunders felt that Inchcape had 'gone astray'. But neither seemed able adequately to convey his views to the chairman.

The unfolding deterioration in our relationship was compounded by Inchcape's tendency to rewrite history in his own image. I, so absorbed in and so enjoying the job itself, did not let this daunt me and, perhaps more important and unfortunate, did not, through a sense of loyalty, share my concerns with colleagues in general.

With the public unravelling of the crisis at Burmah Oil in 1975, Inchcape, its non-executive vice-chairman, suffered gruelling public exposure. Tragically, as the attacks on his reputation continued, he escaped into alcohol. My secretaries, Betty Fairclough and Pat Scrimshaw-Wright, manipulated the diaries, kept people and telephone calls at bay and would alert the trusted commissionaire to provide a discreet escort if required. There were occasions when Inchcape's aggressive outbursts, often almost incoherent, could be heard in the outer office and the doors to our suite had to be kept closed.

At home I unburdened to Mona and to our old friend Gordon Bisset, who was sufficiently detached to provide a cool head. But I felt I had no option but to be loyal to and supportive of Inchcape, for to have exposed him would have reflected badly on P&O, and, of course, he was to be the next leader of the UK shipping industry. What misplaced loyalty led me to conceal the problem? I can only say that in the mid-1970s one just did; it was as simple as that.

Inchcape sent me two handwritten notes on 23 February 1975. The first asked that a paper explaining stockholders' perks on the ferries should be put to the Executive Committee and to the board. This small marketing ploy, to match concessions by competitors, had been referred to by an acquaintance and he had been caught out by not knowing of it. Of course this was regrettable and in an ideal world should not have happened. An error, yes, but certainly not what Inchcape called 'another example of your cavalier approach'.

The second note was more serious. 'In view of trouble over your article in FT of 21 February', Inchcape wanted to 'avoid repetition of this type of article'. In fact the piece, by *Financial Times* journalist James Ensor, was well-researched, well-written and positive about P&O's future. Ensor had interviewed me, and what may have piqued Inchcape was a reference to A. B. Marshall as 'a boardroom rebel [who] proves his point'.

The significance of the two memos lay in their tone and construction. The first was reasonably civil, if rather petty in content. The second was aggressive and in no way within the context of advice and counsel. The handwriting suggests that the first was penned in the morning and the second in the afternoon. It was becoming increasingly clear that Inchcape was of little value after lunch.

Ten weeks after the article had appeared, and after I had assured Inchcape that there was absolutely no foundation for his concern, Robin Sanders reported to me with some dismay a conversation with the chairman at the inauguration of the Montrose Offshore Base. Sanders had been pressed hard to acknowledge that I was jealous of

Inchcape's position and that, to ensure I got all the credit, had deliberately set up the February *Financial Times* interview without his knowledge. Inchcape said that Cromer and Crichton had written to him to complain.

On 2 May, unfortunately a Friday afternoon – the worst possible timing, Inchcape asked for a meeting. I played it by the book. I asked for clarification of the Inchcape/Sanders conversation in Montrose which quite properly had been reported to me. I had found it uncomfortable that he should inform Robin of criticism of me by non-executive directors. I had not been aware of the letters from Cromer and Crichton and asked to see them. 'There were no letters,' said Inchcape, 'but all the non-executives have complained about the *Financial Times* article.' Why then, I asked, had he not advised me at the time, rather than raising the matter with our public relations man two months later?

I also expressed concern that he had agreed to our finance director, Oliver Brooks, joining the new Burmah board without telling me. 'I don't tell you how to run *Canberra* and you don't tell me how to deal with the board. I have been around the City a long time you know.'

I was distressed about the strains between us. I insisted that, surely, we were batting on the same side. Inchcape cut in: 'You have always been suspect. I stood by you when you slaughtered Peter Parry and I wasn't going to have another case with Harry Beazley.' When I protested, he conceded that my twelve-month-old judgement had been sound in both cases, but he clung to his own misinterpretation of the facts by claiming that *he* had been instrumental in saving Beazley, 'because we [himself and Crichton] knew that you and Adams were trying to get him out'.

Having been almost capsized on this tack, he returned to my suggestion of six months earlier that I should take over the chair of the Executive Committee. 'You wanted to use my appointment in GCBS to seize power, to get me out and get control yourself. They [the City] are not going to allow another Burmah nor another Nicky Williams. Everyone in the City regards you as a wild man – I have been around and I know.' I asked who in the City. 'Flemings, Barings, Hambros.' I asked why. 'I don't know, but probably because you make quick decisions.' I asked if any such quick decisions had gone wrong. He blustered for a moment, then said: 'IOS [International Offshore Services] for one.' I reminded him that Inchcape &

Co. considered the sale price 'ridiculously high'. This threw him into further disarray. Much later, when presenting the 1979 accounts as chairman and CEO, he struck a truer note: 'We took the view in 1974 that this [off-shore] sector of the industry was going to become seriously over-tonnaged and we were able to sell our UK-based operation before rates collapsed.'

As for my being dubbed a wild man by the City, had I not been on the board of Commercial Union for over five years and was I not chairman of its UK Committee and a member of its Finance & General Purposes Committee? I too had 'been around' in the City. I was in touch with a very wide range of City people. I was a governor of the London Business School with Lord Plowden as chairman and Jim Ball as principal, and I was a member of the City Advisory Panel, working with Sir Leslie O'Brien, Governor of the Bank of England. Hardly wild; sober, perhaps.

Inchcape pressed on: 'You did your best to hold up my appointment – it took you six weeks after the battle was over – we have never trusted you.'

'You have referred frequently throughout this interview to we – who are "we"?' I asked. There was a pause before he replied: 'Andrew Crichton and me.'

I asked why this had taken two and a half years to emerge.

'I know you don't like Andrew and he was equivocal over Bovis.'

'No one could have been more unequivocal than Crichton – let the record stand,' I protested, and stated that I considered Crichton to be a baleful influence within the board.

He again referred to 'that McKinsey paper' which 'purported to be my terms of reference'. He ignored the fact that he had been very fully consulted and that, with him in the chair, the board had approved both his and my job descriptions. 'I don't like these formal documents and will be putting a paper to the Chairman's Committee to discuss the workings of the Executive Committee and by implication the CEO.' I submitted that if recommendations were to be made I should have the opportunity to contribute. 'They won't be recommendations – they will be decisions.' I reminded him that as an appointed member of the committee I had a right to participate and that the committee had no authority in such matters, only the board had jurisdiction. It seemed then appropriate to call it a day.

Why had I not terminated the meeting immediately I realised his condition? Inchcape's outbursts always followed the same pattern; building gradually to a crescendo then falling, probably through exhaustion, to a diminuendo. Had I walked out, undoubtedly I would have been accused of refusing to listen to his 'counsel and advice'. I judged that the best I could do was to remain studiedly calm.

On the morning of Monday 5 May, Inchcape handed me the papers he proposed to put to the Chairman's Committee on the following day, including a draft memo dated 25 March 'covering improvements in the working relationship between Inchcape and ABM'. I immediately welcomed the opening statement: 'The CEO to keep the chairman fully informed on all matters ... so that the chairman has early warning of all likely events good and bad. The chairman to keep the CEO fully informed of all he hears in the City or elsewhere likely to be of importance directly or indirectly to the P&O Group.' I skimmed over the rest of the memo which might have been regarded as innocuous had it not been for a draft covering note for the committee. I was so disheartened by its content that I asked for another meeting later in the day.

I put it to Inchcape, as I had done on a number of occasions, that it was manifestly untrue and unjust for him to say in this note that I had 'demanded' that I take over the chair of the Executive Committee (the change had in any case been *suggested* in November, seven months earlier, and had not been pursued when he said he wished to retain the role). He repeated, as if it were still a live issue, that it showed I was attempting to push him out and that it was only by having him in the chair of the Executive Committee that I had been stopped from 'misleading his non-executive chairman and directors as had happened at Burmah'.

Inchcape abruptly conceded that as I had so many objections he would not put the paper to the Chairman's Committee, but would report verbally. He then told me that, as the meeting would be an informal one confined to non-executive directors, it would be inappropriate for me to attend.

Two days later I received 'Notes on the meeting of the Chairman's Committee'. Not only had Inchcape reneged by handing over all the papers to the committee, but he had added another item to the agenda – the allegation that I objected to Eric Drake's appointment to the board, to become effective on 1 June 1976. The truth was that I had most warmly welcomed the prospect of Drake's joining when it was mooted early in 1974. I heard nothing more until Inchcape's reference to an exchange of letters between himself and Eric Drake about dates for meetings during 1976. My 'objection' had been that on such an important matter the chairman might at least have mentioned to his chief executive that, after two years' silence, we were now going to be able to appoint a senior figure to the board. This was translated into: 'If the managing director now feels he does not want Eric Drake to be elected then that's too bad because he is coming and ABM will have to live with it.'

On 12 June 1975, Inchcape responded to my memos of 6 and 12 May, which had set the facts straight on the most important issues raised in his earlier Chairman's Committee papers. His distortions of the truth were quite disturbing. He refused to see either justification for what I did or truth in what I said. It seemed to me that he had, as prosecutor, judge and jury, decided on a hanging verdict.

Apart from stubbornly declaring yet again that the sale of IOS had been a bad mark for the new P&O management, the main issue was a repetition of the allegation that in December 1972 I had tried to prevent him becoming chairman and 'plotted' with others so to do:

> Your note is correct but as it had been agreed that I should be
> appointed immediately after the Inchcape bid had been cleared,
> a special board meeting should have been held before, or on
> the first working day after Christmas, to elect me as chairman.

This begged so many questions. Did it imply that rejection of the Inchcape bid was a formality or that the bid itself was not genuine?

It emerged that Inchcape considered Donald Anderson had the chair in his gift. His was certainly an important influence in defeating the Bovis proposal, but DFA in fact had no standing other than as a retired elder statesman.

We all wanted the situation to develop whereby Inchcape could become chairman of P&O, but as a public company we had to treat his own company's bid seriously and could not anticipate events. Schroders did not give their formal advice on the bid until 19 December.

Inchcape alleged that I had no personal contact with him at the time, but my diary records that, although Inchcape was bidding for P&O and had, therefore, to be kept at arm's length, I met him twice in November, on the 21st and 30th; I spoke to him and wrote on 19 December and, on 3 January 1973, we met to discuss the agenda for the next day's board meeting at which he would be elected chairman. Denys Brown and I were in touch with his office throughout this period. There was no shortage of constructive contact. I simply did not understand the allegation that when Crichton had come to see me it was to 'ensure' that Inchcape was going to be appointed.

Inchcape's memo went on to say it had been decided that the Chairman's Committee would be reconstructed to consist only of the chairman and the non-executives, 'but will not be a formal board committee'. Yet 'I see no reason to form a special Salaries Committee as the Chairman's Committee will deal with directors' emoluments. . . .' So much for trying to introduce professional management and ensure good corporate governance.

Then he raised the 'alleged' split of responsibilities between chairman and chief executive. At the board meeting on 10 January 1973, under Inchcape's chairmanship, a Company Organisation paper had been approved and thus established our formal working relationship, including an outline of the chairman's responsibilities:

The chairman, elected by the board, has three main functions:

– To act as a constitutional monarch, representing the board in relations with the stockholders and the outside world in general.

– To act as a counter-weight to the managing director by focusing and conveying to him criticisms or suggestions from the board as a whole, from leaders of opinion in the City and from stockholders.

– In addition he will undertake specific responsibilities as may be arranged and will generally provide advice and counsel to the managing director.

For the student of management technique, it is interesting to note our relatively simple, one might say almost naive approach. But these were early days in the realm of job descriptions for top management, let alone for non-executive chairmen.

Two and a half years after the board had put this blueprint on file, Inchcape raised it as something that he 'had never liked' or *by implication* approved. Throughout, he had been dismissive of anything which smacked of the theory of management. He had always operated by intuition and patronage, and deplored what he called the 'throwing out of history'. A McKinsey-type executive committee running the company on a day-to-day basis in accordance with defined levels of authority and responsibility was not for him. 'It's not necessary, everyone should know what to do without having to write it down.' Yet in the brave new world of 1973 he had been involved in defining and establishing those guidelines for management and corporate governance which were designed to meet the complex issues of the day. Management and I, as chief executive, had done our best to operate within that remit and it was destructive for the chairman now to imply that he had never really understood what he was taking on.

As the exchange of memos continued I was becoming somewhat anxious. On the morning of 20 June, Lewis Collins, the very proper company secretary, remarked: ' Sandy, it seems to me that the chairman is gunning for you.'

I sought advice from Rowley Cromer with whom, as I have said, I had a good working relationship and who was well aware of the strain of being chief executive to Inchcape's chairman. His response was that when the going got rough I should relax a bit and not feel that I had to solve everything myself. He was remarkably frank about Kenneth Inchcape: he did not think he had maintained his early promise in business, rather he felt he was over-conscious of his status and 'perhaps we shouldn't be surprised; after all, his grandfather created P&O', but throughout he was sympathetic: 'He's had a difficult time and he is conscious of his inadequacies.'

Cromer was quite clear as to his own concept of the function of a non-executive chairman and thought that Inchcape was making it very difficult for me to operate. He was to spend the following weekend with Inchcape and 'would endeavour to get to the bottom of this'. Cromer emphasised repeatedly that, as far as he knew, Inchcape fully supported what was certainly the view of all the non-executive directors (apart from Crichton, for whom he could not speak but whom he regarded as 'carrying no weight') that 'you, Sandy, are doing a first class job as chief executive.' We discussed the possibility of some other form of management structure which might give Inchcape more of a role. Cromer demurred: 'He doesn't have the knowledge.' For the time being I was encouraged, but his parting words flagged my fate: 'You know, Sandy, it's very difficult for me to support you against him. After all, I was at school with him.'

There was some respite when Inchcape was on holiday for a few weeks, but in mid-July we had another stormy meeting. He did not appreciate my detailed rebuttal of the inaccurate facts in his memo of 12 June: 'You would be well advised not to press the point on IOS as this does not show you up well.' Then, amazingly, he returned to my letter of 19 December 1972, in which I had written:

Finally it is I know of great importance to your colleagues on the Board and to myself to know that you are going to remain with us. The early lead you personally gave at the end of August has enhanced your position throughout P&O.

'Because of this paragraph I circulated it round the City because we considered it showed up that you could well be plotting with Morgan Grenfell to get another chairman in,' he said, telling me that he and Crichton had had a meeting with Hambros and Barings at which the suspicion was expressed that I was negotiating with Morgans and 'we sent Crichton to see you to ascertain what was happening.' My immediate response was 'Rubbish.' We had a ready-made, viable chairman-in-waiting and whatever lobbying Hambros or Barings, or even Morgans, might be doing in the City and through the press the thought of anyone other than Inchcape as chairman simply did not arise.

The examples I have given of the strain put on our relationship by his drinking are by no means the most extreme, and my relief when he finally became much more disciplined about his habit was overwhelming. Inchcape's involvement with the GCBS – particularly during his presidency from March 1976 until March 1977 – must have influenced this restraint. It certainly eased the pressure on me and we managed to develop what I felt was a tolerable *modus vivendi*, always subject of course to the now familiar ups and downs. I was prepared to concede that those long months of tension must have been an aberration and that there was no reason why our delicately-balanced working relationship should not hold. Indeed, as I have said, the first half of 1978 was an exceptionally constructive period. Many illustrious names in world shipping were in difficulty – Furness Withy, Salen and Ocean among others – but we were still very much in business and beginning to climb out of the trough.

The dénouement of August 1978 was a bolt from the blue. It was said that in the 'serious situation' resolute action was required and Lord Inchcape was taking over as chief executive. Profits for the half year were reported at £1.8m. Yet, having 'thrown in the kitchen sink', and as a result of action already planned, already taken and to be continued through the remaining months of the year, full-year profits for 1978 were reported, just after I finally left, at £18.4 million. In 1979 profits recovered to £38.7m and in 1980 advanced to £47.1m.

Jake Saunders had been so concerned at the deteriorating atmosphere that, early in 1979, he contemplated resignation. I was glad he did not go then, for he was an enormous support during my last months. However, 'sickened' by the vicious way in which Inchcape and Crichton behaved, he offered his resignation when I left. Inchcape persuaded him that to withdraw so soon after my departure would be damaging to the company; Jake resigned in September 1979, as the board turned inward again. I dropped him a note of appreciation for his friendship and support and remarked on the low-key manner of his departure. He replied: 'Neither low nor high key would have been of my choosing, but low was not unexpected, perhaps because there's little lofty left!'

In January 1980, Cromer retired. Denholm was appointed a deputy chairman and two new non-executives were introduced, to be followed by the appointment of Jeffrey Sterling in February. Denys Brown and Harry Beazley were both pensioned off later in the year.

The Energy saga came to an end in 1980 when Inchcape reported at the AGM on the sale of Beatrice and the other North Sea and US oil and gas interests. The prices secured were generally acknowledged to be excellent. The fact that the oil price had risen sharply *after* the decision to sell had been taken did not detract from the validity of that statement. But all those close to the process knew the extent to which P&O had been favoured by fortune. The directors had been prepared to sell for a pittance – merely recovery of expenditure. The improvement on the target price reflected neither skill nor understanding on the part of a board ostensibly enjoying top quality oil and financial expertise.

In March 1981 Inchcape, having 'completed' the job which he had taken on in September 1978, stood down as chief executive and that great survivor Adams took over. Little was done that had not been in process or at least planned, but, understandably, the period was represented as one in which 'a firm grip was taken' and decisive action implemented to staunch losses, 'dispose of dogs', and so on. The results were helped as much by the solid performance of the shipping and construction businesses built up during the years since 1972 as by the windfall from the sale of energy interests.

Drake and Crichton retired in June 1981 and, two years on, the board looked very different.

In 1982, Inchcape announced at the AGM, at which profits for 1981 were reported at £41m, that he would cease to be chairman after the annual meeting in 1983, but would remain on the board as deputy chairman. Ian Denholm would be appointed executive chairman, Adams and Brooks would retire and three managing directors, Leach, Hall and Paris would be appointed. This harked back to the 1960s when Donald Anderson presided over a number of managing directors.

But this structure was never to be tested, for Trafalgar House, under Nigel Broackes, stepped in with a full-scale bid for P&O. A tragi-comedy then ensued. Inchcape withdrew his resignation and all proposed management changes were cancelled. It was evident that the reinstated team, 'called from retirement' and led by a chairman who had not succeeded in establishing personal credibility, would have a problem resisting Trafalgar.

Denholm, a decent man describing himself as a simple Glasgow ship manager, made it known that he did not now regard himself as the appropriate choice to succeed Inchcape. The latter is said to have gone to Henry Benson at the Bank of England to seek help. The Bank, surprised that Inchcape should have had so little confidence as to come to such a pass, suggested that he look no further than Jeffrey Sterling who had been on the P&O Board for eighteen months and who still, in Bank of England eyes, trailed clouds of glory following his masterly rescue of Town & City Properties. Inchcape was reported to be less than enthusiastic and it was abundantly clear that he had not taken the time to find out about his colleague's attributes. However, I understand he got Roland Escombe (his one-time fag at Eton and a member of the P&O board since 1980) to float the idea with Sterling who took twenty-four hours to respond that he would do the job provided Inchcape ceased to be directly involved with the company.

Inchcape and Brooks departed later in the year, as did Derek Hall. Sterling became chairman on his chosen terms in November and Adams stayed on until the middle of 1984, by which time the Trafalgar bid had been withdrawn after P&O had succeeded in having it referred to the Monopolies Commission.

By 1985, Rodney Leach, Malcolm Paris and Ian Denholm had gone and a new team was in place led very largely by executives whom Sterling had brought over when he merged Sterling Guarantee into P&O in 1984. The early years of this new look were promising – P&O was again being managed professionally.

Inchcape may have had a reputation for success as a seat-of-the-pants operator, but that was in an earlier and very different environment. In 1979, as Rodney Leach put it, 'P&O seemed to go back into the Dark Ages.' Inchcape dismissed modern management methods as complicated, time-consuming and cumbersome. He prided himself on choosing people, considered his personal endorsement to be sufficient and was cruel in his use of power when anyone crossed him. The directors who had been such enthusiastic supporters of the new post-Bovis P&O clung to their own positions, fell into line and accepted the rejection of the style of the previous decade. Such compromises lost them credibility and they did not survive.

What might I have done or not done to rectify or ameliorate the strains? Had I recognised that my relationship with Inchcape was on a collision course I could have confronted the situation in 1975. I was probably in as strong a position as ever at that time. I had delivered on my promises, while Inchcape had suffered a severe blow to his credibility through Burmah and was seen to be in some personal disarray. But I honestly do not recall the thought of 'it's him or me' crossing my mind. He had been my choice as chairman, I still thought we were on the same side and I continued to believe that good performance would convince him that he had nothing to lose and everything to gain. He was both a City and an Establishment figure. Again I played it by the book.

I had been nourished on a strong diet of integrity and the Scottish Presbyterian ethic: do your best, work hard, and you will be rewarded. Seeing that my duty lay in supporting Inchcape, could I have managed the situation and the man more elegantly? No, I could not. I had no problem with his re-hashes of the Executive's papers, with supporting him through his dark patches before the board, the staff, the industry, the City, the press. What I could not support was virtually being called a liar. I had to set the facts straight between us.

Were we alike in certain ways? It seems ridiculous – I the tall, lean, gaunt figure and he the squat turkey-cock. But there were degrees of obstinacy and pride in both. There was initially awe and respect on my side and a broad sense of history. On Inchcape's side there was certainly a sense of history, but with a narrow focus. And there was a subtle chemistry in the relationship. It wasn't antipathetic; at any rate I did not have any such feeling. Of course Inchcape was ultimately responsible for his own actions, but there remains a question-mark over the part that Crichton's persistent and insidious interference played in shaping Inchcape's attitude. I was admittedly establishing myself through my own efforts and there was certainly room for both of us, but perhaps I was getting 'too close'. His continual insistence on the prospect of a Burmah-type collapse may offer a clue. He must have known that such a threat was not real for P&O. However, if it could be so represented then he, Inchcape, could, in 1978, be the hero again, saving the company from a 'wild' chief executive.

Inchcape seemed to win in the short-term, because I lost the support of my executive colleagues and a majority of the non-executives. From the executives, perhaps given the example of 1972, one might have hoped for a more robust response. But no. Personal agendas were to the fore – a convenient smokescreen was that 'it had all been decided – how could I, on my own, stand up?' and in any case 'I couldn't have had much influence . . . I was too new, too old, too insecure.' The attitude of the non-executives was equivocal – at the end of the day they had to make a choice and they chose Inchcape, despite four out of five of them having expressed grave doubts about his knowledge and capability.

Did Inchcape achieve his objective in the long run? His vision faded. The hero of August 1972 and the inheritor of his grandfather's mantle did not have around him enough men of courage and quality. He and they lost credibility. The status and trappings were there for a time and he enjoyed public recognition, in the grand style, when *Canberra* returned with distinction from the Falklands in 1982. But the reality was that the demands upon him were too complex and the burden too heavy. It was a sad and inglorious end.

I see now that what I thought of as solely my, and P&O's, problem must have clouded Inchcape's other interests. He was a far from distinguished president of the GCBS; Burmah Oil was a disaster; soon after he lost P&O he also lost Inchcape & Co. – ousted by a board determined to modernise. Over the next few years he became a rather sad, even forlorn figure. I used to come across him on 'the circuit'. Not infrequently I would see, out of the corner of my eye, a small, diffident figure, circling round the reception to pop up at my shoulder grunting: 'Mmph, how are you Sandy?' Perhaps he was trying to make amends – I don't know. I still wonder if he recognised how wasteful our rows had been, and that his own circumstances might have been so much happier if we had managed to work together.

In P&O Jeffrey Sterling took up the challenge, galvanised the troops, put some backbone into the board and a renewed spirit took the company forward.

The history of P&O has continued to be bumpy. It was for years a classic cycle story. The return on capital has never been consistently satisfactory. Pedestrian, to say the least, in the 1960s, it soared relatively in the 1970s and subsided in the 1980s to another low. Since the mid-1980s the switchback has again been evident. The problems of operating what is primarily a shipping enterprise as a publicly-owned company remain formidable. I was fortunate to experience the whole gamut and to have the authority and responsibility when in the 1970s we moved P&O into a new range of performance.

PART THREE
Portfolio Years 1979–1995

11

Bestobell

I had always said to Mona that I was a shipping man. In part this was defensive – what else could I do? I knew my role and to date it had been a challenging and fairly happy one. As I realised this attitude would be put to the test, I also realised how fortunate I had been for thirty-two years, and particularly for the past ten, to have experienced such a wide range of activities, interests and responsibilities – perhaps an unusually wide range. I was fifty-four and felt that I was approaching the height of my powers. Significantly, anger was now added to my disappointment, and I was determined to succeed elsewhere, not simply for my own satisfaction but to 'show them'.

While the terms of my severance from P&O were under negotiation, I was grateful for the support of a number of friends and business associates. On the home front, Gordon Bisset was sound as ever and John Woodthorpe helpful and rational. Mark Turner and Alistair Frame of RTZ and Edwin Plowden at Tube Investments, Michael Verey of Schroders and Richard Westmacott of Hoare Govett all helped me to face the reality of my situation. Stuart Menzies of Allen & Overy, who had been a tower of strength during the Bovis battle, was again refreshingly down-to-earth in helping me clarify the issues.

Within a few days of the announcement that I was leaving P&O, I had a most welcome shot of encouragement in the shape of a letter from Maersk Mc-Kinney Møller. He wrote: 'This is a tragedy, not only for you, but for the industry' and went on to say that, in order to recognise the contribution I had made, he would like me to join his London board, the Maersk Co. Ltd. Much moved, I replied that, while greatly honoured, I must first sort myself out.

Then John Broadbent-Jones came into the picture. John – counsellor to chairmen and headhunter at the highest level – had worked with me to secure senior appointments in P&O's Energy Division, notably that of Alan Sykes, and we had made a habit of meeting periodically to 'shoot the breeze'. When we met for lunch, a long-standing engagement, John's first words were: 'Sandy, if I read the tealeaves correctly, you may be looking for some help shortly.' 'Yes John – tomorrow,' I replied. 'The difficult takes time, the impossible a little longer – I don't think you are in either category.'

After a few minutes' reflection over a glass of Chablis he said: 'What would you like? I believe I could fix you up as chief executive of a shipping company – but you may feel that's rather close to home.' He had Ellermans in mind, and although I had a warm regard for Dennis Martin-Jenkins, the chairman, it *would* have been too close.

'What about a nationalised industry?' he asked, and immediately answered his own question. 'No, not yet, you've got another private sector job in you before you should take that on – it's frustrating and demanding, however much you may feel you want to give something back to society.'

Then John pulled a third possibility out of his hat. 'It may be a bit late, but would you be interested in a mini-conglomerate – engineering, consumer goods, paint and so on – very widespread, sort of Empire company following the flag to Australia, South Africa . . .? But we're looking at a short list on Friday this week and I'd have to know in twenty-four hours if you want to throw your hat into the ring.'

This third possibility certainly engaged my interest, and when John told me that the company was Bestobell, formerly Bells Asbestos & Engineering, my interest quickened. I had known a number of the Bells executives in Calcutta, where the company had a good reputation, and I was attracted by its extensive international interests. John explained that a chairman and chief executive was required following a breakdown in confidence between the current non-executive chairman and the recently appointed managing director. It had been clear that one or other had to go and the decision was, marginally, in favour of keeping the latter. With the appointment of an executive chairman the present incumbent could 'retire' with some grace, while Donald Spencer, the managing director, was confident that in a relatively short period he would convince a new chairman and the board of his capacity to be an effective chief executive.

Although I was less than enchanted by the parts of the business and the locations of which I knew little – paints, 'window coverings', pumps, sophisticated electronic controls, steam valves and traps, waste disposal units, aviation components and so forth – and was apprehensive about management and relationships, I believed, broadly, that I had enough experience of how *not* to run a railroad to have a reasonable chance of getting it right. As lunch progressed John continued to make encouraging noises: 'The board has decided to move the head office from Slough to London, so you wouldn't have to alter your lifestyle. . . . I'm sure the salary would be satisfactory, and of course, the chairman has always had a Rolls-Royce.'

I was getting in rather deep, and with only a few days to go before a decision was required, I had to consult Mona. We had already agreed that my break with P&O represented a golden opportunity, perhaps the only one for us, to enjoy three months away, free from the demands of corporate life. When would I be expected to start? I had to meet Bestobell's directors – especially to get a feel as to whether I could work with the managing director. What was the company's financial position? Where did the main opportunities lie, and what might be the threats? Having spoken, we concluded that if Bestobell wanted me they would have to wait. Meanwhile my name could go forward and we would look carefully at any offer that might emerge.

The next day was taken up with my physical departure from P&O, but on the day after John Broadbent-Jones reported that my interest had been welcomed by Phil Dunkley and Pat Gaynor, the Bestobell non-executives charged with the selection of a successor to Sir Humphrey Browne, the outgoing chairman, who was also chairman of British Transport Docks Board (BTDB). So the pace hotted up – I took a liking to the people I met and soon there was little reference to other candidates.

Mona called a meeting with Broadbent-Jones. She felt that she had been given scant consideration in P&O days and sought reassurance that Bestobell's proposed move to London would take place sooner rather than later. We wanted a weekday pied-à-terre, ideally within the new office, and she was concerned that the daily travel to and from Slough should not continue for too long. She also asked a number of pointed questions to assure herself that I was not about to enter an antagonistic atmosphere.

For my own part, I was living with the pangs of rejection, as it were untimely ripp'd from the womb of thirty-two years, and felt strongly that the sooner I was back in the game the better for me and the family. Although there were special circumstances, which I will describe later, rapid reintegration into employment turned out to be highly beneficial. I appreciate that there are instances in which a case can be made for not taking the first opportunity – for holding on for a job of the scale and status which you consider you merit. Against that, regrettably, is 'out of sight, out of mind'. Is he being too choosy? Does he really need a job? Better, I think, to get back to work quickly. With application and a degree of luck it will work out well and in proving yourself you will attract attention and make progress. If not, it is easier to move on from a base than it is from lengthening unemployment.

The Bestobell board wanted me to move fast. A compromise of a sort was reached – I would be available in mid-May and would take over the chair after the AGM on 1 June. I had to complete the task of disentangling from P&O – letters, filing, thankyous and so on – and then Mona and I were to be left in peace for a month.

Or so we thought as we left for Scotland. But Sir Humphrey, knowing how desperately we needed a break, nevertheless bombarded me with apologia, with reasons why he mistrusted his managing director and indeed most of his management around the world, and with explanations as to why performance had been so flat. However, he had little to say about what he would have done to remedy these failings. My feeling of déjà vu, although sickening, certainly cemented my respect for my new board colleagues who had clearly made the right decision. Browne compensated for his lack of inches by his immense self-importance. I was angry but not surprised that, although he had agreed that no announcement of my move would be made until the end of April, he jumped the gun.

Betty Fairclough was being treated appallingly by P&O. After fifteen years as my principal secretary, it may have been too much to expect that she would be smoothly absorbed when I departed. Indeed, she made it clear in her usual forthright fashion that she would not want to be. Inchcape and his new appointees adopted a thoroughly unprofessional approach to her terms of severance. I wrote to express my concern and received a reply that was characteristically unhelpful. But I was taken aback to read Inchcape's postscript: 'I was interested to hear of your appointment at Bestobell and send good wishes.'

I had wanted the news kept confidential until the agreed date, partly to give Mona and me breathing space and partly, I have to confess, to surprise Inchcape at a time of my own choosing. Also, I did not want it to be concluded that I had been negotiating secretly

Mona, 1961

The author's children, James, Gillian and Alastair, Grand Canyon, 1979

LEFT On watch with Gunner Windebank RIGHT On *Oribi*'s quarterdeck,
Copenhagen, May 1945

Oribi in Northern waters, screening HMS *Victorious*, April 1944

The Chummery, 10 Lord Sinha Road, Calcutta

Author and Mona on trek, Jalori Pass, Suraj, 1990

LEFT The author on Zemu glacier, 1949 RIGHT Wedding in South Africa, 29 April 1961

Scottish family: the author's mother's ninetieth birthday, 1985

Launch of SS *Ottawa*, June 1964. Left to right: the author, Lady Hunter, Lady Geddes, Angus Mackinnon, Earl of Inchcape, Lord Geddes, Sir John Hunter, Mona

The author with (left) Sir Donald Anderson (right) Janeke and Bo Masden

Cartoon from *The Times*, November 1972

Working dinner in Japan: the author, with Edward Platt of B.P., talks to
Yamashita San (foreground) of Mitsui Zosen

THERE WAS A YOUNG MAN
IN THE CITY!
THE SUBJECT OF THIS LITTLE DITTY!
TO WORK HE WENT
AT P&O!
BUT GOT INCHED OUT.
AND HAD TO GO!
THEN, BESTOBEL BECKONED!
AND HIS REWARD?
TO BE THE CHAIRMAN
OF THE BOARD!
TODAY, IT'S MEMBERSHIP OF LLOYD'S!
AND A SEAT ON THE BOARD OF BOOTS!
WITH LOTS OF HONG KONG
MONOGRAMMED SHIRTS,
AND WARDROBES
OF SAVILLE ROW SUITS!
AROUND AND AROUND
THE WORLD HE FLIES,
FROM HERE TO TIMBUCTOO!
WITH TRAVEL FIRST CLASS,
CHAMPAGNE IN A GLASS.
AND A TICKET FOR MONA TOO!
THE MAN WHO HAS EVERYTHING
(AND A ROLLS ROYCE)
PLUS THE COMMERCIAL UNION CHAIR!
BUT, THE ONE THING HE HASN'T,
AND HASN'T FOR YEARS!
HE HASN'T GOT VERY MUCH
HAIR!

Cartoon birthday card to the author from Roger
Hargreaves, creator of the 'Mister Men'

November 1984 cartoon from *The Times*, when
Commercial Union was hard hit by claims

Dipping sheep with James at home in the 1980s

LEFT With the Queen at opening of Chamber of Shipping, October 1994
RIGHT Mona painting on the terrace at home

with Bestobell for months. However, Sir Humphrey saw P&O as a very important client of the Docks Board and pleaded that he did not want to rock that boat by appointing me his successor at Bestobell without telling them first. It was a specious argument. I was not his nomination; he had already been given his cards. Browne's vanity unleashed a host of interruptions upon our holiday and frustrated my modest attempt to score a point.

I joined Bestobell as deputy chairman in May and immediately set out on a round of visits up and down the country with the heads of the operating units – Alistair Hamilton at Paints, David Stark at Seals and Douglas Denny at Aviation.

Ron Waddingham, my driver, made a significant contribution to my induction. A large man, ex-Royal Marines, he was blessed with a clear sense of values and harboured no nonsense. He drove me from home to the office and back each day, taking up to four hours – the M25 was not then open – and often much farther afield. The job suited him to a T. He took constant pride in his Rolls-Royce, was always smartly turned out in cap and gloves and seemed to have eyes in the back of his head, for as I emerged from each visit he would be poised to open the door of the car for me. Conversations on long journeys were perhaps a trifle unorthodox, but I valued his good sense and trenchant assessment of the qualities of individuals. His loyalty to Bestobell was unquestionable, and his concern for its internal weaknesses was as shrewd as it was genuine. I was reminded of Powell, my driver at P&O, who had prompted me to pay more attention to UK staff on my euphoric return from my overseas tour. Waddingham taught me a good deal about the company's history and culture which, together with my intensive programme of visits, was to stand me in good stead when I assumed the chairmanship.

Bestobell's corporate headquarters were at Stoke House, an elegant listed building in Stoke Poges on the outskirts of Slough. At Sir Humphrey's instigation, a modern wing had recently been added. It was an expensive disaster. Inadequate consideration had been given to ventilation and the offices were intolerably hot in summer. I had an uneasy feeling that the writing was already on the wall – country house headquarters, costly extensions, a Rolls-Royce for the chairman. My early discussions with Paul Lewis, newly arrived as finance director, with Charles Ball of Kleinworts, with Anthony Forbes of Cazenove and with Phil Dunkley and Pat Gaynor were enough to convince me that, although Bestobell might not be an immediate candidate for takeover, something had to be done quickly to improve performance and to set out a plan for development, or we would soon be 'in the frame'. The return on assets was insufficient and Bestobell was trying to do too many things – a mini-conglomerate with insufficient clarity as to its markets and its purpose.

Donald Spencer, my managing director, was a bright, imaginative type, mightily relieved to be out from under Browne. He seemed perfectly happy to have me join and in doing so effectively to demote him, maintaining that he would soon prove himself. He had an appealing, fresh approach – and, in retrospect, a significant streak of naiveté.

As 1 June approached, we held extensive discussions about strategy and our immediate action programme. A distinct advance in Bestobell's share price indicated that something was afoot. As we dealt with the formalities of the AGM and my assumption of the chair at Stoke House, I realised that I was in for a much more challenging role than I had contemplated a couple of months earlier.

Immediately after the AGM, I told the directors that I considered we would face a bid within a matter of days. It seemed that my tenure might be very short-lived. But we did just wonder whether the predator had not missed a trick in failing to move *before* I joined – now I could at least maintain that the board recognised the need for, and had started to implement, change. I had a sense, too, that the company was worth substantially more than the current share price of 140p and I felt quite strongly that there was a quality worth fighting to preserve.

Thus, when I was traced to James Rockley's office at Kleinworts in the City on the morning of 7 June, I was to an extent prepared. It was Owen Green of BTR on the telephone:

> I have to inform you that BTR will be making an announcement at noon today that we have acquired 10% of your shares and that we are seeking a meeting with you which could lead to an offer to purchase the balance at 200p. I would like to see you today to discuss this, and I hope your directors will agree to recommend the bid.

I replied that if BTR intended to bid at 200p then there would be no purpose in meeting. We would regard such an offer as wholly unacceptable.

By the time the announcement was made our share price was leaping ahead, but only went marginally over 200p, indicating that the market judged, at that early stage, that we could well be 'goners'. Indeed 'City Diary' under the heading 'Not Bad for Some' published a fictional 'Extract from Marshall's Diary':

1 June appointed Chair of Bestobell – Nice.
6 June Inchcape announced at P&O AGM a golden handshake of £77,000 – Very nice.
7 June BTR bids for Bestobell. There should be another substantial golden handshake – nice again – but it would be nicer to have a job.

We at once set up an executive team – myself, Spencer and Lewis with Lord Rockley and Harry Noble from Kleinworts and Frank Barlow from Extel. Hugh Butterworth, of our auditors, was in constant touch. Anthony Forbes had advised that Cazenove, as stockbrokers both to BTR and Bestobell, would stand aside – as was then the convention. I was glad to call on my old friend Richard Westmacott of Hoare Govett. His immediate acceptance was certainly an early plus for Bestobell.

But the company was not yet ready. Top management, in particular, was dismayed and alarmed. Knowing that we needed to redeploy resources for an intense and, as we hoped, a long battle, I made a swift management move to ensure that the operating units were in good hands while, together with Donald Spencer and Paul Lewis, I took on the defence of the company. Four senior people were each made responsible for a rough-and-ready grouping of similar units. I told them: 'Win or lose, yours will be a layer of management that won't be required. Win, and we will have a stronger company in which you will be key players; lose, and you will disappear.' It was a challenge they accepted bravely. We might have two to three months, and each business manager had to get his operations motoring so that we could justify a share price higher than that offered by BTR.

Whatever concerns may have beset Bestobell in the recent past, the bid brought everyone together. There was no desire in Australia or South Africa to disappear into the BTR mill and the 3,500 employees in Europe were equally persuaded that continued independence was preferable. Trade unions and local politicians offered support. Even schoolchildren in Slough noted with anxiety that Asbestos Man –

who stood proudly in the High Street to commemorate the firefighting suits produced by Bells for the Fire Service and the RAF during the war – was at risk.

BTR's offer document on 12 July gave us a few more hard facts to work on but not many. Their approach was simple: their growth was compared with that of Bestobell – no contest. They concentrated on the prospects for shareholders in BTR compared with an independent Bestobell performing at its current level.

We played the emotional card, saying to shareholders and journalists that surely the new team should be given a chance. We emphasised the opportunistic timing of the bid, coming 'just before the redirection of Bestobell' which was flagged at the time of my appointment and would result in 'resumed growth and increased profit'. I stated:

> I became chairman on 1 June. I believe the reasons for lack of growth have been carefully studied and clearly identified and that our plans have considerable potential. I am impressed with the quality of skills I have found; I have established a new management structure to enable the focus of action, responsibility and authority to be more clearly defined. The financial terms of BTR's offer are unattractive and the commercial merits negligible.

Finally, to make the point that I had some experience in defending a company, we planted a firm 'NO to BTR' on the cover of the document. We then took the plunge by forecasting an increase in profit of 'not less than 30% over 1978 and an increase of 15% in the dividend'.

July was a warm month. Almost every day I would go first to Slough and then on to London for meetings with advisers, shareholders and customers, sometimes returning to Slough before getting home. I was able to work throughout – I now had an arrangement with Waddingham that he spoke only when invited to do so, and I think he rather liked being given his innings and then being given 'out'. I had a telephone, a tape recorder and always a pile of papers. One of the early casualties of the campaign was the promised London HQ – it soon became evident that there could be no justification for such a major move, and if anyone had to make an uncomfortable accommodation it must be the chairman. Stoke House was also a casualty. We put it on the market and acquired what would become a more cost-effective office in the centre of Slough. These two decisions alone amounted to a powerful declaration of intent to improve performance.

It was vital that our new management structure got to grips quickly and that the priority of delivering the forecast profit was recognised throughout the company. For this we were acutely dependent on our overseas companies. There was no time for me to visit them, but senior management came to the UK, sensed the atmosphere – the smell of battle – and were supportive. A great spirit throughout the operating units enabled us to bring our interim results forward by a month and to announce the figures immediately after BTR, as anticipated, raised their bid to 220p. BTR's first offer had been cash only, but now they were forced to produce a share alternative. Owen Green declared that this was their final offer and that helped to concentrate minds, but a strong stock market performance resulted in the value of the share offer moving up to 242p, making our task more difficult.

Bestobell was David against BTR's Goliath. We again concluded that the company was being under-valued – even at 220p – and that more potential for staff and shareholders lay in independence. We were greatly helped by the Kleinwort team, who under James Rockley's leadership remained cool under fire, laid back even, but I became far more involved than I had intended. My experience at P&O had taught me the importance of letting shareholders hear directly why I thought the bid should be resisted. So a number of teams, in most cases led by me, benefiting from the standing I had acquired in P&O days and my reputation for integrity, visited shareholders around the country.

We saw the Pru and the Scottish institutions, pension funds and investment trusts and called on a number of individuals with significant holdings. At that time the Yellow Book, covering practice during takeover bids, required that, in putting our case, we had to do so on a one-to-one basis. Britannic Assurance was represented by Frank Weaver, the investment director – a tough Birmingham man with a reputation for supporting medium-sized engineering companies. In a bid situation Britannic, like M&G another substantial shareholder, favoured the incumbent management unless in their view something was manifestly wrong. Both, too, were concerned at the way in which conglomerate takeovers were reducing the number and spread of investment opportunities. We were grilled hard, and rightly so, and it was of great significance when Britannic went public on 4 August: 'We would still like to see Bestobell remain independent.' M&G added their weighty support.

I attacked BTR's offer document – having the temerity to question the quality of its earnings. I pointed out with derision that if BTR were to grow at the rate of 43% per annum quoted in their revised offer, their market capitalisation within five years would equal ICI's current position. As it turned out, it very nearly did just that.

We said boldly that, whereas we had been prepared to back our case with a profit forecast, it seemed unaccountable that BTR, offering a share alternative, should not have produced its own forecast. 'BTR may need us – we don't need them.' 'Still *NO* to BTR,' we proclaimed and much more in the same vein.

By this time BTR had increased its holding to some 26% of our stock and, as the end of the bid period approached, press comment on the theme of Bestobell being likely to go down as a gallant loser outweighed expectation that we could survive. One exception was Kenneth Fleet, who wrote in the *Sunday Express* on 12 August:

> If you are still unconvinced of the wisdom of having Britannic on your side, look at Bestobell.
>
> I want to see the current, revised BTR bid (220p in cash or 11 BTR shares for 15 Bestobell) fail for two reasons. One is feeling for A. B. (Sandy) Marshall, evicted from P&O by an ungrateful Lord Inchcape, now executive chairman of Bestobell. He, and I in my own way, kept P&O out of the clutches of Frank Sanderson at the time of Bovis's infamous reverse bid for the company.
>
> I think he deserves better than to have the Bestobell chair shot from under him.
>
> My other, perhaps more logical reason is Britannic's backing. Frank Weaver, secretary and investment manager, sitting on 10% of the shares says: 'We are prepared to stay with Bestobell . . . a sound recovery situation, which BTR is trying to acquire at the bottom of the cycle.'
>
> That should be good enough.

There was no let-up and it was becoming abundantly clear that in the various plants and outlets the workforce was producing the goods, showing tremendous commitment and getting their own views across to local interests from Slough to Edinburgh.

On closing day, Friday 7 August, I awaited the count at Kleinwort's Fenchurch Street office. Bullish noises came from Hill Samuel, who under Michael Valentine (ex-Warburgs and Bovis) were leading for BTR. It was a long afternoon. Then suddenly came a telephone call for Rockley from Valentine. BTR had secured acceptances, which, when added to the block of shares already purchased, would take their holding in Bestobell to 48%. Valentine conceded that Bestobell had won – by a whisker. It seemed that because we were open and determined, shareholders and the public were willing to let the new team 'have a go'. The factors for improvement were there, and we were able to unlock them and bring them forward. The bid was a significant failure for BTR – Bestobell being the first to escape its clutches during a very acquisitive phase.

From my point of view all was turning out well. I had had a crash course in learning about Bestobell's business; the management had recognised its lack of experience in the big, bad world of corporate takeovers and was glad to have my leadership; so in three concentrated months I won credibility and acceptance and was thus able to move on with a team whose respect I had earned.

We savoured the victory, issued congratulations throughout the company and dealt with a flood of messages from around the world. There was euphoria of course, but, at the same time, we appreciated that some 48% of shareholders had not accepted our case, and those who had would be more than interested in our ability to bring to fruition our somewhat ambitious-sounding plans for the next few years. Bestobell was a traditional 'medium-tech' engineering company with a sound enough base on which we were able to build. There was no great support structure, everyone had to get their hands dirty, everyone had to be at the sharp end. Top management had to be involved with industry bodies, trade associations, town councils, trades unions and customers. The experience was broad and the fact that we had to deliver, with BTR breathing down our necks, was instructive and a powerful incentive.

The first priorities were to ensure that nothing had slipped between the cracks during almost three months of diversion, and further to tighten up the operation. We needed to nail down a number of significant contracts to maintain momentum and to sustain the high morale that had been achieved. With that understanding in place I felt justified in having a break and flew to San

Francisco on the 21st, to join Mona and the children – Alastair, seventeen, now becoming very responsible and grown up, Gillian, fifteen and James, twelve. The children could hardly contain themselves as they conducted me to the massive limo which Mona had hired the day before, and they burst with pride as their mother, with astonishing confidence, drove us round San Francisco. We had to use our twelve hours there to maximum advantage, and I was happy not to be in the driving seat.

There followed three weeks of the greatest enjoyment and easy touring. We exchanged our limo for a station wagon and headed for Lake Tahoe; then a glorious climb to Emerald Lake; white-water rafting on the Truckee and good swimming from an almost tropical beach. Our last-minute accommodation in dreadful canvas huts in the Yosemite Valley we remember for appalling graffiti and slinky racoons, but sublime scenery. Death Valley lived up to its name, so hot we could hardly believe it; we swam in hot water and 'froze' at 90 degrees in the air-conditioned hotel, all purple tufted carpets and velvet bedspreads.

On to awful but laughable Las Vegas where, with children under age, we were excluded from some of the wilder shows but enjoyed 'Circus Circus'. In the line-up for breakfast on the Strip the next morning we stood between rows of fruit machines. The odd dimes were passed to James, who had to use his stetson to hold the jackpot of silver which suddenly poured out; he could easily have been hooked.

We saw Bryce and Zion Canyons. We 'discovered' Lake Powell on the Colorado and had a glorious day on the water. Grand Canyon, despite the grotty hinterland with its depressing Indian shacks, justified its billings. Glorious sunset, nerve-wracking trails, Alastair leaping over the rim onto a hidden ledge.

To Los Angeles across the Mojave Desert. Marina del Rey gave us a couple of nights to unwind and clean up in some comfort. We did Disney World, memorable for the space ride which I hated. Mona, first declining to participate, was persuaded not to be chicken but, having reached the head of the queue, had the courage to turn back: 'Why should I?'

I remember that holiday as one of the happiest and healthiest of all, and that is special because we have had many wonderful trips. It was for me the perfect cure after months of corporate activity and in-fighting. For, whatever had been taken from me, the most important element of my life, my family, was intact. My problems had drawn us closer together, and for that I was deeply thankful. I had re-established my values and recognised with exciting clarity how good life could be after P&O.

I was able to earn tolerably well and that, underpinned by a P&O pension (and it is worth noting that over the years the P&O Fund has been a model in its policy, its structure and its management), gave me a degree of freedom and independence. I could exercise choice about what new ventures I should take on; I could choose, too, to put something back. While it might have been enjoyable to have had more income, I believed, genuinely, that salary was not the most important aspect of any engagement.

I had an early opportunity to use my freedom. On return to the UK I found another note from Maersk Møller: 'It seems that you have sorted yourself out pretty well, so I renew my invitation to you to join the Maersk board.' I was proud to accept – I was properly back in business.

After the dust of the bid settled, I contacted Owen Green, now Bestobell's largest shareholder, to explore what form of relationship would be appropriate. I got a brush off. He did not demand, nor did I offer board membership, but the response was, to say the least, cool: 'We will continue to monitor our investment, and together no doubt with other shareholders, will look to you to make good the promises made during the bid.' Until I left in 1985, Bestobell had no significant contact with BTR. This contrasted markedly with the declaration during the bid, that they could see useful opportunities of co-operation. The investment was passive and unproductive – for a time BTR's 29% holding kept a degree of bid speculation in our price, but even that faded.

In November, mindful of the committed support we had received from the overseas companies, Mona and I went to Australia to take a look at Bestobell's substantial interests in Melbourne and Sydney, and en route to visit Hong Kong, Malaysia and Singapore, where we had merchanting activities of some value. In Kuala Lumpur I faced the ongoing problem of Malayanisation. Lim, our manager, was of Chinese origin and had one eye over his shoulder on an escape route to a safe haven in Australia.

Sir Eric McClintock was a good Australian and an excellent chairman of Bestobell Australia Ltd (BAL). The fact that BAL was ostensibly a publicly quoted company, although the number of shares in the public's hands was small, gave him the ability to play the Australian card. I am in favour of a UK company handling its Australian interests in a structure with a significant local content, whether as a joint venture or, more simply, by floating a meaningful proportion of the stock. Bestobell's structure was neither flesh nor fowl, and for such a change to take place BAL would first need a better track record. It had made a useful contribution to the parent company in 1979, but its main businesses were labour-intensive, low skill, and did not provide the basis for consistent, long-term profitable growth. The company had to move up-market. Eric McClintock recognised this, but John Hayter, the managing director of long standing, was not so sure and it took time to make progress.

As touched on earlier, Bestobell had been in a whole range of asbestos-related activities, particularly during the Second World War when aircraft components made extensive use of the material. We had withdrawn from most asbestos work around the world, but the past was catching up and an early task was to cap the company's exposure to claims for industrial injury. During the war and for years afterwards, the dangers of asbestos were not fully understood until the instrumentation to measure fibre content in the air was invented. Desperately-ill people contaminated forty years earlier felt they had nowhere to turn except to their employers, who had been as ignorant as they. With the consistent help of Royal Insurance we established that Bells had had full industrial liability cover through the London and Lancashire, which had since become a subsidiary of 'the Royal'. We agreed a commutation which relieved Bestobell of the outstanding claims and, more important, all future claims. This was a relief to us and, I am sure, to the claimants who now had Royal Insurance behind them rather than a medium-sized engineering company with limited resources. The devil of these long-tail claims which have so affected the insurance market, particularly in the USA, is that in the past the underwriter was effectively taking on risks of which he had insufficient or, indeed, no knowledge – such as creeping pollution, computer glitches and asbestosis. No wonder the concept of the 'deep pocket' has developed so markedly.

Gradually we sold or closed the smaller and less profitable Bestobell enterprises, streamlining both our product lines and our structure. Douglas Denny, extremely well-balanced and a man of great integrity, headed Aviation and, together with Donald Spencer, led our expansion in the aerospace business and signalled the future for Bestobell as a specialised engineering and component manufacturer.

General Connectors Corporation (GCC), based in Los Angeles, was sole supplier of specialised ducting to Boeing for the 747 programme. (Incidentally, another Bestobell company, this time in Blackburn, Lancashire, made extruded window seals for the same 747 programme.) They also supplied important componentry to a number of the military aircraft builders. An extension of GCC's plant to Toulouse to give our ducting a European face, which we hoped would be attractive to the Airbus Consortium, was a costly failure. The French were adept at non-tariff barriers and the Germans saw no reason to give us credit for our site in France, insisting that we were still subject to the British quota. We worked hard to get F16 fighter components for manufacture by Bestobell Australia as 'off-set' contracts, but it was an artificial concept and not of sufficient scale or longevity to justify the investment in plant and skilled staff.

A more successful move was made in the USA in Manchester, New Hampshire, where we acquired Armtec, another aerospace manufacturer. Under a calm, competent Ed Allman, from whom we bought control, Armtec made Edison fire-detectors, later developed to provide alarm coverage for the after-burners of high-performance military aircraft and components for NASA's Apollo programme. An intriguing aspect of the Armtec plant was to watch the women operators weaving and threading the wiring in harnesses for aircraft engines and for the motor industry. They were in fact using the dextrous skills so long employed in textiles on which Manchester's past prosperity had been built, before that industry moved south to the Sunbelt.

Our African businesses were at the low-tech end of the spectrum. In South Africa, and more so in Zambia and Zimbabwe, they operated in virtually closed economies with little competitive pressure. This did not encourage innovation or investment, although the Zimbabwean company, which could import little, was particularly ingenious in turning its hand to anything that showed some possibility of profit. I had to ask myself whether 'old Empire' agency businesses could survive in the modern competitive world. They had to be able to source and sell what their customers wanted and the ties of 'sole supplier' were becoming restrictive. The value of belonging to a UK-based group was increasingly suspect. It was good for everyone when we moved towards more independence throughout Southern Africa and I was glad when, in the mid-1980s, all these companies were bought out by their managements.

It took time for Bestobell to cure the hangover deriving from lower quality business. Bestobell Australia had secured a number of high-value management contracts, including insulation of the cooling towers of the Castle Peak power station in Hong Kong. But their unfortunate inability to turn away traditional insulation jobbing contracts at home continually led them astray and, indeed, threatened the stability of the whole Bestobell group. Eric McLintock had handed over the chairmanship to a retired ANZ bank executive, Max Sandow. Throughout his short tenure, relations were fraught. BAL was not doing well. Together with the new chairman there was a new managing director who was able, but needed time and support. Sandow spent much time criticising his predecessor, trying to justify BAL's performance by pointing out problems elsewhere in the group and finally by negotiating privately for a New Zealand corporation to make a bid for BAL. I had to fire him.

At head office I had recommended that after four years' apprenticeship with me as executive chairman Donald Spencer would be ready to become CEO again and I looked forward to working with him in this new relationship. To my dismay, which was shared by his colleagues, he did not have the strength and balance to hack it. He responded to pressure by becoming hyperactive, which compounded his problem. Finally, the only way we could persuade Donald to ease up was to let him go. I have always been sad that he did not succeed. He was an enthusiast, an optimist, and he had a genuine if sometimes almost juvenile keenness.

In 1985, after Spencer's departure, strains with Australia and a stretched management in the UK, Bestobell again needed a period of intensive care and attention. We brought in a temporary chief executive, and it was logical that a chairman with a longer tenure ahead of him than I would have should have the responsibility of overseeing the appointment of a permanent CEO. It was time to move on. I had become chairman of Commercial Union in 1983 and its demands upon me had increased. It was a challenge I enjoyed. Shortly before I was to leave Bestobell, I was invited to join the main board of Royal Bank of Canada. This appointment arose in part through my Canadian connections on the British North American Committee and fitted neatly into my portfolio of non-executive interests. I handed over the chair of Bestobell in September 1985.

There was a déjà vu postscript to the Bestobell story. Eighteen months after my departure BTR struck again, this time through Meggitt, a BTR surrogate which enjoyed the luxury of a 29% launch-pad. The new team was unable to resist, but happily a number of Bestobell's specialist aerospace and controls businesses have since played a significant role in Meggitt's development.

12

British North American Committee

The British North American Committee (BNAC) was founded in 1969. Its purpose is 'to study and comment on the developing relationships between Britain, the United States and Canada . . . , to promote clearer understanding of the economic opportunities and problems . . . [and] to promote better understanding through the collection of facts and their widespread dissemination.' This mission statement was alive for the membership and provided parameters for the committee's work. The group embraced approximately sixty from the USA, twenty from Canada and forty from the UK; business men and women, academics, and labour leaders. American members have included distinguished Democrats and Republicans 'resting' between administrations – such men as Bill Simon, Jim Schlesinger and Fred Bergsten.

Between bi-annual meetings, member task-forces and the secretariats in Washington and London follow up and develop papers for the full committee. This process may lead to a publication or a committee statement. Members are expected to contribute actively and I have always felt that the benefit one secured was in direct relation to one's input.

When I accepted Richard Dobson's invitation to join, George Goyder, who was the honorary secretary, said to me: 'I hope you will have as much enjoyment from this association as I have had over the years and, remember, if you feel passionately that the committee should tackle a subject, persevere, because what we need is to identify issues which will be of importance in the future and about which we might be able to exercise influence now.'

One morning, jet-lagged in San Francisco after flying in from Australia for a committee meeting, I went for a walk with Ian MacGregor. He reflected that, in the early days of Thatcherism, there seemed a danger of unthinking tycoons taking too much out of the system for themselves. Perhaps BNAC might pool thoughts from the three-nation perspective – an early identification of the fat-cat syndrome and one with which we might well have persevered.

BNAC has never been a lobby. It has concentrated on establishing facts, explaining how members with wide experience in our three countries are, and will be, affected by them and suggesting what our membership and our countries might do to mitigate problems and influence developments.

I was involved in a number of working groups and led the task-force which oversaw publication in 1982 of 'Conflicts of National Law with International Business Activity – Issues of Extraterritoriality', a contribution towards resolving the growing strains over the extraordinary outreach of US anti-trust legislation.

I had also been closely engaged, harking back to George Goyder, in trying to develop a committee initiative on South Africa. It seemed to me, and others, that if our members, from three countries, from the very different disciplines of business, labour and academia and representing a reasonable spread of age, could agree a statement of principle and suggest a route forward it would carry significant weight.

The record of the June 1984 meeting states: 'Most of the membership agreed with Sandy Marshall's analysis and proposals, some of them to their surprise.' Harold Samuel, then of the US Labor organisation AFL-CIO but, earlier, under-secretary of Labor in the Carter administration, had been a member of the US Thomas Committee which had produced a severe indictment of the South African government and recommended punitive measures against it. He initially took a very strong position against my theme of its being essential to keep bridges open, to help to build the economy, to give labour a stake in the country's success and thus an interest in peaceful evolution. At the end of a great debate and much further discussion over the weekend, a remarkable convergence of view was established and it was, I believe, to the regret of both of us that we did not achieve a committee statement. It was a casualty of time-pressures, and we missed a window of opportunity in 1984 when it could have been influential.

Originally, meetings were held at locations felt to give an adequate sense of peace, withdrawn from everyday commercial bustle. Winter at that splendid establishment, The Breakers, West Palm Beach, and summer at Gleneagles were first choices. However, as communications improved, isolation was not possible. More important, it was felt that being readily accessible would attract the cream of outside speakers and that was proved when we met in London, for the first time, in 1985. By then I had been appointed co-chairman, alongside Bill Turner, a leading Canadian member.

Geoffrey Howe, my MP and at that time foreign secretary, opened the meeting on 'Private Sector and Government Roles in Transatlantic Economic and Commercial Relations'. This gave him scope to tackle a wide range of subjects, a number of which remain unresolved today – the EEC's Common Agricultural Policy, the threat to the US motorcar industry posed by the Japanese, inflation, barriers to world trade (both tariff and non-tariff) and instability in foreign exchange rates.

Another member of the cabinet, David Young, spoke on 'Effective Training – the Role and Limitations of Government'; Sir Terence Burns, chief economic adviser to the Treasury spoke on 'How unstable has the International Monetary System become?'; and Robert Elliot of the International Institute for Strategic Studies spoke on SDI (Star Wars).

I remember that during the discussion following a review of recent developments in the UK given by Ken Durham, then chairman of Unilever, fears were expressed 'that Mrs Thatcher might throw away the results of all her work in an effort to stay on.' The year 1985 is worth noting.

To follow the distinguished speakers and some spirited debate, we had arranged a social programme which caught the imagination of members. The prime minister gave us a reception at 10, Downing Street. Mona and I tried to ensure that as many as possible were introduced to her, but that no one should monopolise the PM – although a number tried. Not only was Mrs Thatcher interested in each member, she impressed everyone with her understanding of the array of issues raised, from US labour policy to the CAP, from takeover activities to biotechnology. She captivated labour leaders from the USA and somewhat liberal economists from Canada; a retail chairperson from Texas and a rising oil tycoon from the UK. The Brits were honoured to have been able to secure such a special invitation, and proud of the importance which Margaret Thatcher attached to the committee's work.

Our formal function was held at the Mansion House. To the consternation of some we had stipulated black tie and it seemed appropriate that Mona and I should meet the guests in the anteroom. The evening took on a life of its own. With a master of ceremonies announcing names in stentorian tones, a few of our overseas friends were so overcome with the splendour of the chambers and the drama of their entrance that the ladies attempted to curtsey. Protocol was only restored when the Lord Mayor processed into the Indian Chamber before his 175 guests.

We had music, the loving-cup ceremony and more meaty speeches than usual. I had pondered how to bring the three elements of BNAC together with some relevance to the past and the present and found the vehicle in reflecting on the award of the Freedom of the City to General Dwight D. Eisenhower in 1945:

> Forty years on from the last terrible war in Europe, we have, all of us, remembered the events of 1945. On 12 June that year, General Eisenhower attended the Guildhall where the Freedom of the City was voted to him and he was presented with a Sword of Honour. He then came here to the Mansion House, where a luncheon in his honour was given by the Lord Mayor.
>
> 'The treasures of free men', Eisenhower said, 'are the freedom to worship, equality before the law, liberty to speak and to act, subject only that they trespass not on the similar rights of others.'
>
> These were sober but also heady days as we began to think of peace, reconstruction and a better world. The hopes expressed then have not all been realised, but we should not undervalue that which has been achieved. First reconstruction, then growth and, largely within a framework of peace, relatively free trade and, throughout, basic trust and goodwill between our peoples. Eisenhower, forty years ago, had a message for us all, Canadian, American, British: 'No petty differences in the world of trade, traditions or national pride should ever blind us to identity in spiritual, priceless values. If we keep our eyes on this guidepost then no difficulties along our path of mutual co-operation will be insurmountable.'
>
> In some small way the British North American Committee is the epitome of this precept.

Two years later, when it was time to hold the winter meeting in Washington, the Americans showed that they too had tradition, history and access. We dined in the State Department with George Shultz, the Secretary of State, as host. This was particularly pleasing as George had, until moving into the administration, been an active member of BNAC and also because on the following day President

Gorbachev was due in Washington for the first summit meeting with President Reagan and there were, to say the least, many issues between the two superpowers still outstanding.

Time was tightly controlled so discussion was staged. Bill Turner introduced George Shultz as a distinguished alumnus; Michael Palliser put the British question; Paul Martin, later Minister of Finance, the Canadian comment; and Bill MacDonough, of First Chicago Bank and, later, of the New York 'Fed', a contribution from the USA. Shultz actually exceeded his brief and was both amusing and informative on Cold War politics. I expressed our thanks and the Secretary of State was whisked off to finalise the draft communiqué on the Reagan/Gorbachev Summit.

On the next evening we dined in Congress with Majority Leader Thomas Foley, who shared with us some of the art of running a Democratic majority in the House of Representatives under a Republican President. At the working sessions we had heard from a number of senior members of the administration and one who, already well-known in military and defence circles, was to make even more impact as National Security Advisor to President Bush, General Bent Scowcroft. At that time, in late 1987, he spoke about the deployment of Cruise and Pershing missiles, about the 'Zero Option' and the upcoming START negotiations. He talked of a 'breathtakingly ambitious' programme to bring these to fruition, but emphasised throughout that the purpose of negotiations was 'to enhance the stability of the nuclear balance'. In the light of developments since, much of the thinking and particularly perhaps the language, seems dated, but then it was serious stuff.

Late in 1985 the finance ministers of the G7, exercised about the world financial scene, signed the Louvre Accord. At a meeting in Los Angeles shortly afterwards, there was fierce debate on the Accord's principles between our eminent economist members and our equally eminent businessmen before the committee sent a message of support to the leaders of our three countries, President Reagan, Premier Mulroney and Prime Minister Thatcher. We welcomed the agreement and urged the leaders to reinforce steps to deal with exchange rate volatilities, developing country debt and the international trade problems exacerbated by these distortions. This rather rare pronouncement by BNAC was well received, perhaps, in part, because the recipients were unused to accolades. Unfortunately the problems which it addressed do not seem to have been resolved.

On that occasion we also took in the Getty galleries and at drinks one evening I met again Dr Armand Hammer of Occidental Oil, with whom I had crossed swords in my tanker days. He had been brought along by Tom Symons, Vanier Professor at Trent University and one of the most distinguished Canadians of his day. Both Joe Baird, another BNAC member, and I might have offered Tom some comment on his choice of guest – Joe had had a torrid few years in the hot seat as CEO of Occidental and had scant regard for the ubiquitous and manipulative doctor.

I found the role of chairman challenging and enjoyable and fortunately I did not have to turn a blind eye as had one of my predecessors. On the first day of a meeting members sit at a hollow square, in alphabetical order, and there was an occasion on which a rather dull dissertation failed to keep the attention of three distinguished gentlemen sitting under 'S'. Those whose attention was not wholly absorbed by the speaker were amused to see Lords Seebohm Selkirk and Sherfield dozing gently together.

Interest and intervention is what the committee is all about and it is infinitely preferable for the chairman to be put to work in orchestrating discussion, than to have the miserable task of flogging a dead horse when the subject does not fly. A severe case of just such a problem occurred in 1988, when I had asked the Chief Secretary of the Treasury, one John Major, to speak on 'The Management of a Market Economy in an increasingly globalised International Scene'. Simon Webley and I had briefed the Permanent Secretary at the Treasury, Peter Middleton, extensively, both on the composition of the committee and the subject matters of interest to the membership. I was looking forward to introducing one of the rapidly rising stars of the Thatcher government. John Major arrived in Bournemouth after an all-night sitting in the Commons. He had ten minutes for a sandwich and cup of coffee in the course of which he said to me with some satisfaction: 'You'll be glad to know that on the way down in the train I tore up the Treasury brief. I've made some notes and I'm sure I'll give you something more to your members' liking.'

His address was the sort of report one might expect at the AGM of a minor Conservative association. As the lack of response was to show, he completely undershot his audience. I exercised the chairman's prerogative and posed a number of questions; I attempted to provoke members into reaction, but the heavyweights stayed silent and for the only occasion during my five years in the chair I had to terminate the session well before the appointed time. Two years later at another winter meeting in Los Angeles, Britain had a new prime minister and I was able to say: 'After all, my boy *has* made good.'

It was important to bring the Canadian dimension into full communion and a meeting was arranged in Montreal in December 1989. It was a bitterly cold weekend, but it was a successful and constructive gathering. At a dinner arranged for the committee by the Beaver Club, Bill MacDonough and I, representing the non-Canadian interests, were afforded honorary membership. When the club was formed in 1795, membership was limited to those who had over-wintered in the North. Bill Turner was our principal sponsor together with Alastair Gillespie, wearing the founder member's medallion handed down by his great-great grandfather. Allan Taylor of Royal Bank was in support and Pierre Jeanniot, then of Air Canada and now IATA, was a formidable master of ceremonies.

The inauguration remains a signal honour. Relatively few outsiders are inducted and I believe it may be regarded as some recognition of a contribution to understanding between our nations. A side benefit of membership is that one has a specially struck copper plate, embossed with one's name which hangs in the top restaurant at the Queen E Hotel. When I used to dine there, on Royal Bank visits, Charles, the maître d', was always happy to wheel out the salver.

The strength of BNAC membership has fluctuated with, at times, more apparent strength among the British contingent than the US, or the reverse. I felt that the Canadian membership was throughout of a consistently high standard, although for a time the unions took a blinkered view of the opportunity which the committee offered and refused to join. One can, of course, appreciate that Canadian businessmen find a group such as BNAC useful in maintaining contacts and influence. But what of the US membership? For some years the British worried. A number of distinguished industrialists retained nominal membership but rarely attended, some attended but made little contribution and some seemed to regard the committee only as a stepping-stone. Others, quite simply, stayed on long after they had ceased to be involved in business.

The British had some of the same problems and I tried, with great help from colleagues, not only to secure top industrialists, academics and union leaders, but to identify rising stars and to arrange that, without tension, room was created for them. In these tougher times for senior management, there have been many cases of top executives losing their jobs in a variety of circumstances. While a good company background is desirable, membership of BNAC is by invitation and personal, so such an individual is encouraged to remain a member for up to two years. If he is 'reincarnated', as is happily often the case, he is welcome under the new hat. Similarly, so that the committee does not lose the benefit of someone retiring from full-time employment, a two year 'afterglow' membership is a felicitous way of keeping the membership dynamic. Such arrangements, under an active executive committee and with strong leadership have done much, today, to maintain a powerful tripartite membership.

I tried throughout my time to make sure that we did not fall into the trap of taking ourselves too seriously. A significant contribution to that end was made by the involvement of wives and husbands. There were some memorable evenings of song and dance in San Francisco, New Orleans and in Florida, while I recall with particular pleasure Willie Weir leading some enthusiastic if not very competent members in an eightsome reel at Blair Castle and my farewell at Scone Palace when, thanks to Alan Tuffin, General Secretary of the Postal Workers' Union, the pipes and drums of the Post Office played for us.

On a more significant level, however, I arranged that we address the question of the continued relevance of the committee. The EEC member countries were being drawn increasingly closer in trading and political terms and developments in Eastern Europe were suggesting a new shape for Europe itself. Canada and the US had created their own Free Trade Zone and were looking to include Mexico. Was there still a special relationship to be nurtured? Was the Committee functioning effectively in its chosen role of identifying problems likely to affect relationships, performance and opportunities in the three countries? No punches were pulled, no options excluded. A penetrating and honest appraisal concluded that there is a continuing role for a group of BNAC's unique constitution and a compelling justification for the committee to use that composition and its experience to identify and explore issues of concern to our three nations and to pass on to our successors both understanding and appreciation of the values which we share.

13

Commercial Union

As a director of P&O, Denny Marris had seen me at work, but when I joined him for lunch at Commercial Union, where he was a deputy chairman, I had no idea that I was being vetted by the chairman Ronnie Brooks and his colleagues. The outcome was, however, my first outside non-executive directorship – evidence of growing recognition in City circles. At the age of forty-five in 1970 I was considerably younger than the other twenty-five directors – merchant bankers from Barings, Kleinworts, Lazards and Schroders, investment trust managers, diplomats, academics and one executive. I was the only director from industry or commerce. The fortnightly meetings had a brief agenda:

(a) Minutes of previous meeting
(b) Results (for a period ending some weeks earlier)
(c) Any other business

Some of the more irreverent referred to these meetings as 'Matins' and others suggested the notice might as well have read '12.45 for 1 o'clock,' because lunch was always excellent.

Directors from the financial institutions formed the Investment Committee. Before the days of concern about insider trading, much of the value of the committee to the investment manager was from gossip picked up over the weekend. There was an assumption, not wholly peculiar to management, that much of the business of the company was too specialised and therefore too difficult for the non-executive director. As a result little was done to explain problems or issues – the board was a place at which statutory figures and formal reports were presented. Discussion was not expected.

Soon after I arrived, it was proposed that Commercial Union should bid for the property company MEPC, to enhance the asset base and improve earnings through attracting property expertise. I was, of course, a tyro and probably would not have made much valuable contribution to the debate, which seemed to be conducted by an inner group of directors. There was little attempt to involve the juniors. It was a case of finding one's own way around.

I determined to get to know the company, and with the encouragement of the executive, Gordon Dunlop, John Linbourn and Bob Sloan in particular, I met the management in head office and in branches up and down the country. I was travelling extensively on P&O business so made a point of calling upon CU people in Australia and New Zealand, in Canada, Singapore and the Far East, in the USA and South Africa, even Swaziland. I developed an appreciation of the scale of the business and the quality of the staff, together with some understanding of the dynamics of worldwide insurance.

By the mid-1970s, I was beginning to be of some use. I attended fortnightly board meetings, chaired the UK Committee, sat on other committees and still visited overseas offices whenever possible. My director's fees brought me the princely sum of £96.01 net per quarter. Gross fees were £875, income tax £711.30, National Insurance contributions £50 and pension contributions £18.

Gordon Dunlop had been appointed chief executive of CU in 1972, with Francis Sandilands becoming non-executive chairman. I do not recall being consulted about the appointment; it was simply presented for confirmation. I would certainly not have opposed it – Gordon was a relative newcomer to the insurance business and had already shown a willingness to think differently, to look outward and to work extremely hard. When I became CEO of P&O later in the year I felt a kindred spirit.

Gordon drove Commercial Union on an expansionist path. In the USA he was determined, by acquisition and internal growth, to secure a meaningful market position. There were inevitable clashes with some of the newly-acquired managers and the growth he demanded tended to come from undisciplined underwriting. Perhaps it should not have been a surprise. The new chief executive in Boston, Lawson Swearingen, a Bible-thumping native of Louisiana, had been a free-wheeling broker. Losses escalated, and Gordon took direct control from London. It was a disaster in commercial and people terms.

I was developing a style in P&O and had a team working with me in whom I had confidence and to whom authority was delegated. I felt I needed to *know* everything but not to *do* everything myself. It seemed to me that Gordon was becoming a one-man-band and on more than one occasion I went across the piazza to see him. I suggested that he should show the board that he too led a team and had confidence in it. Despite our friendship, I got short shrift: 'If you don't like what I'm doing you go and see the chairman.' To my regret I did not take his advice. I do not know what the relationship between Sandilands and Dunlop was at that time. The chairman's duty is to offer counsel and advice to his CEO. Perhaps it was too late. Gordon developed a scheme to take CU offshore to enhance its international scope, and to escape what he regarded as the restrictive jurisdiction in the UK. For most of us it was a scheme too far.

Yet it was a shock to be summoned, early one June morning in 1977, to an emergency board meeting at which the chairman would report that he had asked for Dunlop's resignation. The decision had been taken by the inner group of directors and the rest of us were assumed to be ready to support it. I was unhappy at the way it was handled, but ready to accept the inevitability of the decision, given my growing breakdown in confidence. I wrote to Gordon that in personal terms I was distressed, that it seemed a waste of talent which we could ill-afford and that I thought that history would show that he had done much to bring CU into the modern world.

I was going through something of the same trauma in P&O, but believed I was handling it rather better, and when the P&O débâcle unfolded in 1979 my colleagues at Commercial Union were very supportive. I had by then been on the board for almost ten years and, as I moved on to new fields, I continued to build up my knowledge of CU's business and its staff. The trading position was difficult, in very large measure because of over-exposure in the USA. The issues were complex. There was marked optimism within the senior management in America contrasting with, in some cases, near despair in the UK. These were difficult years for Commercial Union.

In 1982 Francis Sandilands, who was due to retire in two years' time, began discussions about succession. I think he felt that the position was straightforward – Jack Emms would slide effortlessly from his appointment as CEO into the chair; indeed this intention had been conveyed to Jack. However, it became evident that not all directors were content.

I was clear that, in principle, it was not good practice for chief executives to 'retire upwards' to the chairmanship. Others were not totally convinced that Jack Emms, however worthily he had performed as CEO during a difficult period, was cut out for the job.

When concern began to colour relationships, Francis showed some impatience. Discussions gathered momentum and the critical decision was taken that Jack Emms would *not* be offered the appointment. I was then prepared for a candidate to 'emerge through the usual channels' and expected that a City Establishment figure would be nominated.

To my great surprise Francis telephoned me one evening to ask if I would be prepared to succeed him. The other non-executives had apparently, unbeknown to me, focused on two candidates from among their colleagues. In the end, consultation with top management indicated a marked preference for me. Although deeply immersed in the City, I did not regard myself as of the Establishment. Indeed P&O, Tube Investments, Bestobell and Boots had already taken me into different fields. I had, however, tried to learn the insurance business. I was not simply an attender at board meetings, and I had not been afraid to take a position during some of the many difficult situations CU faced in the UK, USA and Australia.

Succession in 1984 could be arranged to fit with Bestobell's plans although, clearly, CU would have first call. With some apprehension, but also excitement, I accepted, stipulating that I would retire when I became sixty-five. I did not want there to be any suggestion of withering in office or clinging to power. The then vice-chairman Nicholas Baring wrote to me at the end of October, and, treading on delicate ground, asked if I could so arrange my affairs as to be available to assume the chairmanship in March 1983, twelve months earlier than at first envisaged. Supported by the other directors, he suggested that the gathering problems, particularly in the USA, were such that an early handover had merit and that there would be advantage in applying 'your fresh mind' to the issues. I felt able to run in double harness at CU and Bestobell for a period. Francis, for whom this was a rather bitter pill, was gracious and helpful.

The formal announcement was made on 25 November. We prepared for penetrating questions from the press and analysts: 'Is Sir Francis's retirement connected with the acute financial problems in CU?'; 'Surely in these difficult times it is vital to have a chairman well-versed in the insurance industry? Mr Marshall has no such experience'; 'Has there been a boardroom struggle?'; 'What special qualities will Mr Marshall bring?'.

My response was ready: 'I have been on the board for twelve years; I have knowledge of CU people and respect for their professionalism; I am not starry-eyed; strategic thinking is improving, but we have some way to go. I have made a success of recent years; I have international experience and have negotiated with governments in Washington, Moscow, and Canberra.'

The press gave me a resounding welcome. The *Daily Telegraph* proclaimed: 'Sandy Marshall has landed the toughest job in the insurance world.' The *Daily Mail* referred to me as one 'who combines ability with popularity to an unusual degree', and went on to say: 'There is a certain blissful irony, though Mr Marshall is far too nice to say so. From his new office, high in CU's HQ, he can look down on the black building next door – P&O's head office.' CU had just announced an underwriting loss of £180 million for the nine months to the end of September 1982. ' "It is not an easy scene we are operating in, that's for sure," said Mr Marshall.'

One of the most interesting letters in a large sack of mail was from John Woodthorpe, who as well as being a friend and neighbour was a partner of McKinseys. He added to his congratulations a penetrating analysis of the UK insurance industry and the proposition that in my tenure as chairman I might preside over what he regarded as a necessary restructuring involving large-scale consolidation. This suggested, given the then straits in which CU stood, a surprising degree of confidence in my capabilities. His vision, too, turned out to have been accurate if his timing was some years too early.

At the beginning of 1983 my business activities were at a peak: I was chairman both of Commercial Union and of Bestobell; I was vice-chairman, and soon to be chairman, of the Maersk Company; a director of the Boots Company and soon to be vice-chairman; I was a director of Tube Investments, chairman of the UK South Africa Trade Association and soon to be co-chairman of the British North American Committee. I was also involved for intense periods of activity in a number of charities and appeals. It was a busy time, but I was buoyed by the challenges. I was fit and operating from a strong home base.

The bare figures covering my tenure at CU tell a story of crisis in the early years being turned into reasonable stability in the later years:

	£		£
1983 profit	93 m	1987 profit	170.1m
1984 loss	(72.8m)	1988 profit	201.8m
1985 loss	(58.8m)	1989 profit	150.5m
1986 profit	119.1m		

US business dominated the first years. Ill-considered appointments to top management had resulted in impressive growth in geographic coverage and in premium income. In one year CU's gross premium rose by almost 23%. Unfortunately the market grew by only 2%, so we found that, inevitably, we had picked up a lot of the rubbish discarded by other insurers. Yet, in the course of visits to the field in the South East, Mid West and Chicago I appreciated how difficult it is to control activity and cost in the branches. An indication from head office of a wish to acquire more business can lead to compromise in underwriting standards; tightening-up can be achieved by maintaining the premium, but, for a 'good' client, increasing cover. It needs understanding and commitment throughout the company. Head office must run a tight ship and be seen to add value.

An early move by Cecil Harris, who had succeeded Emms as chief executive, was to replace the top US management with home-grown management, principally Tony Brend, plucked from Australia and made a main board director to afford him added status. He picked further key personnel and soon began to make a difference – leadership had been lacking.

Given our size and track record however, it would be difficult to live profitably in this enormous, very competitive and over-insured market. We were followers in the market and had little influence. We had a good name in Massachusetts and in some other areas, but no significant national presence.

Our competitors were also going through difficulties, and we responded to various suitors and initiated discussions with others, the object being to see if we could joint-venture our US interests. We would sweeten the pill by contributing some measure of international business. The problem in reaching any meeting of minds was the black hole of our domestic US results. We simply did not know how bad they might be. Thus we could not be sure that our reserves were adequate and the other parties inevitably made a worst-case assumption. Nevertheless we kept a number of balls in the air –

Equitable Mutual, Allianz of Munich, with whom we had a long-standing and supportive relationship, and Hertford.

To compound our woes, hurricane Alicia in August and extraordinarily cold weather at the beginning of winter resulted in huge claims. Yet I suggested in my annual report statement that 1984 should give us good grounds for securing an improvement. There was a long way to go. It was a difficult time and put enormous strain on both board and management. There was tension and criticism, but it was then that management really accepted that they needed the directors to understand and to be supportive. It took time, but papers became more informative, there was more discussion, more patience on both sides. Gradually the non-executives began to feel that they were being shown a true bill of goods, that there was a chance that we would not have to face an apologia each month and that their opinions and comments were appreciated.

But, despite progress, a number on the board favoured withdrawal from the USA, and, until we had more reliable data and improved control systems this had to remain an option. One of the sceptics was Christopher Laidlaw. He had, I think, been disappointed at not himself becoming chairman and it was not surprising that he resigned in 1983.

The quality of data was really the root of the problem and when we came to finalise the 1984 accounts I was faced with one of the most difficult situations a chairman could have. There was fundamental disagreement between management and our auditors, Coopers & Lybrand, on the reserving policy in the USA. A tough Cecil Harris and a cool John Linbourn argued the company's case – the culmination of massive work with our US managers and much negotiation with regulators in Boston.

Coopers took a hard line, which, if accepted, could have fractured our already fragile stability. I had a rather stormy meeting with the senior partner, Brandon Gough. I was by no means the rational detached chairman; I was partisan, I demanded that we look at CU as an ongoing business, I maintained that we knew our business and had a plan, that the auditors did not have the information to justify the scale of provisions they were demanding and were obviously going for belt, braces and hope. I insisted that any talk of qualifying our accounts be dropped. To my immediate satisfaction, if somewhat to my surprise, Brandon Gough withdrew. It was a fine point. He faced a real dilemma, but I am glad that his judgement was to back our case.

The first years had indeed been rough and there were many analysts and journalists who had more or less given up on us. Neil Collins of the *Sunday Telegraph* wrote in November 1984: 'If the rot has been stopped at CU nobody outside the company can see it.' There was the rub and there was, for an extended period, nothing to do but bear it – we could offer no more hostages; we had to deliver. Meanwhile, takeover speculation was rife. Rumours were generated when, despite every precaution, someone heard of talks we had had with other insurers on the possibility of joint-venturing our US interests. Even prudent reinsurance arrangements were seized upon as indicating a readiness to throw in the towel. I was quoted: 'It takes time [in the USA] for changes to come through. To say that we should have acted earlier is not constructive, we have been taking action for the past eighteen months, cutting back unprofitable business.'

As the year passed and we improved risk analysis, claims data and management systems, understanding and confidence in our reserving systems grew. We also understood better where we had come from. I realise now that had we known in 1985 what, with improved management information, we knew in later years, I would have been unable to argue so strongly with the auditors. But we still had to put up with external criticism and there was also some dissatisfaction within the company. Those parts of the business which were performing well saw their good work being dissipated by horrendous losses in the States. But we won the time needed and we managed our way out of the problem. With less realism and less dogged determination we might have crumpled and effectively lost a business which was certainly in a very delicate state, but which had within it the potential for recovery. Some of those who contributed greatly to this total management effort retired before the fruits ripened, but they must have taken pride in the way in which their successors picked up the ball and ran with it.

Tony Brend, who had done so much to stabilise the US company, came back to the UK at the end of the year to succeed Cecil Harris as chief executive. We had added weight to the board with the appointment of Martin Jacomb, then of Kleinwort Benson. It was sad when Harry Fowler's time to retire came – as an American director he was very helpful to me in the early spiky climate surrounding meetings in Boston. He had been a particularly good friend to this country, having joined the British Army early in the war and served with distinction in the Rifle Brigade.

Tony formed a new top management team, and the systems approach brought in by Cecil Harris to ensure firmer controls began to deliver. We ceased to chase underwriting for the sake of premium income. Life assurance was pursued strongly to broaden our base, emphasis was placed on the UK and Europe, particularly France, and gradually the overwhelming influence of the USA was moderated. Instead of being referred to routinely as 'accident-prone Commercial Union', 'struggling CU' and so on, we now began to see 'recovery-stock CU' and 'CU the phoenix'. The marketing slogan 'We won't make a drama out of a crisis' became part of everyday language and helped significantly to re-establish recognition of professionalism and security, not only as fire and accident insurers but in general corporate terms. This was of great value as we developed financial services.

The board had had as hard a time as had management, and it was particularly tough for those whose knowledge of the insurance world was neither instinctive nor experience-based. Full marks to:

– Peter Ramsbotham, late of the foreign service, ambassador to USA until deposed by Jim Callaghan when prime minister in favour of his son-in-law Peter Jay.

– Bobby Brooks of Kleinworts (son of Ronnie, chairman in 1970) a steady, low-key individual who mostly followed but occasionally surprised.

– Freddy Fisher, ex-editor of the *Financial Times*, among the cleverest of the directors but one who I felt always hedged his bets.

– Martin Jacomb, a cerebral thinker and a very powerful contributor – it was immensely satisfying to me to have someone of that calibre on board and in position, I hoped, as a candidate to succeed me.

– Nicholas Baring, the longest-serving director. From the age of thirty-two a director of Northern & Employers and on the CU Board since 1968; by experience and conduct another eminently suitable candidate for the succession.

– Ronnie Hampel, a colleague from BNAC and an executive director of ICI, joined early in 1987. He did not accept that insurance was 'too difficult', which was good for all concerned.

These stalwart non-executive directors helped enormously as we developed our system of corporate governance.

After some years in the chair I suggested to management that we should revisit the question of establishing an audit committee. To my amazement Tony Brend, by then CEO, advised me that he had discussed this proposal with his opposite numbers in the other major insurance companies. Their conclusion was that in financially-oriented and aware companies like ours an audit committee was not required. My view was diametrically opposite. It is in such companies that a strong independent audit committee can provide the most powerful resource for transparency and reassurance. Sir James Ball at Legal and General, doyen of the insurance company chairmen, was of like mind. My colleagues were persuaded, and in short order we led the way with an Audit Committee composed entirely of non-executives, under a deputy chairman, in order to distance me. This innovation was followed shortly afterwards with the establishment of a Salaries – later Remuneration – Committee, again composed of non-executive directors. We were in the van of British companies at this time. It was therefore a neat accident of timing that Andrew Crichton should choose this moment to send me a copy of his memoirs inscribed 'To my old friend' – shades of less constructive corporate governance.

I was thinking about succession when I became sixty-five. Having declared firmly that I would go and still, optimistically, considering that I might then scale-down my commitments, I was also increasingly persuaded that some time-frame should be put around the appointments of chairman and chief executive. Without being dogmatic, and recognising that there are always special cases (my own experience in P&O being one such, because there was unfinished business!), I was beginning to favour the argument that after, say, eight to ten years, a chief executive should have done most of what he came in to do. He should have contributed to change or maintained a steady course, been through a business cycle, developed his management team and prepared successors. So far so good, some might say – now he should enjoy the fruits of his labours. However, there are dangers – technology, practice, politics are all moving rapidly and one needs constant refreshment to keep up. When he 'knows it all' a chief executive can become defensive. So, without drama, the mechanics of moving on merit consideration.

For the chairman the position is not quite so clear. It is his role to think strategically, to be independent, not too close to management. The arguments about defensiveness can still apply and, even if they do not, there is a case for a fresh eye to take a look at any business. The exact timing is not important; my view is simply that a company is better to avoid entrenchment at the top. In 1987, with two and a half years to go to my self-imposed 'sell-by date', it was not too early to start getting my ducks in a row.

Then, in the autumn, there came an amazing coincidence of physical and financial catastrophes. On 17 October Mona and I held a dinner party on the top floor of the CU building with guests drawn from major business connections, government departments and politics. It was a rather splendid affair, although, on a misty evening, the lights of the City and the Tower were not at their sparkling best. In my welcoming remarks I mentioned, specially, Mike and Bee Rosholt of Barlow Rand who were over from South Africa. Natal had just experienced a devastating cyclone, which had done immense damage. I said that while our weather might often be disappointing, at least we did not have to undergo the extremes experienced in South Africa. I went on to labour the point by saying that, in business terms, CU had itself suffered severe conditions over recent years, but that I was confident that the mists were now . clearing.

The party broke up at 11 p.m. Mona and I were driven home by John, the chauffeur. As we got out of the Rolls, he observed that it was rather windy. In the small hours we were wakened. The hurricane which swept so powerfully over south-east England is now part of history. As with so many others, our trees were uprooted, fencing destroyed, no power, no telephone – we were isolated for days. It was a disaster for many individuals and businesses and a severe blow for the insurance industry, but fortunately for CU our risk-averse posture, which had ensured extensive external reinsurance, limited losses to £15 million. That net figure does not, however, reflect the unprecedented effort by CU staff, who handled over 100,000 claims.

There was more to come. Over the weekend immediately following the hurricane the world stock markets were put under immense strain. Black Monday saw prices in free-fall and for a time there was a threat to the world's financial system. We were relieved that the conservative investment policy which we had followed in the UK and the USA proved its value in moderating the impact on CU of these market upheavals.

I have not been allowed to forget my somewhat infelicitous comments about UK weather and CU prospects at the dinner on 17 October 1987.

The last years of the 1980s were years of consolidation and in two areas negative decisions stood the company in good stead. UK management decided to withdraw from mortgage insurance and when the property bubble peaked in 1988, and then entered a prolonged collapse, that decision was more than fully justified. In 1986–8 there was a rush by insurance companies, banks and building societies to buy estate agencies. Vertical integration providing 'one-stop shopping' for house purchase, mortgage, financial services, insurance and investment seemed irresistible. Fortunately, CU decided against this pattern, for it did not generally work well for the participants. It would be nice to say that this represented perspicacity at its best, but in part, a large part, it has to be admitted that our balance sheet was not in shape to take on such commitments at that time.

In cutting our cloth to difficult trading conditions there was a marked scaling-down of sponsorships and promotions after 1983. During the 1970s, CU had sponsored the Masters World Tennis championships, Glyndebourne productions – notably *A Midsummer Night's Dream* – and under Francis Sandilands's influence many artistic and musical occasions. Early in 1983 Mona and I inherited from Francis a special evening at the Albert Hall when CU sponsored the centenary concert of the Royal College of Music. The guests of honour were the Prince and Princess of Wales and it was a memorable experience to sit alongside them in the front row of the Royal Box – indeed to stand beside them as the National Anthem was played and the whole assembly turned, faces raised towards us.

As 1990 approached and with CU in better shape I again took soundings among my colleagues about succession, not without some regret. For a time I developed severe withdrawal symptoms, but I stuck to my plan. Martin Jacomb, who was favoured by a number of directors, said quite firmly that he would not be available if Nicholas Baring wanted to do the job. That settled it – Nicholas, as a result of a redeployment in Barings, was no longer fully engaged there. He would do the CU job very well indeed. I handed over to him after the AGM in March 1990, leaving the company a very different animal from the one I had taken on in 1983.

The insurance industry – for so long closed, defensive and inward-looking – was by now evolving swiftly, partly as a result of the market and partly as a result of regulatory pressures. I do not say that there was not more to do – there was still a residue of the old attitude that insurance is unlike any other industry and requires a lifetime to understand its complexities. But quality staff, a smaller and better-informed board, an improved balance in the business, both geographically and in terms of focus, with expanded life assurance and investment services added to general insurance, and a culture of transparency with employees and customers, all helped to ensure more professional and confident management.

While my time with Commercial Union makes a good story, another insurance association was a disaster. Membership of Lloyd's had been suggested to me in the 1970s, but did not seem right for me, a dedicated, one-company man. When I moved on in 1979, however, my income was coming from a number of different sources and I was paying more attention to personal tax. Through Neil Matthews, who had been so helpful to me as P&O Marine Insurance Manager, and Carel Mosselman, chairman of Sedgwicks, I accepted a renewed offer. Mona was not keen – she had little time for the pompous, self-important and dim 'professionals' whom we came across. However, I was sponsored by Gordon Brunton, chief executive of the Thomson Organisation and married to Mona's cousin Gill. I was introduced to a number of syndicates with apparently successful records, I knew a number of satisfied Names, the tax breaks were attractive, capital worked twice, and so on. I secured approval from Francis Sandilands.

Profits rolled in, but advisedly I treated these as distinct from my budgeted income and distributed them to the family or put them back into reserves. I did not pledge our home or engage in borrowing or guarantees to support my funds at Lloyd's, which demonstrated some caution, although at no time did I think we were at risk in any significant way.

On becoming chairman of CU in 1983, I had to be sure that there could be no, even remote, possibility of a conflict of interest so, with the board's approval, I put my Lloyd's interests with Sedgwicks, who were given full authority and instructed not to consult me. There was some sort of holy satisfaction in such action, but in hindsight, it was a poor decision to grant a third party discretion over what could be one's entire 'fortune'. But, as everyone said: 'It can't go wrong.'

So it seemed for the next seven years. Then it fell apart. So much has been written about the disaster that I will not embark on analysis. While there was undoubtedly fraud and criminal negligence, much of the shambles was due to arrogance, selfish insiderism and sheer ineptitude.

Fortunately the hard-won rescue and rehabilitation settlement of 1996 succeeded and the majority of Names are well out of it. The lack of equity in the settlement and the escape of some of those with the gravest responsibility are unhappy legacies, but a commercial solution was found and I was relieved to survive without excessive damage and at a far better level than seemed possible during the bad years from 1992 to 1995.

14
South Africa

Although family connections were strong and holiday visits not infrequent, some years were to elapse after my exploratory visits to Southern Africa before I developed a further business interest. It was modest at first. With UAL, the merchant banking arm of Anglo American, P&O established a shipbroking office in Johannesburg, with the intention in the early 1970s of securing contracts for the carriage of coal and ore from Richards Bay to Japan and Europe.

John Popper, an enthusiastic man who headed Peninsular Shipping, involved us in a major project being promoted by Dr Wilhelmi, a somewhat shadowy businessman with interests in steel and in mining. These were days of growth and a 'can do' attitude. Certainly to construct a new railway from Wilhelmi's iron and manganese ore mines in the Northern Cape, across South Africa, to a loading facility to be built at St Croix, Port Elizabeth, qualified as one of the more imaginative schemes. Extensive technical studies were encouraging, but contracts for the sale of ore proved elusive and the project collapsed.

Chemicals and gas offered more tangible reward and the Johannesburg team developed business both for Mundo Gas and Panocean. In 1970, however, a significant contract for delivery of propane to Johannesburg was secured by Fred Jackson of Mundo Gas – not through Peninsular Shipping but through a complicated chain of middlemen in Europe. This was a new market for Mundo Gas and one with potential, so it was with concern that we, P&O, were informed in London that the international monitoring authority established to enforce sanctions against Ian Smith's breakaway Rhodesia had reason to believe that a cargo discharged at Lourenço Marques from one of the Mundo Gas vessels, and ostensibly destined for Johannesburg, had found its way to Rhodesia.

Looking back on the whole affair, it has to be recognised that Rhodesia, aided by South Africa, had developed a highly sophisticated sanction-busting organisation. It was not impossible that documentation could have been changed after the tank wagons containing the propane were in the SA railway system and that the end-user certificate produced to Mundo Gas was spurious. At the outset, however, P&O and our colleagues, Lorentzen and Mobil, were outraged that it was being implied that we had condoned such goings on. Worse was to come when Mundo Gas and a number of executives were charged in the Bermudan courts. The shareholders agreed to the company defending itself and its executives, and there commenced a ridiculous legal jamboree. I alerted the Foreign Office to the damage being done to a significant British interest. The ministers and officials pleaded that the matter was sub judice, and in any case was nothing to do with them because it was in the hands of the Bermudan government. The latter made it clear that the shots were being called by London, where I believed it was felt that Britain could show willing by clobbering a relative minnow, in a colonial jurisdiction, while suspect cases, involving major oil companies, were ignored.

Counsel after counsel was engaged from the UK – they were not available in Bermuda. Everyone connected, even in a remote way, deemed it necessary to have at least a watching brief, because such was the atmosphere that there was no knowing where the various cases might lead. Rhodesia was beginning to cost us dear.

Eventually sheer overload brought matters to a head. A pragmatic, if rather shoddy deal, was concluded, involving – although no such admission would be given – the Foreign Office and the Bermudan government. The charges against the company were withdrawn, the executives pleaded guilty and were required to leave the island, with compensation, and the legal luminaries counted their fees with satisfaction while the shareholders counted their costs with dismay.

For years before this, the Rhodesian situation had been a major topic during our family visits to South Africa. In November 1965, the colony's government led by Ian Smith had declared UDI (Unilateral Declaration of Independence). The action was, of course, interpreted by its proponents as the essential defence of fundamental values in the face of the feared imposition of majority (black) rule, and there were many in the UK who sympathised with the views of the white government, even if somewhat uncertain about its methods. In South Africa, itself dominated by racial discrimination, there was, within the white population, almost universal support for the Smith government and wide condemnation of the Wilson administration in the UK, which was regarded as crypto-communist. There was a tendency, too, to ridicule the British way of life as demonstrated by the liberal, free-wheeling 1960s.

Mona's father Leslie was a devoted South African, but his roots were Scottish and in many ways he was the archetypal Scottish export. Despite his commitment to his adopted country, he had retained a sense of history and perspective and it was impressive to hear him take issue among his friends. He recognised the winds of change and was one of few in the White River community to question the morality and viability of UDI, as, indeed, he questioned the reasoning behind the South African National Party's move to leave the Commonwealth. Mona's mother had stood with the Black Sash movement against the pass laws and Mona herself moved in a young group in Johannesburg which, finding the segregation laws ridiculous, treated them with disdain.

We had friends in Rhodesia on both sides of the argument, extreme right wing and progressive liberal. On one principle they all agreed, affection for the people and the land of Rhodesia. There was some tendency, outside, to condemn the white population as a whole, but I always found it both salutary and inspiring when I was able to drop in to Salisbury or to Fort Victoria even when the 'war' was at its worst. I wanted to show that, while we might not support their government, we hoped for a long-term solution which recognised and preserved the contribution which the settlers had made to the country.

Alastair was christened, aged four months, at The Fountains on his first visit to South Africa and thereafter Mona took him and Gillian out more than once for two or three months of the British winter. They were idyllic times with trips to the Kruger Park, Swaziland and the high-veld. James, our youngest child, appeared, the children were growing up and visits were necessarily shorter but just as exciting. There was fishing in the dams, ringing of migratory birds and walking in the bush with Mona's brother, Howard. There were many magic experiences: lions at Shingwidzi in the northern part of the Reserve, which interrupted Alastair's birthday supper, an epic Land-Rover chase when game-catching in Swaziland and thunderstorms below us as we climbed Mount Anderson.

Sometimes on my own and sometimes with Mona, I was able to visit for a day or two en route from Australia to the UK. We were at home in South Africa and I grew to love it. Politics existed in a time-warp and we often suffered frustration, but throughout the bad years we always marvelled at the general goodwill between peoples, which still gives hope for the future.

In 1979, I found, in Bestobell, a flourishing presence in South Africa. The company was well-established as agents for suppliers of specialised engineering components, as a manufacturer of valves and as an insulation contractor.

Later, when I became chairman of Commercial Union, my direct interests in South African business multiplied. CU was expanding life assurance and developing the emerging Black market for both life and general insurance.

Because of Bestobell's high profile, I was glad, in 1980, to take on the chairmanship of the UK South Africa Trade Association (UK-SATA), at a time when the anti-apartheid movement was stepping up its campaign to discourage investment, and indeed to introduce sanctions. I felt that I could make a contribution to rational policy. The UK was the biggest overseas investor in South Africa, accounting for over 50% of all foreign investment. At the same time, the UK was in the top three of South Africa's trading partners with a substantial balance of payments surplus in our favour. This was in itself worth protecting, but the membership of UKSATA, representing most of the major UK companies with interests in South Africa, also felt an obligation to their workforce and a conviction that the most significant contribution that business could make towards a solution of the appalling dilemma and dichotomy of the country was to operate an efficient, competitive enterprise. Favourable economic growth would, in turn, benefit all sectors of the population. There seemed at the time to be a school of thought that the quickest way to bring about change was to pull down the house about South African ears. Who then would have benefited?

The four years during which I was chairman of UKSATA included some of the darkest days of relations with the apartheid regime, but we kept communications open.

It had been important under a Labour government for UKSATA to be apolitical, and we still kept our distance in case we wanted to adopt an independent line, but during my term as chairman we found the Thatcher administration realistic and constructive. I had ready access to Geoffrey Howe as foreign secretary and to Malcolm Rifkind, the minister of state.

At a Ditchley conference in May 1983, I chaired a working party to consider what contribution the private sector could make to the process of change in South Africa. My team included academics from the UK and the USA, businessmen, and our 'statutory' SA black – Enos Mobuza. He had been the schoolmaster at White River where he knew my brother-in-law Howard and was now chief minister of Kangwane, one of the smaller semi-autonomous homelands. Our discussion was circulatory and at the lunch break I felt discouraged. I sat with Mobuza, who had hardly spoken at all; we could help, but the will and the drive had to be from within – could he not offer some suggestion? This was his first appearance at such a conference and he was rather overwhelmed, but he gave me a key, saying that, unless we had a member of the South African government in our group, we would not make progress. The one interest *not* represented at Ditchley was, of course, the Pretoria government. However, Reg Hibbert, the director, persuaded Van Zyl Slabbert to join us. An articulate and persuasive man, he added the missing political dimension, and from differing standpoints we were able to develop sufficient unanimity for me to report a conclusion. We could see no economic initiative having value unless it were taken in the light of positive political action. The government had to set the scene. It was the dearth of such action which was so discouraging and so damaging. It was neither original nor surprising, but the obvious had to be stated again and again.

Prior to the Commonwealth Conference in Nassau in October 1985, I was summoned to Chequers, together with John McQuiggan, the dedicated if somewhat opinionated executive director of UKSATA. Margaret Thatcher wanted to consult a broad spectrum of academics, politicians and businessmen before facing her inevitably hostile colleague premiers who were all, for a variety of reasons – mostly self-seeking, prepared to attack Britain for not taking a sufficiently aggressive stand against the Nationalist government.

I felt that Britain had a different role to play and, when called upon, suggested to the PM that she should recognise her unique position as an instrument for change. Her world standing was at a high point and in South Africa she was recognised as 'our only real friend'. She could not perhaps go herself, but she could, contrary to accepted wisdom, send Geoffrey Howe to tell the Pretoria government bluntly that time was not on its side, that its friends might not be able to hold out forever and that, without some political initiative, confidence in the economy could not be maintained and the growth essential to meet the aspirations of a rapidly increasing population could not be achieved. Unfortunately, I then jeopardised the value of my contribution by suggesting also that she should not ignore the influence of the church, which had such wide support in South Africa. There was an audible intake of breath around the table and a short 'Thank you, Mr Marshall, for an interesting comment – next please, Professor Barber.'

However, the Nassau Commonwealth Conference did produce the Eminent Persons Group (EPG) led by Malcolm Fraser, which made considerable progress in establishing international bridgeheads. It was then largely frustrated by one of those repeated reminders that the SA government could be its own worst enemy. Just as the EPG mission was reaching its climax, commandos launched attacks on African National Congress command posts in Harare, Lusaka and Gaberone.

I was leading an UKSATA delegation to South Africa and, on that same evening, Monday 19 May 1986, ran into Tony Barber, a member of the EPG, at the Mount Nelson Hotel in Capetown. Barber was discouraged. The EPG was pulling out. This was a disappointment after so much hope, but the EPG's message perhaps contributed more than was at first appreciated in pushing forward the process of change.

Dick Lloyd, my ex-P&O colleague and now of Hill Samuel, Keith Stuart of British Ports, Roy Sisson of Smiths Industries and John McQuiggan were congenial and constructive members of my group. We visited the main commercial centres and met politicians of many persuasions. While it was hard work, it was also fun. We shared the chores as well as the relaxation and we gathered much useful information.

We were able again to convey to our hosts, at private meetings and at public press conferences, that there was immense goodwill in Britain and that we wanted to help. Yet a fascinating dinner with the minister of information at the government hospitality house near Pretoria illustrated vividly how difficult it was to bridge the gap between us. The minister was quite unprepared to accept any criticism. He saw no necessity to explain; *his* job was to tell people what they should know.

It was after that meeting that Roy Sisson, the wag of the party, commented: 'It's all downhill now, Sandy.' I know he meant we were coming to the end of the mission, but afterwards I wondered if he hadn't spoken of more serious events. There were bitter days to come before the breakthrough.

A happy outcome of that trip was that Mona and I saw something of James, who was in the Cape during his 'year off'. He seemed to be of no fixed abode and turned up at the Mount Nelson with all his worldly goods in the boot of a clapped-out old Toyota, pulled out some reasonable if crumpled clothing and was eager to make use of the facilities.

UKSATA gave me the opportunity to do something constructive to maintain the UK interest and perhaps to influence opinion-formers in the UK and in South Africa. I enjoyed meeting many who were making a much greater contribution – such men as Denis Worrell, the distinguished ambassador to London who gave up his post to go home to form a new liberal opposition party; Jan Steyn of the Urban Foundation, Chief Buthelezi, Dr Mothlana, and Alan Boesak of the coloured community (who was to fall from grace so spectacularly). Through Ewen Fergusson and Robin Renwick, both powerful ambassadors for the UK, we had access to the South African ministers, from the formidable 'PW' to the more compatible Dawie de Villiers. It was an interesting time.

Mention of Mangosutu Buthelezi reminds me of a meeting during one of his London visits as leader of the Inkatha party. Mona was in town and came with me. We were prompt. 'I regret, Mr Marshall,' said the Dutch lady who was Inkatha's European representative, 'the Chief Minister has been held up at a previous appointment, No. 10, I believe.' Half an hour later, Buthelezi swept in towards the lift, followed by his entourage, each member weighed down with Harrods bags. We managed to squeeze into the second lift with four or five of the Inkatha staff. They were evidently frustrated by this inconvenient interruption of their shopping expedition, but of course were not aware that Mona's somewhat rusty Zulu enabled her to pick up the gist of their remarks. Fortunately, the Chief Minister was courteous and charming and made the discussions worthwhile both from a personal and an UKSATA point of view.

15
Three Boards

During the 1980s, my primary commitment was to Commercial Union, although the demands made by other directorships in my portfolio were growing – in different industries each having its different structure and with different opportunities and problems. It has to be admitted that, from today's perspective, the way in which directors were then nominated might seem somewhat incestuous. Just as Denny Marris, who knew me in P&O, had introduced me to Commercial Union, so Lord Plowden, having seen me in action as a governor of the London Business School where he was chairman, and at CU where he was a senior director, introduced me to Tube Investments (TI) in 1974.

From 1981 to 1991 I was a director of The Boots Company, suggested, this time, by Michael Verey, a deputy chairman both of Commercial Union and of Boots, and from 1985 to 1995 I was a main board director of Royal Bank of Canada. These appointments ran in parallel with Commercial Union and Maersk, of which I was chairman for most of the time and with other commitments to BNAC and UKSATA. I believe that there was benefit to each from such involvement – another window on markets, management practices and, towards the end of the period, increasingly on corporate governance.

In 1974, Tube Investments might well have been a target for the asset-strippers, had that dynamic not fallen from grace after a number of high-profile failures and after the spectacular property collapse of 1973-74. The group was an amalgam of many companies across a wide range of heavy and light engineering – Round Oak Steel, Russell Hobbs, Creda, British Aluminium – all household names. The many executive directors represented fiefdoms – bicycles, steel tubes, white goods. Each would vigorously defend the interests of his sector, often frustrating the interests of others. As at Commercial Union, in my early days as a director the emphasis at board meetings was on reporting the past rather than looking forward.

Yet, under Lord (Edwin) Plowden, TI had style. Heavyweights such as Lord Penney of nuclear distinction, Sir Arnold France, an eminent civil servant and Plowden himself, a mandarin of mandarins, graced the board.

The writing may already have been on the wall, but after Edwin Plowden's retirement in 1976, to be succeeded by Brian Kellett, a long-time TI man and a mathematician of repute, the company showed signs of weariness, a loss of direction and of purpose in the face of the problems of the day such as inflation, union demands and international competition. When they left, non-executive directors were simply not replaced. Shortly, there were only four: Professor Sir James Ball, Sir James Menter, now of Queen Mary College, London, Sir St John Elstub, of Imperial Metal Industries, and myself. The imbalance was not helpful, especially as the chairman was himself executive.

Boots, which I joined in 1981, had some similarities with Tube Investments, but as many differences. A household name, yes, but an ethos of quality and of concerned service lay at its core. The reverse of this coin was, however, a tendency to 'cosiness', an assumption of almost effortless leadership and ultimately of invincibility. It was endearing in a way, but did not augur well in increasingly competitive times.

The board of Boots was close to the business – everyone was a customer (including the directors) and thus had strong views about the front window, Boots the Chemist. Sally Oppenheim, who was the first woman on the board, was responsive to consumer interests (her responsibility when in government); David Sarre to relations with the public and staff; while Bernard Scott was particularly interested in the overseas operations. Involvement in such detail led to understanding and to an ability to contribute on matters of policy.

Boots valued and made use of its non-executives. When I joined, there was already an Audit Committee. A few years later I became chairman of that and also of the Ethics Committee which, first established under David Sarre, oversaw issues of environmental concern, energy conservation, the place of women in management and, always, drug testing on animals. Boots was one of the first to publish a statement of corporate policy on such matters.

TI, on the other hand, seemed to regard its non-executives as ornamental, even a bit of a nuisance. Soon after I took over at Bestobell, we engaged the Boston Consulting Group to assist in analysing the business, to identify distinct profit centres and core activities. I had the temerity to suggest to Brian Kellett that TI might benefit from a similar approach. There were a few thinking executives on the board, but a number were disinclined to admit that a business in which one had spent a lifetime could be better managed, or was absorbing scarce resources and therefore a candidate for disposal. My initiative was not welcomed; TI was defensive.

The chairman sprang a proposal on us to buy the privately-held Lansing Bagnall company. The Lansing fork-lift truck was a first-class piece of engineering, but faced competition from Komatsu and other Far East manufacturers, whose machines were increasingly sophisticated and low-cost. The vendor's market projections seemed to have been accepted as the basis for negotiation on price and premium. I voted against what I thought to be an ill-conceived and poorly presented case, to be subjected to quite severe criticism for not being a good team player.

In Boots, the non-executives were encouraged to see and be seen, in shops and pharmaceutical plants around the world. I ensured that when I was in Australia, the USA or Bangkok I met the Boots people. I was always welcome and I learned a lot. The contrast in TI style was perhaps best summed up by Brian Kellett's response to my tentative enquiry as to whether, in a period when being a director was almost a labour of love (fees after tax were negligible), I might be afforded a modest contribution to expenses when visiting South Africa. I suggested that, in the course of our family holiday, I might make time to see TI steel tubes and the Raleigh bicycle plant in the Johannesburg area. 'No,' said Kellett, 'to make a gesture of that sort would not be understood within the company. I don't think it would be considered worthwhile your making a special visit, but of course if you want to . . .' I went ahead and my interest seemed to be appreciated, locally at least. I had done the same a couple of years earlier, when, on a visit to P&O's oil interests in the USA, I was able to fit in a brief call on Raleigh's new bicycle plant at Enid, Oklahoma. Built for growth (and for tax reasons, I suspect) it had enormous, and it turned out excess, capacity. Raleigh's market could not sustain the investment. It would have been better to promote the brand, but source in Taiwan or Korea.

Royal Bank of Canada (RBC) was a household name too – it handled 25% of Canada's banking business and was a leading international bank. Robin Adam, formerly a managing director of BP, was, in 1985, the sole European director. I was known to a number of the Canadian and American directors through BNAC (and also because of Commercial Union's well-publicised problems). As another European it was intriguing and exciting to be invited onto the board.

Rowlee Frazee, the chairman, explained that meetings were monthly, but I would not be expected to attend every one – 'something like four or five in the year'. Had I taken that literally I would soon have lost touch; so began ten years of monthly trips. On one of the last, in December 1995, the immigration official at Montreal looked up at me:

'What is your business?'

'Banking.'

'How long will you be here?'

'Twenty-four hours.'

'Have you been to Canada before?'

'Yes.'

'More than once?'

'About 120 times.'

Reflecting the federal structure of Canada, there were thirty-six directors and, as with CU, all non-executive bar one. Over the years, the number came down to twenty-five and the streamlining continues. RBC used its directors through a system of regional committees and, in the case of Europe, a subsidiary company in London, of which I became chairman. In RBC the Audit Committee was of great importance. There was also a Remuneration Committee and a Nominating Committee. The Audit Committee met Canada's Supervisor of Banking Institutions for an annual review; it led the board's understanding of directors' responsibility for the bank's creditworthiness and its capacity to handle exposure under the clearing system; and, most difficult for the layman, the whole issue of derivatives trading. Canada was, in a number of ways, ahead of the UK in matters of corporate governance.

Both Boots and RBC took the board to the shareholders. The former held meetings in centres of production or research. In RBC the board was even more mobile, with meetings in the state capitals, in New York and in London, where strategic issues were important.

When it came to succession to the top job in these three companies, there was a marked difference in approach. Change was forced upon TI. The company was bumbling along, trying to retain erstwhile predominance in activities in which competition or technology had overtaken it. In 1983, the non-executives, effectively Jim Ball and I, concerned at lack of grip and loss of direction, persuaded a reluctant Kellett that he should appoint a chief executive and, with some encouragement, he concluded that he should step down altogether. It is strange today to recall that, although a non-executive search committee was formed, we accepted that Kellett should be its chairman.

Peter Main had succeeded Gordon Hobday as chairman of Boots by some process of osmosis, and in 1985 Bob Gunn succeeded Peter. During his reign, he began to think about splitting the roles of chairman and chief executive. Internal candidates were considered for the chief executive appointment but soon the committee – Peter Reynolds, Ian Prosser and myself – was looking outside for someone unencumbered by historical baggage.

It was a long search. We thought it was a plum job with immense scope, but some thought it, frankly, too big; others were concerned about political danger in the conflicting profiles of the retail and the pharmaceutical divisions. Happily, after a year, our preferred choice unexpectedly became available. James Blyth, formerly with Lucas, the Ministry of Defence, and Plessey, is a driver and a doer. We voted for change and he made it happen. What was pleasing was that he found quality at top level in the Boots management which he had not expected. With a little redeployment, a bit of juggling with individual responsibilities, there was only one senior casualty. There have been one or two strategic 'misses', but many more successes and, under James, Boots has gone from strength to strength.

While the successor to Kellett was being sought at TI, I put forward a radical proposition that the role of Group headquarters was not proven. The businesses were too separate; simply presiding over consolidation of results did not justify the structure or the cost; where was the added value? I suggested that we might benefit shareholders and staff by de-merging and floating white goods, specialised engineering and bicycles. In the aftermath of management changes the idea was not followed up, but may now seem to have been ten years ahead of its time.

The management changes included the appointment of an initially reluctant Ronnie Utiger as CEO. After British Aluminium and a stint as managing director of British National Oil Corporation, Ronnie had returned to TI knowing full well that there were nettles to be grasped. He was not a very popular figure with colleagues, but was of undoubted ability. It took some time to persuade him that he could do the job well, that he would attract support and that he would be credible in the City and in the market. Having discharged one of the prime responsibilities of a non-executive, I assured Ronnie of my personal support, but also said he must feel free to make changes in the board to help him through what would be a rough period and that I would, of course, withdraw if he asked. After this selfless offer, it was, I have to admit, a jolt to have my 'resignation' accepted in short order. Jim Ball's resignation was also accepted within days. The important point was, however, that under Ronnie Utiger, TI began to take the required action and has since become one of the few British engineering businesses which are world-class – focusing on sophisticated activities in which they can be market leaders.

TI had not been an altogether happy board experience – in contrast with Boots, where I had ten stimulating years before retiring in 1991.

Both Boots and Royal Bank of Canada attracted upwards of 1,000 shareholders to Annual General Meetings. In Montreal, the AGM was an occasion for a major policy speech by the chairman, reporting on economic and political issues, and was covered extensively by the media. The two chairmen under whom I served, Rowlee Frazee and Allan Taylor, were towering figures in Canadian affairs. For the Boots chairman, after all the preparation which goes into arrangements, anticipating issues and researching answers to questions about obscure matters, the AGM must sometimes have been a letdown. Shareholders turned up to ask about pet food at the Kingston branch or why the shop at Caterham had been closed and, in many instances, simply to pick up the 'little gift' which was available to all at the conclusion. But, for all that, Boots's meetings were probably better than one particular Tube Investments AGM which I remember vividly. The year's results had been appalling, the worst in the company's history, yet not a single comment was made or question raised.

When Allan Taylor's retirement under RBC's age policy approached in 1994, there was much debate about the merits of splitting the roles of chairman and CEO. The bank executive, including the outgoing chairman, favoured continuation of the combined role, citing the structure of other Canadian and American banks. There were as many examples of different structures and, in my view and that of others, a tide moving towards separation. The issue of succession and the form of it was of great importance for the bank and the board over the next ten years, and the discussions held over some months by the Nominating Committee, enlarged by the addition of the chairmen of the other board committees, were frank and constructive. It is not often that opinions are changed in such debate, but in this instance strongly-held views were modified and in some cases altered. Perhaps it was no wonder that the meetings sometimes ran until late into the night before the monthly board, or had to be summoned for 7 a.m. the following morning.

Although I continued to hold the view that separation of the roles of chairman and chief executive would be better for the bank in the long term, and by instinct and experience I favoured the hierarchical, traditional management structure with well defined lines of authority and responsibility, I recognised that there is more than one way to skin a cat. Not having to live with the consequences – I would be retiring from the board in January 1995, just after my seventieth birthday – I had the luxury of being able to make my point firmly, but then accept gracefully the majority decision not to impose a structure on management but to support their commitment to the structure which they had developed. John Cleghorn, the president and an outstanding man, would take over both as chairman and CEO, with senior management forming a 'chairman's office' in which the chief executive would have a casting vote. I am glad that John Cleghorn and his team have shown this structure to work effectively.

My years on the Royal Bank of Canada board covered the emergence of the spectre of Third World debt, when default by a number of state borrowers threatened the stability of the banking system of the West. There were many criticisms levelled at the bank both for having made such loans over the preceding twenty years and then for 'failing to recognise the fragility of the loans'. Of course there was a dilemma – to bite the bullet and write off the loan might be macho, but not altogether in the shareholders' interests. On the other hand, to whistle in the wind and 'talk up' the competence and the intention of the borrowers could encourage them to avoid necessary action to get their houses in order and mislead investors as to the true financial strength of the bank.

In the event it was a balancing act. The hawks and the doves compromised. The banks, when possible jointly, made as high a provision as they could, while resisting pressure from certain governments and non-governmental agencies (NGOs) to forgive. Brazil, Mexico, Argentina, and on a lesser scale but to an even more parlous degree, a number of African countries were all among the basket cases. It was not until the US Secretary of the Treasury developed the eponymous Brady bond that the breakthrough came. The plan established a pattern for capping the losses, but also providing a market for the debt. Together with improved discipline imposed by the International Monetary Fund and a recovery in the world economy, the major problems, which at one time appeared overwhelming, were overcome, albeit at considerable cost to the banks' shareholders.

What was interesting as an external director to observe was the toughness of the executives in recommending the 'punishment' – in many cases the same executives who had been responsible for authorising the culprit loans. This scenario was to be repeated periodically as, in turn, it seemed various blue chip markets turned sour. Oil and gas produced Dome Petroleum; the property market Olympia & York. The lumber industry, agriculture, real estate and shipping all had their problem loans which we sweated through. As the end of the decade approached, high risk, threatening loans to the former tigers of the Orient and to the sophisticated but inadequately managed hedge funds, have caused concern. It is hard to learn.

I saw RBC grow with the acquisition of two major financial enterprises, Dominion Securities and Royal Trust. The integration of each was handled differently but equally effectively. I was glad too, as chairman of the International Strategic Issues Committee, to be involved in the broad thinking about some of the major issues facing the bank. The committee was at first a rubber stamp for management, but I was able to establish a more active agenda and we began to study the various international businesses. We looked at trade finance, at the increasing fragility of Japanese banking and at potential issues arising from moves towards European integration and a common currency. The USA, a major opportunity or threat, was a shadowy area for the committee – management regarded the States as domestic business. There was a tension here, never wholly resolved.

But something was missing, and in my last year I was able to focus on the problem. I had no difficulty with an advisory role for the committee provided we were 'in' on the issues at an early enough stage to contribute advice. But I saw that there could be a more worthwhile role if the committee could advise on the balance of our overall business – where emphasis should be placed or reduced, what major opportunities or threats were on the horizon or indeed beyond it, and so on.

The committee could not make a really effective contribution if it was confined, as first constituted, to international business (quite apart from ambiguity about the USA) and when the overwhelming preponderance of domestic business was very firmly 'off limits'. I therefore felt there was an excellent case for dropping 'International' in favour of simply a Strategic Issues Committee. Its brief on behalf of the board would be to study, report and recommend on issues affecting strategy for the various major businesses in order to develop and maintain an appropriate balance in the overall business. This could, I appreciated, impinge on – for example – the retail franchise in Canada or the potential expansion into insurance. It could, indeed, be said that these were matters for the board itself. Of course decisions would be for the board, but in today's complex conditions, and even with a board reduced to twenty-five, the donkey-work required to take an informed decision would put an excessive and ideeed unnecessary burden on management and on individual directors. As with the other committee functions, I felt that directors would, without abandoning responsibility, be able to feel confident that a committee of independent directors working with management would serve the board well. I was glad that in the final structure, settled as I came up to retirement, the Strategic Issues Committee was established.

Another international matter worried me. Initially, as the pattern of banking activity changed to corporate global finance and as local banks around the world took on more run-of-the-mill retail banking, RBC reduced or even withdrew its overseas operations. South America and the Caribbean were much affected, and even in Europe there was centralisation of systems and management with 'hubs' being created in Miami, London, Hong Kong and Singapore.

Because of immigration regulations in many countries, it became increasingly difficult to place Canadians in overseas jobs, even for training. The old tradition of service overseas, followed by a return to head office with foreign experience, was being lost and with that loss came an inevitable tendency towards 'Canada knows best'. It could be argued that high quality local staff were being recruited and the bank was therefore becoming more international in its personnel. However, when further, centralising, steps were taken towards the end of 1994 with a proposal to move the management of Private Banking from London to Toronto, I was concerned that it would require a positive effort to maintain the commitment and performance of the overseas offices. If all roads for promotion lead to Toronto, the bank remains a Canadian institution with certain international interests, rather than an international bank. Perhaps this is as it should be, but that is a strategic decision to be taken rather than drifted into. I left my colleagues with a paper expressing this worry.

The warm friendship of the RBC directors and many of the staff made a great impression on both Mona and me during my ten years. This was again emphasised at the AGM in January 1995, when I was due to retire. It was a celebration whose outcome could have been tragic. Three days of functions lay ahead of us. At a huge dinner on the first evening, for staff from around the world, I and the other 'retirees' made our farewell speeches and suffered much leg-pulling. Allan Taylor was standing down as chairman, and the meeting on the following morning was marked by well-deserved tributes to him, led by John Cleghorn, while in the evening the new chairman gave another enormous dinner party. Mona had been in very good form throughout and it was therefore confusing and frightening when she fainted dramatically as the guests were being seated. There followed a nightmare, with paramedics, wailing ambulances, and Mona's emergency admission to hospital in the manner of the most lurid television series. Ghastly for her, and I found the strength draining from me as I watched the doctors at work. Yet, after several days of extensive tests and monitoring, the excellent specialists at Toronto General Hospital pronounced themselves satisfied that her collapse had been an inexplicable aberration, and that Mona did not have a heart problem. Jane Lawson, Secretary of RBC, gave us generous support, as did John Evans, a fellow director and former cardiologist, and his wife, Gay. We travelled carefully home and normal life resumed. All the directors and their wives had been concerned, and when, at John Cleghorn's invitation, we returned to Montreal for the AGM in January 1996, 'to complete the retirement process, so rudely interrupted', the welcome for Mona was to a degree touching.

16

Back to Shipping

Two very different associations kept me involved in shipping during the 1980s while my principal tasks were elsewhere, in engineering and insurance.

The first, which must stand as one of the eccentricities of the shipping industry, was the Old Tie Club. Soon after the Second World War, a number of individuals, who had been in Merchant Shipping Control in London and Washington, agreed that their close relationship should not be allowed to wither. Each would go on to positions of authority in their respective countries and an informal network could be valuable in promoting common policy and in defusing any potential problem. The membership included many of the most illustrious names in the international industry.

'Old Tie Club' was suggested by the Dutch, and Bill Weston of Shell sealed it by producing a stock of hideous, stringy ties, surplus after the closure of a boys' prep school. The tie became an amusing and treasured symbol. At bi-annual meetings, friendships were maintained and, through a patently obvious old boy network, I am sure that policy, especially in the liner trades, was influenced. When the EEC was formed, German and Italian members joined the club, but the formal international bodies increasingly provided more appropriate vehicles for consultation and the success of NATO covered the defence concerns. The founders departed.

In the 1970s, Murk Muller of Van Ommeren led a revival. Lindsay Alexander, chairman of Ocean, Bob Crawford of Silver Line and I joined and a number of Scandinavian, French and Benelux people picked up the baton. We enjoyed friendly meetings in London, Oslo, Paris and Hamburg (where, eerily, I was given a German-made model of my wartime *Oribi*), but, as time and cost pressures weighed more heavily, commitment faded. The Old Tie Club was unique, initially influential, but finally anachronistic.

The second association was one I valued highly. I have recorded earlier how honoured I was in 1979 to be asked by Maersk Møller to join his board in the UK. I put in fifteen years as director, vice-chairman, chairman, and then again as director, before retiring at the end of 1995. The Maersk Company Ltd, a subsidiary of the Danish A. P. Møller Group, had been established in the UK since 1954, but it was under Karsten Borch, an engaging and lively managing director that, in the 1980s, it became an innovative and entrepreneurial shipowner.

When I succeeded Sir Andrew Stark, former ambassador to Denmark, as chairman in 1988, I undertook that Maersk, although effectively owned by a single shareholder, would operate as if it were a publicly quoted company. The balance sheet would be important, debt ratios reasonable, we would aim to pay consistent dividends and should seek new business appropriate to capacity and skills. The final say in matters of investment was not wholly in our hands and a number of areas, despite their potential, were declared off-limits, but the company developed formidable skills in ship management and, thus, after establishing itself as the low-cost operator in the group, was progressively given the opportunity of spreading its wings. With RoRos, LPG vessels, small container ships and large offshore craft, Maersk established a significant British fleet. Together with sister companies, it has become a major player in project management work for the oil industry in the North Sea, and in the container trades, Maersk, as agents in the UK for A. P. Møller's worldwide services, has achieved great success – customer-oriented, systems-supported, slim and responsive – the jargon really means something. The watchword 'with constant care' continues as does the objective to have zero deficiencies in operations.

Maersk Mc-Kinney Møller, who leads the Group, is a figure of immense distinction in the international business world. He is both demanding and inspiring. It is a happy recognition of his friendship to Britain that he has been awarded an honorary KBE.

Despite these connections, my invitation to become president of the Chamber of Shipping in 1994 came as a surprise and I was delighted. It was fifteen years since I was in the frame, and to some it may have seemed that I was being hauled back from retirement. But I knew that I could make a contribution. My appointment was a breakthrough for Maersk in industry affairs. Hitherto, although it had been accepted that American oil companies could supply Chamber officers, there seemed to be some resistance to smaller companies, which were perhaps regarded as not 'true blue'.

Maersk Møller had been strangely and unnecessarily concerned about a possible clash of interest when, as was my duty, I sought his endorsement of my presidency. His worries were however resolved when I handed over the chairmanship of Maersk to Juan Kelly, who had many more years than I of active business life ahead of him.

The Chamber of Shipping (the shipowners' association had reverted from GCBS to its traditional name in 1992) draws its authority from the support of its membership and I was glad to have this in full measure. After a six months' apprenticeship to Edmund Vestey, my predecessor, I took over on 18 January 1994, when my first engagement was the Chamber's dinner for some 750 guests at Grosvenor House. As I delivered my address, setting out a theme for my period in office, I was proud to have behind me the house flags of both Maersk and P&O, the latter because Tim Harris of P&O was my vice-president.

I had hoped that Peter Sutherland, then secretary-general of the GATT, would be my main speaker at the dinner. I wanted his authority in international trade matters to emphasise the successes which British shipping had achieved – among the world's premier operators of container ships, cruise liners, ferries and gas carriers. I wanted to raise the sights of government and indeed of some in the industry itself. When Sutherland could not come, I fell back on David Hunt, Secretary of State for Employment, because I hoped that he, said to be close to the prime minister, could provide a coordinating role for the several government departments which ought to be paying attention to shipping but which too often followed their own agenda ('joined-up government' perhaps?). Hunt made all the right noises off the record, but his speech was 'motherhood and apple pie'. While generally supportive, he avoided commitment and ignored the specific points that I had put: we did not seek subsidy but deferral of tax to help cashflow; recognition of the importance of a core British fleet to the maritime service sector which leads the world in marine law, arbitration, design, education and insurance. British shipping sought first of all recognition, and after that fiscal adjustments to put us on a level with our competitors in Europe – in all, assistance which would represent only 0.5% of the Department of Transport's annual budget. We sought a modest investment for a huge national return. No reaction.

It was ever thus – ministers will offer no hostages. We would have been better served by not hoping for pearls of policy, but settling for a speaker interested in the issues and who would speak his mind.

Helmut Sohmen of World-Wide, replying for the guests, was both complimentary and critical. He has been through boom and crisis, and his speeches over the years have been perceptive. Hong Kong, his base, has proved one of the better regimes under which to ride out storms, but then if there are no fiscal penalties vis-à-vis your competitors you need no government help.

Mona, Alastair and Gillian were at the dinner. We missed James, who would have seen some old colleagues from China Navigation. Whether he would have realised, while Helmut Sohmen was speaking, that he was listening to his future father-in-law I cannot say.

The message during my year as president was simple, but needed emphasis on every possible occasion. We pursued a consistent strategy to raise awareness of the importance of a strong shipping industry to the UK economy as a whole. With the maritime unions batting on the same side, together we lobbied MPs and took our case to parliamentary committees, constituences and schools. With the British shipbuilders, I presented our case to government departments and to the European Commission. There were still issues in connection with US policy to contend with, and close attention had to be paid to Brussels. Since the president can be involved in every aspect of the Chamber's work, it is important to establish priorities. There is no doubt that the Chamber is to a great extent judged by the standing of the president and his immediate team. Incidentally, soon after my appointment I had been offered the customary CBE. I declined, as I did not feel an honour appropriate simply for having accepted a job.

I spoke up and down the country and found myself called upon for some unusual occasions. At the National Maritime Museum a gala dinner for fifty Russian 'shipowners' and shipbuilders concluded their week of exposure to Maritime London. As the noise level rose my host suggested that I should speak *before* the main course – a good idea. I had agreed with the interpreter that I would speak in paragraphs – not a good idea. Those who were interested began themselves to translate for neighbours; those who assumed they would see a transcript later, talked on; the noise grew louder and louder; some even burst into song. I began to laugh at the deteriorating shambles. I pulled myself together, and ploughed on to deliver a strong plug for London's maritime service industry. The Russian Minister of Shipping rose to reply. Even I, sitting next to him, could not hear a word.

The centenary of the Commercial Court in 1995 took me to the Guildhall for a more distinguished occasion. The shipping industry has not infrequently found itself engaged before the Court, so I was asked to address the guests as a 'user'. Following the Lord Mayor, the Lord Chancellor and the Lord Chief Justice, I spoke of interdependence of the many parts of Maritime London and international recognition of the Commercial Court as a centre of excellence. While dignified by a fair amount of pomp and ceremony, this luncheon was a very friendly occasion. Lord Mackay, the Lord Chancellor, congratulated me on my address (there was much mutual admiration) and I confessed to him that I had always had an inclination towards the law. Hearing I was from Dunfermline, he said: 'Stevenson & Marshall? Then it must have been your father who gave me my first brief. I remember it well, he didn't want to handle it himself; the client was important but his case untenable.'

My time in office fell under a Conservative government. I had to deal with two Secretaries of State and three ministers. I found John Macgregor businesslike and congenial and I dined *à deux* with him every three months or so. I felt we were making progress, but when Brian Mawhinney took over he did not give us much time and failed to grasp the political opportunity which shipping offered him. The ministers or parliamentary under-secretaries were in the Lords and, however well-meaning, had no clout. Viscount Goschen was twenty-eight when appointed and, with a travel agency in Zambia as his only business experience, was hardly equipped to fight our corner. It is good that, under a Labour administration, responsibility for shipping has returned to the Commons, where it is entrusted to John Prescott, a 'supremo' with some feeling for the sea.

Politicians want instant results and it has been difficult to convince them that eleven years of neglect and discouragement cannot be reversed overnight. During those years of neglect, British shipping had, perforce, to learn to live with the regime – arrangements were made to flag out to more tax-efficient registers, to employ foreign seafarers, in some cases to move management overseas. Companies had made an accommodation and it was not be assumed that these arrangements would be scrapped at the first sign of success in the UK. I emphasised repeatedly that shipowners require stability, some reasonable prospect that policies will not be again reversed in the foreseeable future and above all a really quite simple and straightforward recognition of the worth to the nation of a prosperous maritime industry. Some useful first steps to recover the position were made in 1994–5, with the reintroduction of modest tax-relief, but one had to ask: 'Why spoil the ship for a hap'orth of tar?' – not much more was required to finish the job.

The commemorations of the Battle of the Atlantic and D-day in 1993–4 raised again the role of the merchant navy in time of war. The defence card is not one which can be played today with as much conviction as in the past, but the examples of the Falklands in 1982 and the Gulf War in 1990 show the extremes of the range of scenarios which could develop. In the former, British interests alone were involved and others refused to be drawn into it, while the latter seemed to engage the whole world. From this more recent experience it became possible for the government to declare that no doubt appropriate vessels 'can easily be secured through allied channels or through the external market.' Yes – provided the incidents are of common concern to a number of nations. The government also maintained that an adequate supply of trained seamen would be available to man this paper fleet. The fact that many thousands of those who appear in the records as reserves went home years ago is conveniently ignored in order to generate a spurious comfort. These seamen are ageing, were trained in a different era and cannot be expected, even with expensive retraining, to operate safely in today's sophisticated vessels. Many of the still active ratings under the red ensign are on the catering or entertainment side – almost certainly unable to move easily into the realm of the missile or of the gas turbine.

On 25 October 1994, the Queen came to the Chamber to open its new premises in the City which now replace the St Mary Axe building destroyed by IRA bombs in May, 1992. The photographs of her visit show her laughing and smiling throughout. She was knowledgeable about the issues – ferry safety and the decline in UK ship registration and manpower. She surprised Brian Parkinson, one of the stalwarts on the Chamber staff, after asking him what he did. In reply to his 'Liaison with the Ministry of Defence, Your Majesty', she said 'Oh, STUFT?' (Ships Taken Up From Trade).

The organisation was smooth and the speeches and presentation short. We showed the Queen the Chamber's battle ensign – shredded by the bomb – and the fragments of the forty-year-old painting of her opening the St Mary Axe building. With the agreement of the artist, Terence Cuneo, we had had his large painting reproduced. After tea with the past presidents and their wives, her departure was to loud and prolonged cheers from the families inside and a goodly crowd outside. My present to the Chamber on stepping down was a framed photograph of 'Her Majesty with the Presidents'.

Under Admiral Sir Nicholas Hunt, the director-general, the Chamber team had a good blend of intellectual capability, enthusiasm and commitment. I am grateful for the support and friendship I received from staff and members and, more widely, in government and opposition, among union colleagues, the maritime professions and in the City. Shipping had been an absorbing interest for fifty years and it was a privilege for me to lead the industry as president for a fulfilling year as I came to the end of my business career.

17

A Time to Remember

Fifty years after the climax of the Battle of the Atlantic, a commemorative review was staged off the mouth of the Mersey in the spring of 1993. The weather was stormy, giving the event a special resonance. An unexpectedly large number of veterans turned up for the march past, followed by a service in Liverpool Cathedral. The Chamber of Shipping organised a Centre where veterans could have rest and refreshment and where, with the aid of a sophisticated computer set-up provided by British Telecom, any serviceman or woman could ascertain if a member of his or her wartime unit or ship's company had also checked in. Such was the success of this scheme that the software and the database were kept 'alive' until the following year when a series of further commemorations fell due. As president of the Chamber during this period it was my great privilege to represent the merchant navy.

At the end of 1993, the Corporation of the City of London gave a dinner at the Mansion House to mark the nation's debt to the merchant navy. The Chamber advised on the guest list and I was delighted to secure invitations for three *Oribi* colleagues: Disney Vaughan Hughes and his wife Pam, who was one of the Greenock Wrens in 1944, Derek Laughton and Dawn, and Jack Wilson, now Lord Moran, with his wife Shirley. It was a splendid affair with stirring speeches by the Duke of York and the Lord Mayor, Christopher Walford, both of whom were of a younger generation.

D-day was remembered in June 1994. I joined Rear Admiral Portsmouth for the opening of the Veterans' Centre on Southsea Common, just opposite a wartime haunt, the Queen's Hotel. The huge assembly of framework marquees was three times the size of Wembley Stadium. 'Far too big,' cried some. 'Just you wait and see,' responded Lyn Bourke, the project leader. Having no inhibitions about service hierarchy, she had achieved wonders in the last few hectic days. The navy was impressed by her leadership and we were all glad when, later, Lyn received her MBE.

Neil Rankin, the Admiral, had been captain of *Ark Royal* when I embarked in Copenhagen for passage to UK in 1993 as part of a group of Shipwrights being shown the modern navy, and it was a pleasure to meet again. He was supported on this occasion by a very competent and particularly pretty flag lieutenant. Addressing the old boys he declared: 'You are all VIPs today – Veterans in Portsmouth.'

Two days later we were at the Guildhall in London as guests of Royal Bank of Canada for the Canadian D-day dinner, a spectacular evening of pomp and nostalgia. Vera Lynn sang and there were moist eyes all round. Together with the unveiling of the Canadian Memorial in Green Park on the following morning it made a fitting recognition of the immense Canadian contribution in both World Wars. It was particularly moving for me because *Oribi* had worked well with Canadian destroyers and frigates, while at home, in Dunfermline, my parents had cared for a stream of young Canadian relations and their friends – navy, army and air force. The turnout of royals at Green Park was apparently the largest concentration for years. Mona and I were seated well forward. My campaign medals seemed relatively insignificant in comparison with the batteries of decorations adorning the chests of so many of the current military leaders and, more impressively, those of the more senior veterans. I was glad, however, that Gieves had managed, in time, to mount for me the Arctic Convoy medal which I had received through the good offices of the Russian Ambassador whom I had met at the Mansion House dinner six months before.

King George's Fund for Sailors (KGFS) held a dinner in the Painted Hall at Greenwich on 3 June. As the wife of the president of the Chamber, Mona was expected to lead the City flagday for KGFS, which was to take place on 14 June. Mona wrote a mountain of appeal letters and had gratefully accepted Alastair's offer to take part in the London Marathon in aid of the Fund. He raised over £8,000 of sponsorship and, with the support of a group of friends on the flagday itself, Mona's total was a record. Alastair ran the marathon, his first, on 17 April in an impressive 3 hours and 4 minutes. I had always been a bit off-hand about that sort of thing, but with his wife Sue and Douglas, their very small son, we were on Birdcage Walk to see him go through. The leaders were cheered as they passed but I was quite unprepared for the emotion of seeing Alastair appear down the incline from Parliament Square right on his scheduled time. There were two other runners ahead, one in very shaky condition but urged on by the crowd, then came Alastair, looking grimly determined. Suddenly we found ourselves shouting, 'Come *on* Alastair, good show!' He looked up, saw us waving our flags, grinned and got his head down for the last gruelling stretch to Buckingham Palace and back down the Mall. We were immensely proud. He, wrapped in tinfoil and gulping down some soft drink, seemed amazingly relaxed. He kissed Sue, picked up Douglas and asked where we were going to eat.

On Saturday 4 June the weather was like that of fifty years earlier but even wetter. Mona and I joined Nick and Meriel Hunt for the navy's garden party in HMS *Dryad*, the house which had been Eisenhower's HQ for the invasion. The hill leading to *Dryad* was lined by young sailors and Wrens, already soaked by drenching rain. It was disappointing for the 'ship', as the gardens were in superb condition and now the guests had to squeeze into the house or into stuffy marquees. I was able to catch John Major's eye and, when he asked in what capacity I was there, to say: 'As a veteran of D-day myself and proudly representing the merchant navy.' I thanked him for what the government had done for British shipping in the 1994 budget (roll-over tax relief) and was pleased to have his reply: 'We'll have to see what more we can do.'

The weather certainly added realism to the day. It emphasised the strain Eisenhower must have been under when faced on 4 June 1944 with an adverse forecast for the next thirty-six hours. He alone had the responsibility of postponing the invasion of Europe for a day, gambling that conditions would improve and unwilling to lose the tidal 'window'.

We had to miss beating the retreat at Whale Island, for, while Mona and Meriel were to be guests of the wardroom in the Dockyard, Nick and I were to be at the dinner given by the Queen and the Duke of Edinburgh in the Guildhall for visiting heads of state. Before the principal guests arrived, I found I knew many of the senior officers from First Sea Lord to Chief of the Defence Staff (father-in-law of one of our younger friends). It was inevitable that, fifty years on, none of the serving officers had been in the war and it was a pity that more veterans could not participate. It was essentially a celebration of the allied effort. All those countries which had a presence on D-day were represented: by the Kings and Queens of Norway, Denmark, Belgium, the Netherlands and Jordan; the Grand Duke of Luxembourg, President Clinton, and representatives of the Soviet Union; the Commonwealth in force and the old colonies; President Mitterand from France and President Havel from Czechoslovakia. Seated between

Lloyd Bentsen, the US Treasury Secretary, and a Norwegian admiral, I enjoyed a congenial dinner, but I was disappointed that there were no speeches; perhaps the protocol was too complex.

Massive crowds were expected the next morning for the drumhead service on Southsea Common. From the Royal Navy Memorial we walked past the massed ranks of veterans who had been mustered by the Chamber team and a large contingent of sea cadets. Our progress was at first solemn, but Mona and Meriel looked very elegant, Nick and I tolerably smart and we were soon greeted by rolling applause and ribald comment. By the time we had covered the 200 yards it had become very light-hearted with Mona and Meriel blushing and waving, Nick and I doffing our bowler hats and raising our umbrellas.

Warned off the first row in the VIP stand, we sat in the second and soon made room for my friend Lloyd Bentsen and his colleague Warren Christopher. From this prime location we watched the heads of state pass, some scurrying, some playing to the crowd. Hillary Clinton looked chic, the clapping was warm and she flashed a sunny smile in return; more applause for Premier Chrétien of Canada and other Commonwealth leaders. When Prime Minister Keating of Australia was announced there was a marked silence (he had only recently displayed a distinctly republican attitude). This coolness was clearly directed at Keating personally, for the whole stand rose to welcome President Lech Walesa of Poland.

The wind blew keenly. The slow, almost silent, steam past of naval units leaving Portsmouth Harbour, throbbing smoothly down the inshore channel to Spithead, provided a moving, purposeful backdrop as the old hymns rang out over the Common.

On 6 June, the D-day anniversary itself, I was on parade at Northolt by 0630 to join a motley crowd of generals and admirals, officials, politicians and a few veterans, waiting for the government flight to France for the ceremonies in Normandy. The weather was again poor with a low cloud base and we were fortunate to land at Caen before the airport was closed. 3 Div. (my brother James's division when he landed on D+3) was responsible for logistics and they had many complications to deal with as flights were delayed or diverted.

Nick Hunt and I were detailed for the naval service at Ryes while others went to the main function at Bayeux or to Ranville where the airborne assault and the marines were remembered.

The war cemetery at Ryes was as immaculate as always. Families from Canada and the UK moved slowly round the graves, each of which bore flowers placed by the village children. The headstones recorded the names of so many very young men, yet as we examined them we noted that a number of the dead were rather older. These were all army casualties and it came home to us that the invasion army had in large measure consisted of soldiers who had waited since Dunkirk to return to France four years later. I saw Admiral Tony Griffin in the crowd, He had come over on his own and it was touching to be reminded that he had been there in 1944. One of the veterans, who had been a troop commander with the guns supporting the Essex battalion which had taken the hill, looked slowly round and said to me: 'A lot of my boys are here.'

I wrote to my sister-in-law, Janet, on the following day, with the order of service and telling her that I had tried without success to identify someone from James's unit, but I appreciated that he had landed at Sword beach which was to the east. I recalled how low-key he had been about his experience. The service was taken by the senior Church of Scotland chaplain at Portsmouth, Neil Bruce. We talked about James and Edith, whom he had known well when he was minister at Townhill, Dunfermline. I told him of their deaths, two years before, within three months of each other, and how Edith had written to James: 'I can see you now, setting off up the hill, with your pack on your back. The gate will open easily for you, but leave it on the latch for me, and cast an eye over your shoulder from time to time for I won't be far behind.' I thought of my mother also, who had been so robust during the war and still stalwart when she died at the age of ninety-five in 1990.

We moved down to the small village to meet the mayor of Ryes, a short, round man, wearing a tricolour sash. He embraced us all. I said to him: 'Monsieur le Maire, je suis très honoré d'être ici . . .' He interrupted me: 'Pas du tout, c'est nous qui sommes honorés.'

The Royal Marine band from *Britannia*, made available to Ryes because of the regard the organising team had for the mayor, played before the war memorial with its banner 'Welcome to the Liberators'. Then down the hill came a group of thirty elderly veterans, survivors of the Dorsets who had liberated Ryes at 1600 on 6 June 1944. General Neville, company commander on that day, led them. The mayor made an emotional speech, six small girls helped the general to lay a wreath and the veterans marched past a simple saluting base. It was such an unlikely scene – a tiny French village, a marine band in full fig followed by a mixed bag of old boys, medals jangling, many hirpling a bit, but yet a spring in the step because it was very special.

Amidst the emotion there was much laughter, particularly at the lunch which 3 Div. had arranged at the celebrated *auberge* in Ryes. Crammed along long oak tables were all the high heidyins of the day addressing mountains of *pâté*, *boeuf* and *fraises des bois* accompanied by jugs of full-bodied red wine.

In the afternoon we went on to Arromanches for the big march past on the beach. Because, as well as being a 'vet', I was representing the merchant navy, I was in the VIP seats beside the dais from which the Queen and Prince Philip took the salute. Nick and I appeared on the TV news that evening in prime position at the end of the front row. Unfortunately I didn't spot my cousin, Sandy Badenoch, who was marching with the Royal Marines, but if he executed the drill-book 'Eyes left' correctly, he could hardly have missed me.

The day ended with the lowering of the colours as a lone piper played. This almost intimate ceremony was somehow very fitting after the scale of the afternoon's events. The crowds were silent and at the foot of the flagstaffs stood just a small group – the Queen, Philip, Charles and Andrew, the Princess Royal and Princess Margaret, a covey of chaplains and a clutch of officers. Suddenly the clouds dispersed, the sun came out and it was a warm and quiet evening. It was a great privilege to be there and I certainly felt, as I'm sure most of us did, that we were sharing it with those who had gone before.

By way of contrast, I flew, a few days later, by Concorde to Washington and on to Toronto. On the next day the RBC board meeting ran into the late afternoon, but Jim Ball and I still caught the 8 p.m. BA flight, seat 1A, arriving Heathrow about 6 a.m. My diary says that I attended an adult education computer course for two hours in the afternoon and then changed into white tie and tails for the Chancellor of the Exchequer's dinner at the Mansion House. Life went on.

The following week we dined with the Admiral Commanding at Greenwich, and the naval theme continued soon afterwards with dinner on board *Britannia* moored in the Pool of London, again a KGFS function. Many of those present had been part of the D-day events – the Hunts, Robin Ross of the Royal Marines, Neil and Jill Rankin. The evening ended, after heavy rain, with the same marine band as had played at Ryes beating the retreat on the quarterdeck. No location could be more dramatic – the backdrop a floodlit Tower of London and a glowing Tower Bridge.

The week after brought another visit to Canada, this time to Montreal – a 'bounce' trip of twenty-four hours during which I tried not to alter my body clock, with only partial success.

The next date in the twelve months of commemoration was 8 May 1995, fifty years on from VE day. On that day in 1945 *Oribi* was en route from Hull to Scapa Flow. We were, I am sure, happy and relieved, particularly for the civilians of Britain, that the end of the V-1s and the dreaded, impersonal V-2s had come, that the lights would come back on, that those we knew, who had been in the front line in Europe, would be safe. But strangely I recall little feeling of triumph or personal release; we were very much engaged in what was then our normal job.

Tim Harris of P&O had taken over the presidency of the Chamber from me in March, but I was still invited to the celebration of VE day in Hyde Park, where, to everyone's delight, the Queen Mother, at ninety-four, presided and spoke. It was an occasion of rather mixed content, pop music and fireworks, laser beams and children bearing flowers, military bands and a marvellous little vignette as a group of holders of the Victoria Cross and the George Cross marched past – British, Australian, a Sikh, and a Gurkha.

A note from Maersk Mc-Kinney Møller, in response to a description I sent him, read:

> Dear Sandy,
> Your letter was much appreciated. As I have said before, had it not been for the Battle of Britain, for Britain's perseverance and for Winston Churchill there would have been no way for Denmark to regain its freedom – and so I remain forever grateful.
> Warm Regards, also to Mona.
>
> MAERSK

Møller had instructed the Maersk offices and ships around the world to observe a minute's silence at 11 a.m. on the morning of 8 May.

The VJ day events of 19 August overwhelmed me with a wave of pride and feeling. (It would not be unduly wide of the mark to suggest that I was 'in a state' throughout the year.) I remembered so well the wild celebrations on the Clyde on VJ day itself and, behind the partying, our appreciation that this really was the end of the years of hard slogging. In 1995 it was important that, after much apparent uncertainty, the government and the organising committee got this one absolutely right. The pattern and the style caught the imagination of generations. The crowds in London were of all ages.

The day was clear and hot. My first engagement was a reception given by the Queen at Lancaster House in honour of the Chiefs of Staff of the Commonwealth. I assumed that the Chamber of Shipping car would deliver me, but the roads were cordoned off outside the Palace. A purple pass let me through and I strode down the Mall. I had had a new knee fitted only two months before and was therefore limping rather impressively. It was perhaps not surprising that the gathering crowds gave me a cheer.

In the Lancaster House garden there was constant movement as the guests sought shade from a strong sun – Prince Philip and Prince Charles, the prime minister, most of the Cabinet, a great array of black and brown faces from the Commonwealth. The seating at lunch was interesting, for on the Queen's right was the Deputy Commander-in-Chief of the South African forces. Apparently when South Africa rejoined the Commonwealth she did so retaining her prior seniority. Thus an ANC commander, lately of Umkonte e Sizwe, found himself next to the monarch at Lancaster House.

The gathering was a mixture of Sandhurst, Greenwich Staff College and Cranwell, yet was relaxed and had a family feeling – the best sort of Commonwealth occasion. And the young serving officers, some too young even to remember the war, were considerate and gracious towards the older generation. A naval commander who had been working with Lyn Bourke on the Veterans' Centre leant across the table and whispered two 'secrets'. The first was that Prince Philip intended to march with the Burma Star Association in the afternoon parade; the second: 'Don't miss the claret, even on such a hot day. It's the best Lynch Bages from the government cellars.'

The atmosphere was vibrant and we were emboldened by the claret. So I marched alongside the Chief of Staff from Uganda and a New Zealand airman down into the Mall and up the middle of the road to the great area of seating outside the Palace. There the sun beat down on Fijians and Pathans, Sikhs in splendid turbans, sailors, diplomats in morning dress, lady officers and civilians, Red Cross, WRVS, the clergy of all denominations. Ted Heath was there burning like a brazier, Jim Callaghan, John Major and Tony Blair. I took my cue from the Duke of Edinburgh who kept his panama hat on during hymns and addresses but removed it during prayers – a fair compromise which avoided excessive sunburn.

A Lancaster bomber came low over Admiralty Arch up the Mall and seemed to stretch its wings as from its bomb doors it poured a torrent of red poppy petals in remembrance. They drifted on the breeze to settle gently on the crowds, in the trees and on the road and they touched the heart.

We moved to the Queen's saluting base on the Mall. The parade had assembled early and it must have been hard for the elderly veterans, male and female, but how well they tackled it. The regular services came first, small contingents, polished and smart and, as always, I had a lump in my throat as the Gurkhas trotted past behind their pipe band. Then the special VJ veterans, the Burma Star Association, Prince Philip, Countess Mountbatten and John Slim, son of the C-in-C of the 14th Army, Bill Slim. The merchant navy too and the Arctic convoy group, air raid wardens, the Women's Land Army, the London Fire Brigade and the Royal Observer Corps, wartime ambulances, Jeeps and 3-ton trucks. I saw our neighbours, Paddy and Ian Flanagan, Master of the Gardeners' Company, representing the allotment-holders and Richard Brayne who had served with the mountain gunners of the Indian Army. It was impressive and fun and it overran, so that I was very pressed, negotiating the traffic, to meet Mona at Victoria Station.

Nick Hunt had emphasised that we should get to the Veterans' Centre at the Queen Elizabeth Hall before the Queen arrived at 6.15 p.m. Fortunately our driver was even bolder than Mona in these matters – he flourished my purple ticket which was long out of time. I sat forward with my medals glittering, Mona looked regal and to our surprise we were waved through one, two and finally a third checkpoint. As we stepped onto the red carpet a very excited major swooped upon us: 'Who are you? What are you doing here?' 'I'm just a veteran.' 'Don't you know the Queen is due here right NOW?' I started to explain, but the major was in full flight when, fortunately, the Queen's cavalcade hove in sight. Nick rescued us and smuggled us upstairs, where later we were able to laugh with the major.

The riverside and the bridges were thronged, flags and ribbons and balloons everywhere. In the Pool of London rode *Britannia*, gleaming, royal blue. Within the Tower there was a reception for thousands who had been involved in the organisation. We spent time with the Dean of St Paul's, Eric Evans, with Christopher Walford, the Lord Mayor, with Pat Brennan and Terry of the Chamber team. Pat was concerned about my standing for so long and indeed my knee was tiring by this time, so with aplomb and perseverance she secured admission for Mona and me (as a 'disabled VIP veteran') to seats facing the river for a firework extravaganza. I chatted to two ministers, Howard and Heseltine; Mona asked a man sitting next to her if he had been at the parade in the afternoon. 'Yes, not marching this time but in the box.' He was the chairman of St Dunstan's, blinded at the age of twenty while leading his platoon in Tunisia. 'What a pity you can't see these brilliant fireworks.' 'Yes, I can imagine them though, I remember the Coronation fireworks in 1937.' They talked long and easily and when Vera Lynn's voice came over the loudspeakers he remarked how much she had meant to us all during the war. Mona turned two rows behind her and was able to bring Vera Lynn forward to shake his hand.

We left to look for our car up by the Merchant Navy Memorial. The Lord Mayor came out of the Tower gate with us, slid into his enormous official vehicle and swept off up the hill. Suddenly Mona and I were alone, setting off up the cobbled hill with a mass of people behind the barriers on either side. We stepped out, but I suppose I was limping and I was certainly using my walking-stick. My medals clinked and sparkled. There was a ripple of clapping and out of the darkness and the silence a small boy called: 'Thank you for fighting.' I raised my stick and we walked on. I have so regretted that I did not go over and shake the boy's hand, but my eyes were full and my lip trembling.

It had been a remarkable day of memories and inspiration. I reflected on the many strands of my life which it had drawn together; my own childhood and that of our children – all three now independent and happy; wartime navy; the world of shipping; the City and a varied business life which engaged me in virtually every part of the globe. All these have moulded and developed me. With Mona at my side I am conscious of my good fortune and glad that, throughout, I have taken the adventure.

Appendices

P&O GROUP FLEET

as at 1 February 1974

Bulk Shipping Division

	type	dwt
Ardlui	tanker	214,180
Ardshiel	"	214,085
Ardvaraig	"	214,128
Ardvar	"	214,029
Busiris	"	39,488
Erne	"	20,955
Maloja	"	19,948
Malwa	"	39,295
Mantua	"	19,859
Opawa	"	65,903
Orama	"	66,972
Ottawa	"	93,231
Talamba	"	59,820
	total	1,347,025
Atherstone	bulk	43,965
Duhallow	"	43,234
Fernie	"	74,422
Meynell	"	127,346
Eridge	obo	72,692
Grafton	"	73,704
Heythrop	"	73,800
Hinakura	"	150,100
Irfon	"	152,453
Jedforest	"	152,994
Kildare	oil/ore	260,412
Lauderdale	"	
	total	1,225,090

Anglo Nordic (owned 50% by P&O)

	type	dwt
Nordic Courier	obo	41,931
Nordic Ranger	bulk	47,007
Nordic Navigator	obo	71,183
Iron Clipper	bulk	40,352
Nordic Conqueror	oil/ore	260,308
Nordic Clipper	obo	152,657
Nordic Crusader	"	159,250
Nordic Patriot	bulk	127,283
Nordic Rover	"	40,530
Nordic Regent	"	40,560
Nordic Talisman	"	72,027
Iron Parkgate	"	72,030
	total	1,125,163

General Cargo Division

	type	dwt
Amana	cargo	4,739
Amra	"	13,921
Armanistan	"	11,181
Antrim	"	10,267
Aska	"	13,921
Baharistan	"	11,432
Baluchistan	"	10,348
Carpentaria	"	9,229
Chakdina	reefer	14,800
Cumberland	"	14,207
Donegal	cargo	10,207
Essex	reefer	12,550
Farsistan	cargo	13,204
Floristan	"	12,417
Galway	"	12,781
Gorjistan	"	13,150
Hertford	reefer	14,932
Huntingdon	"	14,620
Jelunga	cargo	14,800
Jumna	"	10,134
Kohinur	"	14,480
Kypros	reefer	14,515
Makaria	"	4,890

General Cargo Division (cont.)

	type	dwt
Discovery Bay	container	29,129
Moreton Bay	"	29,125
Osaka Bay	"	48,500
Managed for OCL		
Botany Bay		29,129
Encounter Bay		29,129
Flinders Bay		29,129
Jervis Bay		29,129
	total	174,750

Passenger Division

	type	grt
Arcadia	passenger	29,871
Canberra	"	44,807
Cathay	"	13,531
Chitral	"	13,821
Himalaya	"	28,047
Nevasa	"	20,160
Oriana	"	41,910
Oronsay	"	28,136
Spirit of London	"	17,370
Uganda	"	16,907
	total	254,560

European & Air Transport Division

	type	dwt
Manapouri	reefer	11,931
Manora	cargo	13,319
Mataura	reefer	11,705
Melita	cargo	3,850
Merkara	"	13,165
Morvada	"	13,165
Mulbera	"	13,091
Nigaristan	"	14,083
Nurjehan	"	12,087
Nurmahal	"	12,170
Kohistan	"	14,800
Otaio	reefer	13,725
Otaki	"	12,750
Pando Gulf	cargo	11,470
Albatross	cargo	959
Avocet	"	973
Dorset Coast	"	1,277
Lairdsfox	"	823
Lairdsglen	"	1,847
Lancashire Coast	"	1,027
Norbank	"	1,743
Oriole	"	412
Ortolan	"	453
Petrel	"	528
Pointer	"	1,151
Roe Deer	"	1,775
St Clement	"	510

European & Air Transport (cont.)

	type	grt
Earl of Zetland	RoRo	548
Lion	"	3,333
Norwave	"	3,540
Panther	"	4,400
St Clair	"	2,864
St Ola	"	750
Ulster Prince	"	4,270
Ulster Queen	"	4,270
	total	41,725

General Holdings Division
for P&O Australia Offshore Services

	type	grt
Lady Cynthia	service	987
Lady Norna	"	545
Lady Laurie	"	535
Lady Rachel	"	987
Lady Sarah	"	932
Lady Vilma	"	932
	total	4,918

Energy Division
for IOS Ltd

	type	grt
Lady Alexandra	service	1,067
Lady Astrid	"	482
Lady Beth	"	499
Lady Camille	"	480
Lady Catherine	"	477
Lady Cecilie	"	500
Lady Christine	"	770
Lady Fiona	"	773
Lady Florence	"	480
Lady Jean	"	1,067
Lady Joyce	"	1,075
Lady Karen	"	500
Lady Lisbeth	"	1,067
Lady Margaret	"	480
Lady Mariann	"	461
Lady Miriam	"	866
Lady Mona	"	481
Lady Pamela	"	866
Lady Sylvia	"	1,067

Bulk Shipping Division (cont.)
Operated by Anglo Nordic

	type	dwt
Anco Norness	tanker	25,920
British Norness	"	260,900
Carbo Dragon	"	25,720
Frances Hammer	"	63,486
Henning Maersk	"	36,340
Karen Maersk	"	36,340
Nordic Enterprise	"	134,400
Nordic Leader	"	45,026
Nordic Mariner	"	44,970
Russel H Green	"	63,442
Nordic Rider	bulk	34,585
Nordic Runner	"	34,200
Chemical Explorer	chemical	28,628
Chemical Venturer	"	28,628
Stolt Norness	"	18,139
Stolt Sydness	"	18,236
Nordic Louisiana	sulphur	27,898
Nordic Texas	"	27,957
total		954,815

Panocean (owned 50% by P&O)

	type	cbm
Post Runner	chemical	13,320
Post Rover	"	24,000
Post Ranger	"	20,680
Post Challenger	"	24,500
Post Champion	"	24,500
Post Charter	"	24,500
Post Chaser	"	24,500
total		253,910

	type	cbm
Gazana	LPG	30,000
Gambada	"	30,000
Garmula	"	52,000
Gambhira	"	14,090
total		126,090

General Cargo Division (cont.)

	type	dwt
Pando Point	cargo	11,470
Patonga	reefer	9,777
Piako	"	10,290
Registan	cargo	11,200
Remuera	container	32,236
Serbistan	"	11,140
Shabristan	"	12,417
Somerset	reefer	10,256
Sussex	"	14,680
Strathardle	cargo	12,552
Strathbrora	"	12,604
Strathconon	"	12,638
Tabiristan	"	14,158
Tabor	"	5,008
Taupo	reefer	11,868
Tairea	cargo	11,302
Tekoa	reefer	11,868
Teesta	cargo	11,292
Tongariro	reefer	11,866
Trebartha	cargo	11,292
Trecarne	"	11,866
Trefusis	"	14,235
Treneglos	"	12,268
Trewidden	"	14,270
Turakina	reefer	12,701
Turkistan	cargo	12,362
Westmorland	reefer	11,858
Wild Auk	"	10,790
Wild Avocet	"	10,790
Wild Cormorant	"	9,168
Wild Curlew	"	9,168
Wild Flamingo	"	8,500
Zaida		6,785
Zira		6,634
total		852,036

	type	grt
Dunra	pass/cargo	4,867
Dwarka	"	4,851
Karanja	"	10,294
total		20,012

European & Air Transport (cont.)

		grt
St Magnus	cargo	1,220
St Rognvald	"	1,035
Stormont	"	1,040
Ulster Merchant	"	1,208
total		17,981

		grt
Dragon	RoRo	6,141
Eagle	"	11,609

Energy Division
for IOS Ltd (cont.)

		grt
Lady Valerie	service	480
Lady Vivien	"	1,075
Master Jason	"	74
Miss Anna	"	83
Miss Debbie	"	83
total		16,496

224 SHIPS IN SERVICE
including partly owned and managed

SHIPS ON ORDER
as at 1 February 1974

Bulk Shipping Division

	type	cbm
Gandara	LPG	22,500
Garbeta	"	22,500

		dwt
British Trident	tanker	260,000
Mitsui 1046	"	414,000
Doxford 733	bulk	152,000
Horton 184	product	31,000
Horton 185	"	31,000

for Anglo Nordic

		dwt
Mitsubishi 1764	tanker	407,000
Mitsubishi 1765	"	407,000
Mitsubishi 1766	"	407,000
Nordic Clansman	"	262,500
Nordic Commander	"	262,500
Nordic Chieftain	obo	159,250
total		1,905,250

for Panocean

		grt
Post Challenger	chemical	24,500
Post Champion	"	24,500
Post Charger	"	24,500
Post Chaser	"	24,500
Post Endeavour	"	24,500
Post Energy	"	24,500
Post Enterprise	"	24,500
Post Express	"	24,500

for Panocean (cont.)

		dwt
Post Ranger		20,680
Post Rover	"	24,000
Post Runner	"	13,230
total		253,910

for LNG Carriers Ltd

		cbm
LNG Challenger	LNG	87,600

General Cargo Division

		dwt
Strathdare	cargo	15,000
Strathdevon	"	15,000
Strathdirk	"	15,000
Strathdoon	"	15,000
Strathduns	"	15,000
Strathdyce	"	15,000
Wild Fulmar	reefer	8,500
total		98,500

European & Air Transport Division

		grt
St Ola	ferry	850

General Holdings Division

Lady Vera	service	987

33 SHIPS ON ORDER

PRINCIPAL TRADE INVESTMENTS
as at 1 February 1974

Associated companies	Country of Incorporation	Percentage of equity
Bulk Shipping Division		
Anglo Nordic Shipping Ltd	Bermuda	50
Associated Bulk Carriers Ltd	Bermuda	50
Damodar Bulk Carriers Ltd	India	40
Inter-Continental Carriers Ltd	Bermuda	17
Mundo Gas SA	Panama	30
Naess Nippo Shipping Co Ltd	Bermuda	33
Panocean Shipping and Terminals Ltd	Great Britain	50
General Cargo Division		
Australind Steam Shipping Co Ltd	Great Britain	38
The Mauritius Steam Navigation Co Ltd	Mauritius	28
Overseas Containers Ltd	Great Britain	30
General Holdings Division		
Australport Services (Vic) Pty Ltd	Australia	33
Brisbane Mechanical Services Pty Ltd	Australia	50
Brisbane Stevedoring Services Pty Ltd	Australia	50
Cathay Holdings Ltd	Hong Kong	31
Great Northern Wooldumping Co Pty Ltd	Australia	33
Gray Dawes Westray (Holdings) Ltd	Great Britain	50
Samuel Hodge & Sons Ltd	Great Britain	27
Inship Pty Ltd	Australia	50
Newstead Wharves Pty Ltd	Australia	50
Sagrod Liberia SA	Liberia	50
Sydney Mechanical Services Pty Ltd	Australia	47
Sydney Australport Pty Ltd	Australia	37
United Ship Services Pty Ltd	Australia	33
E Wood Ltd (paint manufactuers)	Great Britain	35
Other trade investments		
Hall Thermotank Ltd (engineering)	Great Britain	33
Southern Pacific Properties Ltd	Hong Kong	11

P&O PRINCIPAL SUBSIDIARIES
as at 1 February 1974

Bulk Shipping Division

Bermuda
Charter Shipping Co Ltd

European & Air Transport Division

(Ferrymasters Sector: Road Haulage)

Belgium
Europa Express NV

England
Ferrymasters Sealand Ltd
Ferrymasters (Ireland) Ltd

France
Ferrymasters SARL

Germany
Ferrymasters GmbH

Netherlands
Ferrymasters Holland NV

Northern Ireland
Anglo Irish Transport Ltd (75%)
Ferrymasters Ltd
Northern Ireland Trailers Ltd

Scotland
Northern Ireland Trailers (Scotland) Ltd

Freight Forwarding Sector

Belgium
Global Transport Bureau BV

England
Anglo Overseas Transport Co Ltd
E Higgs (Air Agency) Ltd
Pandair Freight Ltd
Turner Edwards & Co Ltd

France
Société de Consignation Maritime Franco-Britannique

Germany
General Steam Navigation Co GmbH
Nordsee Hafenbetrieb GmbH

Netherlands
Continex NV
General Steam Transport Co

Scotland
Airsea Freight Co Ltd

Road Services Sector: Liquids

Belgium
NV Solventra SA (81%)

England
Thomas Allen Ltd
Coastal Roadways Ltd
Eastern Roadways (International) Ltd
Eastern Roadways Ltd
Jarvis-Cranmer Transport Ltd
John Forman Ltd
John Forman (Hull) Ltd
A S Jones & Co Ltd
Henry Smither & Sons Ltd (80%)
Storemasters Ltd

Scotland
James Hemphill Ltd

Short Sea Shipping Sector

England
Coast Lines (Services) Ltd
European Unit Routes Ltd
General Steam Navigation Co Ltd
General Steam Navigation (Trading) Ltd
North Sea Ferries Ltd (80%)
Southern Ferries Ltd
Tyne-Tees Steam Shipping Co Ltd

Northern Ireland
Belfast Steamship Co Ltd

Scotland
North of Scotland, Orkney and Shetland Shipping Co Ltd

General Cargo Division

England
British India Steam Navigation Co Ltd
Container Fleets Ltd
Federal Steam Navigation Co Ltd

General Holdings Division

Australia
P&O Australia Ltd
Brisbane Wharves & Wooldumping Pty Ltd
Bulk Handling & General Services Pty Ltd (73%)
The Darling Island Stevedoring and Lighterage Co Ltd

Bermuda
International Offshore Services Ltd

England
Anderson Green & Co Ltd
Bethell Gwyn & Co Ltd
Birt Potter & Hughes Ltd
Birt Potter Westray Ltd
Bishopsgate Insurance Co Ltd
The Falmouth Docks and Engineering Co (77%)
R&H Green and Silley Weir Ltd (77%)
The New Medway Steam Packet Co Ltd
P&O Oil Holdings (North Sea) Ltd
Sealine Services (Marine Supplies) Ltd
Silley, Cox & Co (77%)

Hong Kong
Mackinnon Mackenzie & Co of Hong Kong Ltd
Mackinnons Godown Co Ltd

India
Mackinnon Mackenzie & Co Private Ltd

Luxembourg
Devon International SA

New Zealand
P&O (NZ) Ltd

Pakistan
Mackinnon Mackenzie & Co of Pakistan Ltd

Passenger Division

England
Eastern & Australian Steamship Co Ltd

USA
P&O Inc

P&O FAMILY AND BUSINESS SHIPPING CONNECTIONS

James Marshall = Mary   *sister to*   Thomas Shaw   James Mackay
                                         1st Baron Craigmyle   1st Earl of Inchcape

Margaret Badenoch = David Marshall   *cousin to*   Alexander Shaw = Margaret   2nd Earl of Inchcape
                                    2nd Baron Craigmyle
                                    Chairman P&O 1932–1939

Mona Kirk = Alexander Badenoch Marshall   Donald Shaw
                                    3rd Baron Craigmyle

Alastair   Gillian   James

Anderson Green (Managers of Orient Line)

BI

Mackinnons

BI and P&O merged 1914

Chairman P&O and BI 1914–32

Mackinnons sold to P&O

Inchcape & Co.

Burmah Oil

3rd Earl of Inchcape
Chairman 1973–83
(*Chairman Inchcape & Co.*
Vice-chairman Burmah Oil)

Mackinnons & BI

Trident Tankers

P&O

Orient Line

P&O

P&O

Lord Geddes

Ford Geddes
Chairman 1971–72

Sir Donald Anderson
Chairman 1960–71

A.B. Marshall
CEO 1972–79

Sir Andrew Crichton

R.B. Adams

A. Mackinnon

cousins

cousins

Legend:
Family Relationships — ———
Shipping Connections — ———
Other Shipping Links — - - - -

P&O BOARD MEMBERS February 1971

Sir Frederic Harmer
Deputy Chairman
(*ret'd 1971*)

C.A.W. Dawes   J. MacNaughten Sidey   A.D. Marris   A. Mackinnon   Terence Bird
                                                   (*ret'd Nov. 1971*)

H.T. Beazley   J. Mitchell   R.E.B. Lloyd   P.E. Parry

Appendix 4

SPEECH GIVEN BY THE AUTHOR ON BOARD *CANBERRA*,
NEW YORK, 15 SEPTEMBER 1978

In the present situation of the international shipping industry you may wonder if a reception of this type is appropriate. A distinguished US senator offered what may be an appropriate thought: 'Mankind needs the repetition of the obvious more than the elucidation of the obscure.' It is vital that we find co-operative solutions to our problems, and this seems a good opportunity of making a contribution.

The United States, as the major trading entity, generates, finances and affects most international trade directly or indirectly. Although the US merchant fleet sadly – and we Europeans mean sadly – no longer approaches the scale or power which it held up to and immediately after the Second World War, US maritime policy, or, to be honest, in some areas the lack of it, touches on all of us engaged in maritime affairs.

We Europeans would like to see a strong US merchant marine – competitive in commercial terms; able to command attention through performance and able thus to influence policy. In that direction lies the principal hope of co-operation in our common interest.

There are, however, no really clear views of US policy at this time – perhaps the maritime interest seems so relatively small to some as to be of minor importance. On the other hand, because it is small, and in some respects uncompetitive in commercial terms, it is felt in some quarters that it needs stimulus through further subsidy or even protectionist measures.

Of the two, subsidy, however debilitating, is the lesser evil. A former British Prime Minister said in another context – but I suggest pertinently – that protectionism is an expedient not a solution.

We look for a clear lead to clear policies, because we believe it important to work together to maintain the free enterprise system and freedom of choice. But why have we such difficulty in getting together?

The thrust of US action over many years had been to foster competition and to protect the consumer or user by government regulation – regulation primarily based on considerations of a huge domestic market and a huge mass of producers and consumers, and it is certainly not for us to question that general philosophy. But the European philosophy for shipping is one of self-regulation by the industry, combined with continuous consultation and co-operation with the users – the shippers and importers. Such co-operation between operators themselves and between operators and users is not permitted in US trades, and effectively, therefore, there is denied the possibility of constructive moves to rationalise services, to secure cost-effective and optimised operations. In times of enormous investment and high operating cost, a modern shipping service needs sophisticated planning. Yet, because of US law, there have even been attempts to prevent European lines consulting with shippers in Europe.

The Shipping Act of 1916, when US shipping itself was strong, already recognised the need for modification of anti-trust law – exemption, subject to some restraints, for the international shipping industry. It is a pity that, drifting away from that commonsense application, current practice should be so perplexing, even, one might say, destructive – just when the whole structure of the industry is severely beset by economic and political threats.

Oversupply of shipping: in the sixties and seventies confident expectations of steady, steep, upward trends in world trade stimulated the fragmented world shipping industry to re-equip and expand – each time with more productive units. Encouraged by modernised shipyards and by governments grasping new employment opportunities, excited by banks anxious to lend on fashionable 'floating real estate', the numbers of new speculative ships in service and in prospect rose on an unprecedented scale.

Then came the crash of 1974–5 – first tankers, then bulk carriers felt the pressure of reduced trade. Then the spillover affected all types of shipping as orders were renegotiated, as trade slowed further, congestion eased and freed-up ships, and as shipbuilding nations, old and new, fought their own battles for survival. Employment was sought wherever possible. Where better than in trades weakly organised because of inability to consult and co-operate? Instability is the enemy of reliability and profitability, and many of our western trades are now becoming unstable.

This leads to the threat posed by the Soviet Union – now operating the world's largest fleet of general cargo ships and rapidly developing increased capacity of container and roll-on/roll-off vessels – a fleet of over 9 million tons of such tonnage, effectively under one central control, with a state purse behind it and not subject to compelling economic criteria as are our western companies.

Some of the most significant penetration by the Soviets is in US trades (weakly organised as I have noted) – the North Atlantic, Trans Pacific to Australia and the Orient, where Fesco, the Russian liner company, has captured some 17% of the traffic.

The Soviets nave no cargo to bring to these routes – they are cut-throat cross-traders. Around the world the threat develops – the Soviet Union generates only about 2% of world general cargo, with a capacity to carry over four times that amount. Why? Economic reasons or strategic?

Then there are the developing nations: an airline, an Inter-continental hotel – a shipping line. The UK and the traditional maritime nations continue to recognise these aspirations and indeed, after a somewhat tentative beginning, we have a pretty good record in recent years of assisting them. But it cannot all be done at once. So we have significant threats on top of an already bleak trading scene.

For thirty years much of US trade has been carried by free enterprise western shipping. This has been, perhaps, a reasonably comfortable if not fully recognised position and, of course, this country has shouldered many other burdens on behalf of the western alliance during the period. But continuation of this position is at risk. Private enterprise can tackle commercial pressures in the traditional way – shortening down, tightening up, coming again when the storm is over. Non-commercial pressures beyond the ability or capacity of the private operator to deal with are another matter. The continued expansion of the Soviets into western trades for political as well as economic purposes is something which must be, can only be contained through joint action by like-minded governments.

Again, instability by excessive building of ships for national, probably social reasons is a problem for governmental action, not something which private enterprise shipping can counter.

Ultimately, it is for nations to decide what form of shipping industry they require. I believe that in our western world it is best provided on a free enterprise, if you like capitalist basis. Yet the pressures are severe and it may be that, if no solutions are found and given the scale of investment required today, there will be increasing reluctance to commit private capital to an industry subject to such unquantifiable, uncontrollable political risk. It would be ironic indeed if the outcome were after all to be a slide into state shipping enterprise in the west with all that that implies in terms of less than optimum use of resources, less cost-effective operation, reduced international trade and more political tension.

In addressing you in these terms, ladies and gentlemen, it is not my intention to be alarmist or threatening. One simply knows that in our western democracies it takes time to develop political will and to shift policy. I believe, genuinely, that the great units of the USA and Europe may be so engaged with differences of opinion and interpretation of the minutiae of shipping affairs that we may fail to tackle the real threats to the system. It is not too late but it may be close run.

I hope that the current investigations in Washington designed to re-define maritime policy will not get bogged down in interagency debate, and that talks taking place in London this week between US Government and European officials will address the vital issues. From discussions in Washington yesterday, I know how much your representatives and members of the administration, a number of whom we are delighted to see with us here this evening, are striving to define and chart the right course. I hope that what I have said may assist others of you, leaders in your own field, opinion formers, members of a democratic society, to add your contribution to that effort.

As I said when I opened, this country's involvement and interest in world trade affects us all and I offer no apology for putting these views before you. They come from a country and a company with much history – most of it sharing with you a basic common commitment to enterprise and freedom.

Glossary

SCOTLAND

clapped	frozen
guddle	tickle (with the intention of catching trout)
high heidyins	top people
hirpling	limping
kenspeckle	conspicuous
tawse	the 1.5 inch strap used for punishment in school
timeously	in good time

ROYAL NAVY

Asdic	sonic device for detecting submarines
green 45	45 degrees on starboard bow
iron-deck	upper deck amidships (destroyer)
KGFS	King George's Fund for Sailors
Pompey	Portsmouth
pusser	peacetime
RNR	Royal Naval Reserve
RNVR	Royal Naval Volunteer Reserve
slop chest	naval stores of personal nature for sale
tiddly	smartest
trot	a line of ships, usually at buoys

INDIA

age-wallah	literally, man who goes in front
babu	clerk, particularly Bengali
bundobast	arrangements
burra sahib	the No. 1, the boss
chokra	junior, new boy
chowkidar	caretaker
chula	stove fuelled by charcoal or cowdung
chummery	bachelor quarters
dak bungalow	postal service bungalow available for travellers

Dewan	chief minister
dhobi	washerman
ghats	jetties
gherao	surround and detain
gompa	Tibetan monastery
hartal	strike
kitchen bat	rudimentary Hindi speech
koi hai	old India hand, particularly of Calcutta and Assam; literally 'Is anyone there?' (I need another drink)
lama	Buddhist priest
loti	jar
mali	gardener
peon	messenger
punkah	fan
PWD bungalow	Public Works Department bungalow
sirdar	leader
syce	groom

SHIPPING

bareboat	ship charter where client is responsible for full repairing and manning
break-bulk ships	traditional cargo ships (i.e. before containerisation)
cbm	cubic metres: measurement of capacity of e.g. gas carriers
CofS	Chamber of Shipping (which for a period became GCBS)
dwt	deadweight tonnage: lifting capacity of e.g. tanker & bulk carrier
GCBS	General Council of British Shipping
grt	gross registered tonnage: measurement of capacity of passenger ships
line voyage	classic A to B passenger and cargo trades
LNG	liquefied natural gas
LPG	liquefied petroleum gas
OBO	oil-bulk-ore carrier
P&I Club	Protection & Indemnity Association (mutual insurance for shipowners)
reefer	refrigerated cargo vessel
RoRo	Roll on Roll off – usually of ferries
timecharter	agreement to charter a ship for a specified period

| ULCC | ultra large crude oil carrier – typically 400,000 dwt |
| VLCC | very large crude oil carrier - typically 200,000 dwt |

P&O AND BI

ABC	Associated Bulk Carriers Ltd
BI	British India Steam Navigation Co. Ltd
BSD	Bulk Shipping Division
D Class	passenger/cargo ships in BI fleet
E&AT	European & Air Transport Division
ED	Energy Division
GCD	General Cargo Division
IOS	International Offshore Services
OCL	Overseas Containers Ltd
P&O	Peninsular and Oriental Steam Navigation Company
PD	Passenger Division
POAL	P&O Australia
PSD	Personnel Services Division

GENERAL

ANC	African National Congress
APV Ltd	UK engineering company
ASTMS	Association of Scientific, Technical and Managerial Staffs
BAL	Bestobell Australia
BNAC	British North American Committee
BP	British Petroleum
CEO	Chief Executive Officer
CU	Commercial Union Assurance
DTI	Department of Trade & Industry
e&oe	errors and omissions excepted
EPG	Eminent Persons Group
FMC	US Federal Maritime Commission
GATT	The General Agreement on Tariffs and Trade
Molotov cocktail	glass bottle filled with petroleum spirit
OECD	Organisation for Economic Cooperation and Development
OPEC	Organisation of Petroleum-Exporting Countries
OTC	Officers Training Corps
PPE	Politics, Philosophy, Economics (Oxford degree course)

Pru	The Prudential Assurance Co.
RBC	Royal Bank of Canada
RTZ	Rio Tinto Zinc
topping out	ceremony to mark advanced stage in construction of a building
TI	Tube Investments
UKSATA	United Kingdom South Africa Trade Association
UNCTAD	United Nations Conference on Trade and Development

Index